Troopers' Tales of the British South Africa Police

John Berry   Alan Stock

TSL Publications

The Great War in Africa Association

First published by the British South Africa Police Regimental Association (United Kingdom Branch) 2008

Published in Great Britain in 2024

By Great War in Africa Association, TSL Publications, Rickmansworth

ISBN: 978-1-915660-78-7

Copyright belongs to John Berry & Alan Stock, and unless otherwise stated, to the United Kingdom Branch of the British South Africa Police Regimental Association (United Kingdom Branch)

All rights reserved. No part of this publication may be reproduced, stored in a retrieval system or transmitted in any form by any means, electronic, mechanical, photocopying, recording or otherwise, except brief extracts for the purpose of review, without written permission of the publisher and copyright.

Language has been retained for historical reasons.

Some Tales have not been published before. Others have appeared in *The Outpost* the magazine of the British South Africa Police.

For permission to reproduce Trooper Seward's reminiscences our thanks are due to The History Society of Zimbabwe and its Hon. Editor, Michael Kimberley. These were originally published in *Heritage of Zimbabwe*, the Society's Journals, in 2002 and 2004.

Thanks to D.S. Johnston, M.B.E. (3967) for his kind permission to use the section on his B.S.A.P. days from his proposed Memoirs.

Thanks also to Hugh Phillips (4770) for permission to reproduce extracts from *The History of the British South Africa Police* concerning Lt Col. Seward.

Apology is made for standard of some photographs. This is caused by scanning from old magazines with poor paper quality.

In some of the early Tales variations in spelling of place names occurred. Such spellings have been retained.

Stories from *The Outpost* collected and made available by Alan Stock (6063) together with his valuable editorial advice. Alan was editor of *The Outpost* from 1966 to 1984.

Contents

The Chronicler's Tale	4
Tpr. Bigg's Tale	7
Tpr. Boultbee's Tale	13
Tpr. Ball's Tale	20
Tpr. Stenning's Tale	31
Tpr. Napier's Tale	34
Tpr. Killick's Tale	41
Tpr. Pole's Tale	47
Tpr. Mullin's Tale	59
Tpr. Griesbach's Tale	66
Note on H.G. Seward	79
Tpr. Seward's Tale	81
Further Note on Lt. Col. H.G. Seward	169
Tpr. Johnston's Tale	153

Illustrations

Mounted Trooper 1909	6
Ghostly Trooper	11
M'Kombi Rebellion Trooper	23

Photographs

Modern Trooper	5
B.S.A.P. Patrol Inyanga	19
Tpr. Ball, Umtali	24
Sgt. Major Ball	28
Lieut. Ball	28
Sgt. Major Ball, WW2	29
B.S.A.P. Pack Mule	56
Tprs. Mullin and Style	60
Lieut. Seward	108
Tpr. Johnston's Photographs See List on Page	152
Map Southern Rhodesia	104

THE CHRONICLER'S TALE

Introduction by Alan Stock
Editor of The Outpost 1966 – 1984

Editing the B.S.A. Police Magazine, *The Outpost*, in its closing decades carried a few additional responsibilities: photographer, sports commentator, book reviewer, crossword compiler and one of the most time-consuming duties – disguised as 'The Chronicler' – hosting the regular 'Old Comrades' pages of the magazine. This was where former members of all vintages renewed fleeting as well as life-long friendships, shared experiences and, no doubt, added a wrinkle or two to their stories to compensate for the other wrinkles they could do nothing about.

General topics and specific events debated in Old Comrades had a way of snowballing but so did the contacts (and magazine readership) as long-lost members of the Force were encountered in some distant corner of the globe, current addresses were revealed and the 'do you remember' chorus began in earnest. It was not always easy for The Chronicler to find time to encourage the snowballing by responding to the letters old comrades sent to the magazine. It was also a trifle hazardous if one's grasp of Force history was delicate. Fortunately there were a few outstanding former members with both the time and the enthusiasm to rally to the cause of reworking the Force's history. More of them later.

And it was not only Force history that came under the venerable magnifying glass. There was much more than a glint in the eye of the former trooper who took exception to the magazine's cover photograph in June 1967 which showed a 'modern' mounted trooper on duty outside the B.S.A. Police Pavilion at Bulawayo's International Trade Fair.

'The animal on display is a terrible monstrosity to be shown as a troop horse and I feel the picture must surely have been taken as a "gag". After studying its different points, I decided it must be a new breed: Equine-ox for instance! The forelegs are standing at attention while the hind legs are terribly cow-hocked. And what about the tail, dangling very close to the fetlocks? Is this a new fashion? The forelegs show cloven hooves, as also does the near hind, while the off hind looks as though it was wearing a large sized poultice. It is a very sad picture indeed and no advertisement for my old outfit.'

That particular correspondent, George Ball, had served in a great number of mounted 'outfits', as is revealed in his life story below, so he is more than entitled to his opinion.

Modern Trooper at Bulawayo International Trade Show being inspected by President and Mrs Dupont, and the horse which incurred the ire of ex-Trooper Ball

Ex-members were not slow in expressing their criticisms or their support for successors. There was the time when the Editor was so imprudent as to make an oblique reference to 'old men with walking sticks, muttering that things were not like they used to be' and suffered consequences that left no alternative but to apologise and adopt the age-old servitude of 'your humble servant'.

In the late Seventies, the last few years of the B.S.A. Police before its transition to the Zimbabwe Republic Police, contributions to *The Outpost* and the Old Comrades column of ancient photographs, memories and biographies of former members became more frequent than in the past. They came not only from the members themselves but also from their next of kin. It could have been that confidence in the National Archives was diminishing – that the writing on the wall was likely to obscure the intimate commentaries on ages past (to convolute a metaphor) – but at the same time there remained the simple trust that the B.S.A. Police Regimental Association with its branches throughout the world would do its best to record and protect the official and the informal history of the Force.

Troopers' Tales and the modest books that have preceded this latest collection are an expression of that trust. Some of the stories appeared in *The Outpost* while others appear in print for the first time. The first tale is not strictly that of a Trooper but sets an imaginative scenario for much of what follows, where 'atmosphere' was often absent in our troopers' reminiscences. The daughter of the Chibi Native Commissioner wrote 'Salute to Adventure' in the early 1930s. Her grandson was serving in the Force when it was published in *The Outpost* in June, 1975 – in an issue saluting, appropriately perhaps, International Women's Year.

The first trooper here telling his tale verbatim died nearly a year before I became editor. The fact that his story only came into my hands much later bears witness to the durability of a friendship forged at the turn of the century – between him, Ned Boultbee, and our second raconteur, George Ball. Both former policemen trooped all over the world in the sixty years following their apprenticeship in early Rhodesia and the classic tale would have them accidentally meeting up at a North American rodeo or some other foreign battlefield. That didn't quite happen but … enough of introduction. Let the Tales be told:

Alan Stock
June, 2008

A Trooper of the B.S.A. Police, c. 1909, from an original by 'Snaffles', (C.J. Payne), in the possession of W. Hughes Halls, M.B.E. (939)

BIGG'S TALE

Salute to Adventure
By Neyererwi, believed to be a daughter of the Chibi Native Commissioner who wrote this tale in the early 1930s.
The Outpost, June 1975

If you wander in the bush country north of the Lundi River you may chance on an old deserted road, almost obliterated by the years. Long ago it had quickly and eagerly sprung into being, battered into existence by the tread of many feet – the tread of Mr Rhodes and his young mounted men, that roisterous rollicking band who had set out on the Great Adventure over half a century ago.

Men, horses, wagons, guns and equipment. All these had battled and bustled along its path. All in a hurry, all intent on a new life in a new land, a new 'North West Passage'. It was a rough track, smoothed out somewhat by 12 miles of wagons – so they say. Selous' Road! Selous' Drift! How it stirs the imagination! Selous' Drift on the Lundi River …

Sitting in the greenish blue gloom of that silent place, you try to visualise the scene of long ago, the curtain rising ahead of the Pioneer Column coming into camp on the banks of the Lundi River in 1890.

All is still and deserted – as it is now and very much as it was those fifty years ago before its peace was disturbed: the mopani bush with its saddle-shaped leaves: the flowering vines: the gnarled lianas, grey and shining, for all the world like giant anacondas coiled round and round naked tree trunks: the orange-coloured Bauhinia: the harsh cry of the geese flying up and down the river: the hippo blowing bubbles … All these things remain unchanged. And now the brave laughter of the past as the men come in sight of their promised Eldorado. Watching, listening to the silence which is never silent, you can almost hear the shouts of command and the jingle of the horses' bits: you can almost see the khaki-clad band on the opposite shore. A little more imagination and there are the red and black wagon teams straining as they enter the water. Then come the merciless lashings, the struggle on the soft sand and the final pull from the water with all hands to the wheels to aid the enduring beasts who, right through history, have played their patient part in the mapping of Africa. Later there is the relaxation of the camp fires, lulled by the curling spirals of smoke: the simple food, the songs and laughter. Finally there is the deep sleep of exhaustion.

How long did they camp on the Lundi? How long did they take to cross that difficult drift? Did they build the cairn of stones – some four or five feet high – on the southern bank? A lone sentinel, it still stands on the edge of the drift, a silent monument to the past.

Perhaps the Pioneers did not build the cairn. Could it have been laboriously erected in 1891 by that despairing band of settlers and prospectors, some 15 in number, who were held up on the banks of this river in the heavy wet season of that year. Imagine their predicament – a vast stretch of turgid brown water, sullenly lifting itself down to the sea, in front of them while behind them another such barrier (the Nuanetsi), equally wide, equally baffling, equally impassable. History knows little of this party except the stark fact that all died somewhere on the north bank of the Lundi River in the vicinity of Selous's Drift. The pile of stones – whoever laboured over it – remains just as it was left more than fifty years ago.

And the Pioneer Road? Even today at first glance it would seem as if nature had cried stop to the all devouring bush, for their road is still very definitely a road today although practically unused since the last Post Cart lurched its way along it. At the turn-off into the river bed the ruts of the wagon wheels are such that it might have been used only last wet season. The undergrowth has never reclaimed its territory along the avenue cleared by the newcomers and where the wagons came down to the river, and on the Nuanetsi side, the track is still negotiable today.

On the southern bank of the river, back in the bushes, are the remains of stone terraces, now densely overgrown. Forcing a way through the jungle you mount the two outer rings of boulders to come upon a large flat surface. Here are the remains of two or three old huts, collapsed now and lying in fragments. Nearby, scattered to the four winds now, is a litter of broken glass, the last remains of a heap of bottles which once, so legend goes, almost equalled the size of the huts. This was the old Post Halt and here, alone in the bush and the silence, lived at least one white man. And it was for this spot that despatch rider James Bigg headed on his way south with important documents.

Picture young Bigg – a merry lad, perchance. In the mind's eye you see him galloping his horse up hill and down for hours on end, through sunshine and rain and the deep gloom of the hilly Chibi country. The clip of his horse's hooves bounce back from the great Msoro-we-Woto mountain, echo as he braves the Naka Pass. Hard as nails, young Jimmy hurries – always hurries – to the post on the other side of the river. There he is welcomed by the man who lives alone in the heavy African silence, that paradox of lions and hyenas, booming hippo and the eerie call of the wild dogs: a man alone in the wild relentless veld, warding off the 'pestilence that flyeth by night' and the fever from the river swamps.

Came the day when Despatch Rider Bigg could no longer mount his horse. One can only guess the story – fever, exposure; the almost drunken construction of a rough grass shelter; intense weakness and then – the end of the Great Adventure.

Bigg, in his delirium, is back in England. It is August – full of summer sounds and summer scents. With him in a shady walled garden is his sweetheart. Happy secrets are everywhere, in the green fields and in the lanes at dusk while church bells sing eventide. Shadows float on the placid English sea and there is the gentle beauty of home sunsets – quite different from the garish spectacle staged here. All this kaleidoscopes through his brain, overlaid by the unending hypnotic throb. Is it only his pulse or is it a mocking African drum, beating its triumph over another victim?

Who can tell what Jimmy thought or what he felt? One can only guess. He slips into his last long sleep at the side of the road he travelled so often, under the great mimosa tree on the Naka Pass.

It is only lately that his grave has been located. He did not sleep alone. There are two or three other graves at different points along this same road – nameless graves of men from among that early band of pioneers. All fell prey to the 'witch who knows no truth', who lured them on to seek fame and fortune in a new land and whose ultimate reward was no more than six feet of convenient earth.

Two of these newly discovered graves must be those of James Inglesby and Charles Wilson, both of the 1890 Column. They died and were buried where they fell beside the road in 1891.

Thoughts drift back to Jimmy Bigg. There he is with the nameless occupant of the Post Halt, thrilled with excitement as he explores the mysterious fort which stands on the north bank of the river. Thirteen years ago, this lesser Zimbabwe, with its walls, in places, eight feet wide, was in a good state of repair. Its black herringbone pattern was perfect. Now it is slowly crumbling to decay, ransacked by successive treasure seekers. It has been excavated and excavated again. Today little African children build toy houses with the flat black stones of the chevron pattern.

The unknown trooper of the Post Halt reappears on the stage of one's musings. Was it he who went at a gallop to young Bigg's side? Did he sit there through the long night watches, listening to the dying despatch rider's babblings of home? Did he, watching the last spark of life flutter away, wonder if this was the end or merely the beginning of the Great Mystery? And standing there beside the dead boy's grave under the scented mimosa tree with dismay and helplessness in his heart, did he fire the salutary volley and speak aloud, to break the desperate silence, the last farewell to a departed comrade? We shall never know – time has buried the narrative.

Now the trooper is returning to his shack, walking his horse and with his own head lowered in awe of the parting. Death cannot be shaken off like the dust of a mortal journey and as he sits, looking out into the gathering dusk, the silence is deepened by the murmur of the river and the rustlings of the *Mukuru*, the magic tree-lizard, that baffling inhabitant of the lowveld. The mysteries of life, of death, of Africa – especially Africa – colour the trooper's melancholy...Africa, in whose immensity he was enveloped and enriched, who moulded his character but was always master: Africa, who never sleeps. As the sun sets and the last bird-twitters are stilled, a new life awakes.

There is the river leviathan waiting his appointed time to feed, and he is Africa. There are the lions and the fleet-footed buck, hunter and hunted, lurking in the shadows, and they are Africa. Out there are the myriad 'legand-wing' insects who take up the nightly tale. They too are Africa. To a million whirring insects would the unnamed trooper have listened, perhaps reaching the conclusion that strikes us all:- Africa and her night insects are one, mysterious and invisible: it is as though no other life had ever been.

That pile of broken bottles tells a poignant story – the story of a man living alone with fear, a fear bred of solitude and silence and a fear that at all costs must be overcome. Nightly, by the red glow of the camp fire, he might with brave shiverings have contemplated the unknown. Drowning in the loneliness he might have been haunted by the spectre of sudden and

horrible death or some other stark and lingering disaster. To all his conjecturings would be added the interminably rhythmical beat of the African drum – the drum which, as the hours spun out, seemed to become the life-giving pulse beating in the very veins of the listener's body. But what if the drums should suddenly cease?

What manner of life did that solitary trooper live at the Post Halt? Where was his recreation? A little shooting, perhaps; a little fishing; a little watching the setting sun – the hills turning rosy in the after-glow, grey-blue mists rising from the river, glimpses of brown bodies melting into the blue-green gloom, the scarlet-breasted honey-suckers making their last swift dart – and then the dark.

All this over half-a-century ago and now the honey-sucker has turned to powdered dust. And the unknown trooper is dust too. *Tout Casse. Tout Lasse. Tout Passe.* All except the Lundi River and he still goes lilting on his way just as though nothing had ever happened at all.

Note: James Bigg, Tpr 121, BSACP, attested 4.1.1890. Died 24.9.1890. He was a post rider at Setoutse. Tpr Victor Morier has written:

'At one of the post stations, a wagon brought in the body of a young member of the Police who was a post rider carrying the mail from one station to the next. The poor fellow was very bad with fever when I passed him at Setoutse three days ago. I gave him all the quinine I had left. After I had moved on he was put by his companions into a passing wagon, hoping to get to Victoria but he died just as he got here (Lundi). We have just buried him. We made as deep a grave as we could by the roadside...He belonged to C Troop. I have carved a cross on a tree over the grave and put up a little fence. It looks very decent and the spot is very pretty'.

Courtesy Gibbs/Phillips HISTORY of the B.S.A.P.

BOULTBEE'S TALE

Edward Frederick Boultbee, OBE
Trooper (340)
British South Africa Police

Letter to Trooper George Ball.

'Dear George,
I ought to have replied to your two letters a long while ago, but I have been far from well and had to spend a few weeks in Hospital, and have been taking drugs ever since, which have knocked seven bells out of me.

In one of your letters you asked me to let you know what I have done since we parted at Inyanga, so I have made a brief list of the main events. I have not given details of the odd trip on a tramp as an ordinary seaman & as I am afraid I could not possibly remember them all, I have had quite exciting times & very dull ones, I suppose that is life.

What have you being doing all this time?
Well all the best
Yrs
Ned'

After you were transferred from Inyanga, I spent the rest of my time in the B.S.A.P. there. During the last three months of my service I developed fever and black water, at the end of my service I returned to England for a few months.

1905, I joined the North West Mounted Police, spent most of my time in southern Alberta, after finishing my service took a whirl at all kinds of jobs, including cow punching, navying and various other things too numerous to mention, sometimes plenty hungry, sometimes bloody cold. Started a horse ranch in a very small way down on the Montana border.

August 1914. I joined up in the first Canadians, i.e. Princess Patricia's Canadian Light Infantry. Commissioned in the Northamptonshire Regiment, December 1914. Severely wounded at the battle of the Somme 1916, while serving with the Machine Gun Corps. Spent 18 months in hospital then seconded to the R.F.C. and then the R.A.F. when it was formed.

Repatriated to Canada August 1919 for just over a year, tried to pull the ranch together, no good, too many years of drought. So packed up. Got into my car, a Chev, and trekked west to B.C. via Montana, Idaho, Washington and then to Agassiz, B.C. Spent the winter there, horrible, very wet.

Joined the first Canadian Air Force in the spring of 1920. Helped start the Aerial survey of Canada, flying over the north, my job was Navigator and photographer.

Next I went to England found it very hard to get jobs, the best offered was a doorman at a theatre in the West end of London at 30/- per week, this was through the Officer Employment Bureau, most insulted!!!! Went back into hospital for wounds, had a hell of a job to get out, thought they were going to keep me there for ever.

After that rented a cottage in the country, poultry farming. Made a little money, hated the job, also had the job as Mathematical Professor, coaching lads for the University.

Next thing started an antique shop in Bath which lasted me six years. 1930 depression practically put me out of business. Bought a place in Norfolk and amused myself shooting in season, sea fishing, and professional boxing. I formed the East of England Council of the British Boxing Control of which I was the Chairman. Incidentally I was an Official Referee and Inspector.

1938. I took a course under the Home Guard in Civil Defence including everything connected with it, passed out number one. Lectured on Civil Defence continually until sometime in 1939 was appointed Civil Defence Officer for South Norfolk and Controller. Carried on for five years. Oh, the part I enjoyed most was that of unexploded bombs. Reconnaissance Officer under the Royal Engineers. Very interesting and very tiring, but always excitement, which appealed to me.

Cracked up in 1943, then took an active part in the Home Guard.

1946. I came back to Rhodesia. Collected and started the Umtali Museum which the Government had now taken over as a National Museum of which I am Hon. Curator.

This seems about the end of my endeavours to make a living. Incidentally I have been married twice and have been a widower for seven years. Now for the Big Divide, maybe interesting. Quien Sabe.

Ned

The M'kombi Rebellion.
As seen by a Trooper who participated in it.

The M'kombi Rebellion in Portuguese East Africa along the Border of Southern Rhodesia, North Inyanga, 1902-1903.

Chief M'kombi rebelled against the Portuguese in 1902 and the Rebels when cornered by the Portuguese used to slip over the Rhodesia Border, thus preventing the Portuguese from capturing or defeating M'kombi's Impis. The Rhodesian Government was very disturbed at having these Rebels circulating round the Natives in that area of Rhodesia, as they were very closely related to the Rebels by blood, and were making them very restless, with quite a chance of the rebellion spreading to the Natives of Inyanga District, which would have made a very widespread upheaval.

The Government decided to send a small mobile column under the Command of Col. Jack Flint, composed of B.S.A.P., B.S.A.N.P. and about 500 Native levies.

The B.S.A.P. were from Bulawayo and Salisbury, also the B.S.A.N.P. (Black Watch).

I happened to be one of the Salisbury contingent – about 30 odd of us. We were suddenly paraded, had a special Medical Examination, were hastily equipped and sent by train to Rusapi, where we detrained and marched with our wagons to a point about a mile north of the present B.S.A.P. camp at Inyanga. It was in July and the nights were very cold, we each had only a waterproof sheet, blanket and cavalry cloak (dark blue with red lining); for the next six months we slept on the ground with the above items to keep us warm. Every other day we had a good issue of rum at night, and the alternating nights – lime juice. I preferred the rum at nights, it warmed one up to get to sleep.

On our arrival, Col. Jack Flint inspected us, and on account of the difficulty of getting supplies up to Salisbury from the south we had been issued with any clothes available; our hats were convicts – a gray sloppy, flat-topped headpiece of no shape whatever. Col. Flint was very irate that his men should be equipped as convicts. However, in a very short time we were all in rags, and were allowed to grow beards, we looked like a bunch of brigands, but our rifles, bayonets and bandoliers were always in good and clean condition.

The B.S.A.P. were armed with Lee Metfords.
The B.S.A.N.P. were armed with Martini Henrys.
The Native Levies were armed with Sniders.
We also had two Maxim Nordenfelts .45.

During our march from Rusapi to Inyanga I narrowly escaped being shot by a Native sniper. It happened as follows – we had mounted men in front, then the wagons, and mounted men in the rear. On each side we had men on foot going through the bush, keeping in touch with each other by sound. One early morning, and it was quite cold, I had a white sweater (very foolish of me, as it made me too conspicuous), I was on the extreme left, the bush was very thick, and I had lost touch with the man on my right, so I sat down on a rock to listen. Suddenly a shot from close by in the bush, and a pot leg shot hit the rock I was sitting on within 2 ins. of my manhood. I got very angry and hunted in the bush, but could not find him. It is very hard to find a native in thick bush. The man on my right soon turned up and I told him what had happened. We searched, but never saw hide nor hair of him.

From our position at Inyanga we made regular patrols along the Border and, if not on this duty, were continually practising attacks on Kopjes. This was done by one Section advancing up the kopje and another Section, who had taken cover, firing rapid fire at the supposed enemy at the top of the kopje. Having advanced at a given signal, the advancing Section fling themselves on the ground, taking cover, if any, and firing as rapidly as possible, whilst the other Section advanced.

This action was carried on until we got near enough to the top, when the two Sections joined together, then we got the order 'fix bayonets' and the order 'Charge', and we went up the kopje crest as fast as our weary limbs allowed us, yelling blue murder. What with patrols and these continual exercises, we were a mighty body of ragamuffins; our clothes got worse and worse; our shirts and trousers in rags, and many of us had our toes protruding from our boots.

Food was very poor, continual bully beef and dough cooked in hot ashes. We gradually improved our sleeping conditions, which hitherto had been on the open veldt, by making small grass shelters, but Inyanga can be mighty cold at night in July. I cannot remember how long we were there – it was several months before we were separated, the Bulawayo crowd went back to

Bulawayo, most of the Salisbury crowd were left at Inyanga under the command of Lt. Gwynne.

We were never actually in action with the Natives, but they attempted to set fire to the Camp, and a lot of our ammunition exploded making a lot of noise. There we were, our grass shelters on fire, flames everywhere, we back to back with bayonets fixed, wondering when we should hear their yells and taste their assegais. However, that was all there was to it.

I remember the Regimental Orders which were read out.

    1. That we were on special Action in continuation of the Boer war, and entitled to the King's Medal of the Boer War.

    2. A special letter was read from the King of Portugal thanking all the B.S.A.P. who had participated in this Rebellion, and promised us the Portuguese medal.

I don't know if any of the B.S.A.P. received it, as shortly after the King was deposed, and a Republic formed, and all Royal Honours were done away with.

The night before the Bulawayo crowd left us for their trek to Bulawayo, we all went to the little canteen at the permanent Police Camp about a mile away, and had a regular binge.

Amongst the Police in those days we had some queer customers, nearly all had taken part in the Boer War. There were many who had taken part in the 1896 Rebellion and Mashona Rebellion, and several Pioneers and Jameson Raiders. One of the characters had taken an oath that the Boers would never take him prisoner on his feet. On the occasion when Lord Methuen was captured, it was the B.S.A.P. who acted as scouts for his column. When Lord Methuen decided to surrender, the B.S.A.P. were the only troops left with him, and this aforementioned character found himself in an awkward position being still on his feet. He searched the saddlebags of officers' horses and found two bottles of whisky. He put them down the hatch one after the other. He could not walk and the Boers had to carry him. He was a Jameson Raider. On this last night, before starting for Bulawayo the next morning, he got quite a skinful and, having no more cash, solemnly took off his boots, which I remember were a fine pair of Black Cavalry Riding Boots, and put them up to auction. I bought them. He somehow or the other got back to our Lines and lit a candle which was over his head, went to sleep and the candle-grease dripped onto his head. It was a wonder it did not set the grass shelter afire. The next morning he paraded mounted, candle grease all over his hair, and spurs on bare feet.

I have tried to trace any B.S.A.P. who took part in this Rebellion. The only one I have been able to trace is George Ball, who came to this country on the same Contingent with me on the old Dilwara Troopship in May, 1902.

He is still alive and a respectable old grandfather now, having served in both the big Wars, I believe very creditably, he lives in Nanaimo, B.C.

Some months after the Portuguese had got the M'kombi Rebellion under control, we managed to capture several of his chief Indunas who had crossed over into Rhodesia. We had several disappointing episodes, as the rebels were always warned by Bush telegraph, when we attempted to catch them, but this time our patrol didn't leave until everyone was asleep, and arrived at daybreak at the Kraal on top of a kopje, before the rebels were awake. They had stacked their rifles up against a hut and, as they came out still rubbing their eyes of sleep, the first thing they saw was our Patrol with levelled rifles pointing at them. No use for them to make a fight of it. I was one of the escort of two B.S.A.P. and two B.S.A.N.P. who brought them into Umtali. They were attached by their necks to a long wagon chain. Later on M'kombi surrendered to the B.S.A.P. and was given asylum in Rhodesia; I believe at Umtassa's Reserve, where he eventually died. The natives were well-armed with modern rifles, mostly picked up after fighting in the Boer War.

As an aftermath to this Rebellion the natives in the Inyanga District were very restless and in 1903 a Rebellion was expected. The Police at Inyanga were reinforced, a last stand Fort was built, and plans were made to bring the few settlers into Camp, they were mainly from the Dutch Settlement, and we supplied them with ammunition, which they were always short of. It was estimated that we were surrounded by an Impi of 5,000. It eventually fizzled out, but for a time, it was very tiring, especially as we seldom got a proper rest, being on night picket practically every night. War dances were going on all night in the surrounding Kraals. What a din they made!

There may be a few of Col. J. Flint's Flying Column alive, but I can only trace Geo. Ball. Should anyone who took part in the operation and, if alive, he must be getting quite old by now, I should like him to write to me. I stayed in the Police until 1904 when I got Blackwater Fever and had to leave as I was left very groggy.

The next year I joined the N.W.M.P., and served five years.

Captain E.F. Boultbee, OBE
Ex Trooper No 340 B.S.A. Police

P.S. I understand that all records of the M'kombi Rebellion were lost in a fire which took place at Salisbury B.S.A.P. Barracks in 1905.

Letters written around 1960 to his contemporary, Trooper George Ball, and passed on to 'The Chronicler' by George after Captain Boultbee's death in Umtali in 1965. Not previously published.

National Archives, Zimbabwe
B.S.A.P. Patrol at Inyanga, 1903

A BSAP Trooper during Nkombi rebellion of 1902-3.

BALL'S TALE

My Life Story
Trooper (345) George W. Ball
British South Africa Police

I was born on 10 March 1883 in India at Belgaum, Bombay Province, which place is situated in the ghats (hills) near the Goanese Border. My father was a colour sergeant in the 87th Princess Victoria's Royal Irish Fusiliers and, along with a colour sergeant of the Seaforth Highlanders, was chosen to guard the Heir to the Throne (later Edward VII), at the Grand Durbar held at Delhi. I would like to mention that the two regiments above were the only ones in the British Army to wear two collar badges. My mother often told me that when the troops were moving to a new station the women and children followed behind on bullock wagons, catching up with the regiment when it camped for the night. My people had been in India for 16 years with the Fusiliers. Then came the time for transfer back to Great Britain. At that time I was two years of age. Our troopship had to call at (?) for sealed orders which were given to the ship's captain and the OC Troops and were to be broken open at a certain point. This was done only to learn that they were to proceed up the Red Sea to Suakin.

There the troops were to go ashore, capture the port and proceed to the relief of General Gordon – which they did while the troopship remained in the harbour for a few days. Previous to the men going ashore, the warships bombarded the city, throwing their shells over our ship. Invariably, troops for 'home' service from the east had with them a number of deranged soldiers and our ship was no exception – the poor fellows being in cages on deck. Mother told me in after years that it was terrible to behold their antics when the shells were coming over. At last the ship's captain received orders to weigh anchor and proceed to England, eventually reaching Southampton where all the women and children were transferred to quarters on the Isle of Wight – to await the return of the regiment two years later. What a joyful homecoming, our father was safe and sound. During the desert fighting, it was the habit of the enemy to feign death. After one engagement, my father and another sergeant were walking over the battlefield when an apparently 'dead' man jumped to his feet and slashed at Dad with a sword. But in the nick of time his friend deflected the blow, leaving father with a cut on his head. Then, I can well imagine, the native was sent to his 'happy hunting ground'.

Our next move was to Ireland where we went into barracks at Cavan, sojourning there until Father was 'time-expired', and then moved to London. Even though my father had been educated at Charterhouse, then in the City of London, a time-expired soldier took any job and so he became a warder at Pentonville Prison. We lived a block from City Road of 'Angel' fame – and I have since been told that this district was then in a state of terror owing to its being in the centre of the Jack the Ripper horrors.

We moved from there to Paddington and Father became a Commissionaire for William Whitely – about the age of eight I was enrolled in a gymnastic club and stayed steady with it for ten years, becoming quite proficient, especially in the art of boxing – leaving school at the age of 14 I worked for William Whitely, trying several times to join a Unit for service in South Africa, but, 'no dice' – then in the early spring of 1902 I saw a notice in a paper calling for recruits for the B.S.A. Police and it was not long before I was at the office whence I was told to obtain various references and send them in, which I did. After a long fretting period I received a letter from Major Hopper saying I had been accepted, even though I was only 19 years old and would receive notice of the sailing date, and was I the happy 'kid'.

Particulars soon came from Major Hopper telling me to join the Party at Waterloo Station on July 4th –02. Arriving at the rendezvous I found the rest of the chaps (about 20) and soon we were bowling along to Southampton to sail next day on 'Dilwara'. The passenger list consisted of ex soldiers returning to Africa also a party of sailors from R.N. who to me, a landlubber, looked very 'funny' – all big men with moustache & beard wearing (of all things) straw sailors hats – they were on the way to join gun boats on the Zambesi. I chummed up with a young fellow named Ned Boultbee who became a Captain during World War 1 and afterwards was curator of the museum at Umtali. Ned was also a good boxer and as soon as we entered warmer waters a boxing tournament was soon on the go, Ned winning his event, while I managed to get the light & middle weight bouts – then I was asked to fight a sailor for the heavyweight, but being a bit 'leery' I asked to be shown my opponent – one look was enough – one blow from this chap would have knocked me overboard. The voyage was very pleasant and towards the end my friend and I were asked to report to the office of the ship's R.S.M. (grenadier) – we did so and he congratulated us on our behaviour, while aboard, and he foresaw a good future for us, and looking back, now, I think we both did 'not too badly'.

'The evening we landed at Cape Town saw us on a C.G.R. train headed for Salisbury – it was a very fascinating journey, seeing all the 'block houses' still occupied by the troops and passing through places bearing well-known war names. At last the train halted at Bulawayo where a B.S.A. Police sergeant came aboard and said we were to detrain, after which he marched us to the camp and settled us in a large hut for the night. The next morning with all our gear, we paraded alongside a wagon on which we piled our stuff – an African driver appeared and proceeded to hook up two teams of mules, some 'boys' placed several boxes on the wagon – then – we found out Bulawayo was the 'end of line' and we would have to walk to Gwelo which was the other 'end of line' from Beira. I guess we all felt pretty glum about that news – but brightened up when 10 bare backed remounts were led out, which had to be taken along, we were all eager to lead one, as it promised future rides, but there were only 10 lucky(?) ones – the order was given to move off and the motley outfit got underway. After leaving town, the 'cavalry' mounted and 'lorded' it over us poor footsloggers and when time came to make camp, some smart guys claimed space under the wagon for sleeping quarters. The next morning we were off, the mounted portion still gloating, but – came night time they were only too glad to turn the 'nags' over to us other chaps and by the following night they all hated the sight of a horse and were content to 'hoof it' – but – they all had a very funny style of walking!

We were told before starting out that our road went through the Gwaai forest, which was thickly populated with lions and the night we camped there, all us white boys were very apprehensive – during the night the air was filled with the most horrible shouts and screams and in two shakes of a lamb's tail there were 20 men all doing their best to get to the centre under the wagon, no doubt each having fearful thoughts, which were soon dispelled as an 8 span donkey went by – the driver still screaming his head off.

All in all, I enjoyed the trip very much, but cannot recall the number of days it took, but we made Gwelo safely – entrained and soon were bowling along to Salisbury to begin a new life. Upon arriving at our destination we were taken over by some N.C.O.'s and marched to camp – eft – ight –eft – ight.

Next morning, we met the Q.M. to receive our issue of clothing and equipment and were shown how it should be worn. What a 'fist' we made of the job, but we 'made it'. The following morning, we and others were on Parade at 10 a.m. only to be kept waiting and waiting in the hot sun and us greenhorns were becoming paler and paler, not to mention 'wobbly', when an officer came hurriedly on to the Square, he turned out to be the M.O. and he gave those in charge a real blasting for having us green troops out there at that time of day and gave the order for the Parade to be dismissed.

We soon became hardened up and lived to enjoy it. Many a morning in Riding School under the supervision of R.S.M. James Blatherwick, attended by a trumpeter; the latter really seemed to enjoy the proceedings, as his face wore a perpetual grin. Wearing a 'back board' was a real joker, not to mention 'cross your stirrups', 'drop your reins', 'terott' – the stiff back seam of our Bedford cord pantaloons did not add to our pleasure – but – pipe clay was a cure-all in 'them' days. Eventually we 'Passed Out' of Riding School and also became proficient in foot drill – then we figured we were 'it'.

After about two months there was real excitement – trouble up north on the Portuguese border – the P.E.A. Authorities asked for our cooperation against M'kombi – a Paramount chief who was causing them lots of trouble, then 'hopping' over the border to our side – our H.Q. agreed and at once all available men and horses were gathered and they left for Inyanga via Rusape under the command of Lieut. Col. Jack Flint. A couple of weeks later word came to send all dismounted men to Inyanga. I happened to be one of them and the day we marched to the railway station, the rain was coming down – 'cats and dogs' and us 'humping' our kit and wearing 2 bandoliers of 'ammo' – anyway the ride to Rusape was dry and we soon detrained to begin our march to Inyanga, which was accomplished at the rate of about 20 miles per day.

Upon arrival we went into camp in grass huts and patrols were carried out along the Border. Three or four men were assigned to each hut, a 'stretcher' bed apiece with equipment hung about where possible and one night as I lay on my bed reading by candle light there came the report of a 'rifle shot' and at once there was a great uproar, N.C.O.'s shouting for all to 'stand to' on the parade ground, where arms were inspected as well as possible, but all men denied firing a shot; after a time we were dismissed to our huts. Upon relighting my reading candle I discovered the flame was under a bandolier (though, at a reasonable distance) and had caused a cartridge to explode – the leather being only slightly discoloured which I hastened to rectify and you may be sure I kept my mouth shut tight and the mystery was soon forgotten.

To keep us in shape, a kind of riding school was set up on the high ground near the Inyanga permanent Camp – targets were erected and in single file we galloped past on Australian 'walers' and Roman nosed Hungarian remounts, loosing off shots as we approached each target; at first it was a ghastly job, but – with experience, men and mounts made a good showing. After some months and all being quiet on the P.E.A. border, the Mobile Column was disbanded, some men, myself included, were transferred to Inyanga Camp – the balance being returned to Salisbury. At that time it was common knowledge that the King of Portugal had offered to 'strike' a medal and ribbon for our services, but H.Q. declined.

During 1903 I was transferred to Rusape where I met the late A.J. Siggins and after he had retired to Rickmansworth – England, in reply to a letter from me, he asked 'do you remember that Sunday in church?' he was referring to the little church at Rusape where a service was about to start with Archdeacon Upcher in charge – the lady organist took her place at the organ – the hymn number was given out – and the lady started to pump the pedals to play the first verse, while doing so we noticed she was hitching about on the stool, every now and then shaking her skirt or slapping at her legs – the Archdeacon was gaping at her, then he too began the performance of flailing his arms – suddenly the congregation got into the act – the Archdeacon and organist headed for the door, calling out 'make for the outside' which we did in a big hurry, helped on by a swarm of bees. After we had somewhat recovered, us men made an inspection and found the bees had entered the building through a small hole in a corner of a window pane and had swarmed inside the organ only to be disturbed by the organist's vigorous pumping.

The Rusape River had a bad name for crocodiles and we used to ride down stream to a pool below the Falls for a swim and as a safety measure always took a dog along and allowed it to take the first bath; if he returned to shore then we too took a swim and never had a casualty. One time we had to take some horses to our boundary which was the Odzi River and hand them over to a Party from Umtali – upon arriving at the river we found them waiting on the other side and it took quite a lot of haggling before they crossed over to our side, signed for and collected the remounts, then safely made the return crossing and as they moved off a lot of nasty language floated back to us.

The Odzi had for 'crocs' a very bad name and once on a lone patrol I had to cross over on the railway trestle bridge, but first of all I took a heavy pair of socks from my wallets and fixed them over my mount's forelegs to take care of possible slippage, then taking a firm grip of the bridle I stepped backwards on to each balk of timber, the horse quietly following and we safely made the other side, also made the return crossing. I had heard of this 'quiff' somewhere and thought I would try it out; but success is only assured by having a quiet horse of an even temperament. At this time, as A.J. Siggins mentioned in his 'Mankillers' there were quite a number of lions in the district and here are a few incidents which came my way. While on a patrol north of 'Headlands' I stayed overnight at a bachelor's place and during the night there was a great racket going on in the cattle stockade – we were up in 'no time', the farmer grabbed his rifle and loaded soft nose bullets and asked me to carry a lighted lantern, but to keep it behind me; arriving at the stockade I switched the light to the front and peering through the poles found I was face to face with a lion, I don't know who was most surprised;

but anyway 'simba' took off in a great hurry and scrambled over the pole fence.

Another time while at a farm a 'boy' came a running, shouting to his Baas that there was a skelm among the sheep – we hurried off accompanied by a fox terrier – sure enough there were the remains of the feast, but, as it was growing dark we started for home – then – missing the dog, I retraced my steps and found the dog peering into the bush, body rigid and 'pointing' like a bird dog, but the lion hearing my footsteps made off through the bush as I loosed off a couple of shots – no luck. The time when I was most lonely was on a patrol to the Sabi River area; as I lay in my small 'pup' tent, a lion broke into a series of roars, not far off, and to cap it all, almost with his nose on the tent, a hyena gave forth with the craziest 'concert' and was I glad to see daylight?

Just one more about Rusape – I was on patrol with another chap and had to seek shelter at a farm and found there only an old lady and her young grandson, but the lady graciously invited us to stay the night, so, after fixing our horses up, we brought our saddles and blankets in and camped in the kitchen and were soon asleep. During the night the lady woke us up to ask for our pipes as her grandson had a bad toothache, she would clean out the nicotine and place it in the lad's hollow tooth – we did so and again went to sleep, when we were roused by a shot; upon going outside we found the old lady coming to the house carrying a shot gun – she had been awakened by a commotion among the chickens and surprised a large snake, which she despatched – again we slept and come early morning we moved on and late that day we called to see how the lady was making out and found she had skinned a large snake and had the skin tacked on the side of the house, to stretch and dry; we said 'good bye' and as we rode off, we both agreed that there was a Grandma who could look after herself.

My two years service with the B.S.A. Police were very happy ones and during July 1904 I took a V.G. discharge from Colonel Bodle and returned to England, well satisfied with the experience gained.

A few months at home and I began to yearn for Rhodesia, when my brother-in-law asked me to go with him to Canada – we landed in Toronto early in Jan 1905 – there was no work to be obtained, eastern Canadians seemed to hate all Englishmen and when going to apply for a construction job – there outside was a large notice in foot high letters – saying 'MEN

WANTED – NO ENGLISH NEED APPLY'. Children would even follow you on the street shouting – 'sparrows – sparrows – here are more sparrows'. This kind of stuff really made me sick and I still longed for Rhodesia.

While in Toronto I joined a militia cavalry unit (Toronto Light Horse) and camped for two seasons at Niagara-on-the-Lake – Lieut. McBrien was my troop officer and had just finished a stint with the S.A.C., he later signed up the R.N.W.M. Police and rose to become Chief Commissioner.

August 1906 saw me heading west on a harvest excursion train for Saskatchewan where all men were equal; after the harvest season, my friend and I took up homesteads and then headed for Prince Albert to look for bush work, but nothing doing for greenhorns, so we found jobs on farms. Come spring we bought 3 oxen and a wagon and high-tailed it back to the homesteads 175 miles away. What a trip!!, but, we made it and in that district (40 miles N.W. of Regina) I found my girl and this year 1971 we are celebrating our Diamond Jubilee – we have been blessed with 4 fine children – 3 girls and a boy.

1914 saw me enlisted in the 10th C.M.R., the following day a sergeant and in two months I was promoted to Sqn Sgt. Major – later my squadron was chosen to proceed overseas as 3rd Div Cavalry, but at that time cavalry were a glut on the market, so being a gymnast I transferred with my rank to a P.T. and B.F. Unit and took my V.G. certificate at the Aldershot Gymnasium. Some time later I was recommended for a Commission and went to a Military School for Officers – eventually 'Passing Out' as a Lieutenant and received an appointment to the 46th Bn (Saskatchewan), then in France. I joined the Unit in 1916 and we were among the first Canadian troops to take up position on Vimy Ridge. In early 1917 I was badly blown up during a bombardment and reported dead, but was eventually taken out to the advanced Medical Post whence the M.O. said 'another half hour and you would have burst.'

After some time I was a stretcher case to England and after a few months was returned to Canada for further treatment and in November 1917 I was invalided from the Service.

This was a lonely time, I did not seem to know anyone as my old friends were either dead or still serving overseas, so early in 1918 I applied for re-entry with my rank to a training Establishment and was accepted. In July I was selected as O.C. of a 600 man Draft and we proceeded overseas from Halifax as part of a 30 ship convoy – all went well until we reached mid-Atlantic, then one evening after dinner I was strolling the deck with one of my Officers (who was an expert signaller) when he noticed the 'Blinker' system working on a ship to our immediate rear – we stopped while he read off the message being sent to the cruiser escort. 'Have Located Object – Think It Is Submarine' then a pause and another message blinked out – 'Object Located Is Submarine', at once a little 'hell' broke loose, ships in the vicinity opened fire, at the first sound our gun crew were galloping across the 'well' deck to the Poop Deck where their gun was. Lieutenant Ball in 1916 was located, over the hospital (wouldn't you know it?) and at that very moment a door opened and out came a Nurse carrying a pan of garbage, as she walked to the ships side our gun fired and the poor girl was thrown to the deck to receive the contents of the pan in her lap; she scrambled to her feet and lit for the hospital. The convoy was headed for Liverpool – the cruiser gave orders to 'Zig Zag' and we were off like disturbed ducks – then, a little later a signal came – 'Every Ship For Itself' and a couple of days later our ship was off the Bay of Biscay heading up the Channel to disembark in the Thames at Tilbury where we entrained for Witley – Surrey and there I handed over my Draft to Canadian Authorities.

Lieutenant Ball in 1916

From then on, we cooled our heels awaiting return transportation. At that time the Spanish flu was rampant in Britain and Canada – the night I arrived at my home in Regina, I was down with it and was carted off by ambulance to the hospital, where I was when Peace was declared, but I weathered the storm and was boarded out of the Army on July 18th 1919.

The years rolled by and soon came 1939 – but I found I was struck off the Reserve of Officers so on June 24th 1940 I enlisted with the Veteran Guards of Canada and once more the next day I was a sergeant and shortly after became the C.S.M. of my company – we were a real smart lot, guarding P.O.W.'s in different parts of Canada and one time we went to New York to gather up Rommel's Africa Korp and take them to a new camp in the Rocky Mountains and I will say they were a good looking lot – all 17,000.

We had a Company serving in London during the war, while others were in British Guyana guarding shipping carrying 'Bauxite' from the mines at McKenzie up the Demarara River with H.Q. stationed at Georgetown – the camp at McKenzie was riddled with Malaria.

Still seeking adventure I volunteered for service there in 1944 (still as C.S.M,) and early in 1945 we were returned to our Companies in Canada and then came my promotion to R.S.M. Soon after the Armistice (sic) the P.O.W.'s were shipped to England and I was fortunate to make two trips. October 4th 1946 came along and I was demobbed bringing my Army life to a close.

Sgt. Major Ball in World War 2

We stayed in Regina till Oct. 31st 1947 and then moved to Victoria B.C. and found this Island to be a veritable Garden of Eden and we have enjoyed every minute. Our son Brian having a business at Vanaimo decided us to move there – my eldest daughter came here also, so now we have built up quite a clan, one of my girls is at Toronto and the other in Regina.

My wife and I are very active and have a great deal to be thankful for and this year we will have a big gathering to celebrate our Diamond Jubilee. The foregoing, sir, is my story and I thank you for the invitation to write it.

Very sincerely
George W. Ball

PS During my last trip back from England I was on deck watching the shipping and in a 'slip' I saw a boat showing the name *Dilwara*, I could hardly believe my eyes and to a passing ships officer, I asked 'is that the old *Dilwara*?' his reply was 'yes, that's her', she was still in service; how the memories of 1902 flooded back.

Not previously published. Text, including photographs, passed on to 'The Chronicler' by Trooper Ball's daughter, Mrs Brenda Tyrrell, shortly after his death in Canada on 7 November, 1976.

STENNING'S TALE

Arthur James Stenning
Trooper (547)
British South Africa Police

During the years 1903-1905 I served in the B.S.A. Police and in January 1904, I with a number of others was posted to Fort Gwanda ('G' Troop) from Bulawayo. We travelled by train and halted for the night at Heany Junction, the reason for this was that the engines of that time used wood for fuel, which had to be cut in the bush and stacked at intervals along the track. Two or three natives were carried on the train for the purpose of loading this timber on the engine's tender. This could only be done at night.

Fort Gwanda, then a minor township served several nearby gold mines, among them being the 'Jesse', 'Antenear' and 'Eagle Vulture'. From there the railway went as far as West Nicholson mine, the terminus. The train ran down from Bulawayo with mail from home on Sunday, Tuesday and Thursday, and back with mail for home on Monday, Wednesday and Friday, but none on Saturday.

In April 1904 I was posted to Fort Tuli, approximately 85 miles south east of Gwanda. This station was staffed by eight or nine troopers under a sergeant, and a section of Native Police. Shortly after my arrival the station strength was reduced to two Europeans with the Native Police. This change necessitated me taking over the Post Office duties, for which I received 'Extra Duty Pay' of one shilling a day, in addition to normal police duties.

As will be readily appreciated there was very little postal traffic, as apart from the Police there were only two traders in this area, at a store on the other side of the Shashi River. One of them with a wagon and a team of donkeys traded and bartered with the natives at outlying kraals, exchanging coloured blankets, cottons, bead and wire for grain, principally mealies. However a telephone (or telegraph) line ran across country from Palachwi (Palapye), through Macloutsi and Fort Tuli to Fort Victoria. Each morning at 8 a.m. I had to contact the two outstations, testing for two hours, after which I broke the connection in case of emergency, it being our only link with the outside world. An urgent message for our troop went via Palachwi, thence via Bulawayo to Fort Gwanda.

Mail for Fort Tuli came and went by native carriers on foot, there being six of these 'boys'. They travelled in pairs once a week, two 'up', two 'down', and two resting.

Remaining at Fort Tuli for nearly a year I was re-posted to Fort Gwanda and had a brief spell on foot on Township duty. As will be appreciated, all other duties were mounted, the journey from Fort Gwanda to Fort Tuli and vice versa being made by track through the bush, which frequently had the unhappy knack of losing itself.

During the period of Township duty at Gwanda there as much to be done at the railway station during the arrival and departure of trains, but I was never aware of anything in the nature of a junction and was under the impression that the line went straight on to the West Nicholson mine. The East Gwanda mines were not known to me, Nicholson being the end of the line at that time.

One place marked on Livermore's map recalls a certain incident to mind. From Gwanda we frequently made a patrol to a Police Post some ten miles out named Geelong and during one of these patrols I caught sight of some white object about 400-500 yards off the track in the bush. On investigation I found it to be the bivouac of a lone prospector. In the course of a lengthy conversation I learned he had named the spot 'Colleen Bawn', which name appears on Livermore's map.

Most other names on the Livermore map from Heany Junction to West Nicholson are unfamiliar to me and have come into existence since my time, many, perhaps, having been derived from the gangers' cottages which were spaced roughly seven miles apart on this section of line. Incidentally these gangers each had a squad of natives, and some in addition to track maintenance cut and stacked wood for the engines.

An example of the latter possibility is Stanmore which is shown on the map, and which I have reason to believe was the name given by one of the gangers to this particular cottage. In the course of patrols I became quite friendly with this particular individual and in fact stayed with him at this cottage on one or two occasions when off duty.

My next move was a posting to Filabusi Siding in June 1905, and where, as at Fort Tuli, postal duties were included in my responsibilities. This Post served Filabusi itself, the district of Belingwe and the mines there. Mails etc, were carried by a man named Cornelius who owned a Cape cart and a team of six donkeys.

Cornelius would arrive at the siding on Thursday afternoon with his collection for the 'Up' (Home) mail which departed on Friday, stay with me till the arrival of the 'Down' mail on Sunday, when he would depart for Belingwe with the delivery.

At Filabusi Siding I was (with three natives) the sole representative of the Police, and the only other Europeans in the area were a storekeeper named Julius, and two brothers named Chalmers, one of whom acted as Railway Agent for heavy goods for Belingwe which were brought to the siding by three wagons and teams of donkeys, a unit owned by the transport rider whose name I have forgotten.

Of closer relations to philatelic matters was the fact that I was at Filabusi at the time of the 1905 Victoria Falls issue of stamps (S.G. 94-97) and well remember that, although I was not then interested in stamp collecting I sent to the H.O. of the Post Office at Bulawayo for 3 or 4 sets. These were never received probably because being such a small office with so little traffic it was thought I would not need the higher values, or could it have been as a P.O. Official I was not allowed to collect. This I doubt.

However, I did get a supply of the 1d and 2 1/2d values, some of which I brought back on my return to England. In ones and twos these were mostly given away in the intervening years until now I am left with a strip of 5 of the penny value and a block of 4 of the twopenny halfpenny values. What happened to the stamps on my own correspondence from the siding to the young lady who was eventually to become my wife, I do not know – probably 'whizzed' by her schoolboy brother. However long after we were married I found in a picture postcard album belonging to my wife, a card that I had sent her. It bore one of the one penny 'Falls' stamps, beautifully and clearly struck (by myself) with the Filabusi cancellation. It bears the date -17 AUG-05- within the double ring.

Finally regarding Balla Balla. Towards the end of the time I spent in those parts, rumour reached me that on promotion I was to be placed in charge of a new Police Post there. Right or wrong this did not happen as before the event I took my discharge and returned home.

Studying the map has enabled me to live again a very happy and interesting period of my life nearly sixty years ago.

Not previously published.

NAPIER'S TALE

Joe Phelan and The Killarney Gold
Cecil James Napier
Trooper (1421)
British South Africa Police

In submitting this story I want to say that it is absolutely true and that none of the names have been altered as far as I know. Corporal Lawrence told me all the details personally when he was my Sergeant at Belingwe in 1909. All the characters are dead long ago, and I don't suppose Friend's little mine still exists. I believe this was the only gold hold up in the previous history of Rhodesia but there may have been others since those days.

I knew the Caprivi Strip quite well and the man who was Superintendent there at that time was W.S. Chadwick, the author and member of the Bechuanaland Protectorate Police in Francistown at one time. He confirmed the part played by Ben Johnstone, if that is the correct spelling of his name, and the other characters mentioned, and also said that it is true that Phelan was shot and killed during a drunken brawl at their camp.

C.C.J. Napier

Corporal Lawrence, of the British South Africa Police, stationed at Filabusi in Southern Rhodesia sat in the charge office thinking of nothing in particular. It was about eleven o'clock in the morning, in the early part of 1905, when the world was at peace.

He fiddled idly with the papers on his desk, looked through the window at the endless bush and yawned. Life was boring, he thought – no native trouble, no murders, no thieves, no – as he often said – nothing, only a few boring Pass Law cases now and again. He would get through the day somehow, he supposed, and then take his gun for its customary walk at sundown, after a small buck or a guinea-fowl. The office cat jumped upon the desk to investigate the dregs in a tea-cup, and was smitten with an ages old newspaper.

'Darn!' said Corporal Lawrence, 'nothing ever happens.' Then he looked up suddenly.

Hurried footsteps sounded outside. The door burst open and a man entered, breathless, and collapsed in a chair. It was Plaistow, the secretary of the Killarney Gold Mine. The Corporal looked at him thoughtfully. What was it? Was the man ill, perhaps? Late nights and not enough water with it?

'Never mind, old man,' sympathised Lawrence, 'the doctor's only fifty miles away. Have a hair of the dog in the meantime?'

Plaistow gave a sort of half-strangled roar. 'Doctor be darned!' he said. 'It's robbery! Robbery under arms and all the gold…!'

Robbery under arms in Southern Rhodesia in 1905 was an unheard of thing.

Then Plaistow told his story. The Corporal's boredom was shattered and forgotten.

A masked man had held up the Cape cart in which Plaistow had been escorting several bars of gold from the Killarney Mine to the railway siding at Balla Balla from where it was to have been railed to the Standard Bank in Bulawayo. The robber had fired several shots, one of which had killed a leading mule, and when the Coloured driver had jumped down and run off into the veld, his departure had been hastened with a few more shots! The gunman turned his attention to Plaistow. He was ordered to get out of the Cape cart and start walking along the sandy track that led in the direction of Filabusi. Although there was a fully loaded rifle in the Cape cart, Plaistow had no chance of reaching it while covered by the bandit. So he did as he had been ordered, expecting to feel the shock of a bullet tearing through his back at any moment. Once he heard the sound of a rifle bolt being opened and closed, but he kept on walking steadily until he felt he was out of rifle range. Then he began to run and walk as fast as he could until at last he reached the police camp which was all of seven miles from the scene of the hold-up. The unfortunate Plaistow never recovered from his ordeal, and died a few years later in a Bulawayo mental institution.

Back at Filabusi, Corporal Lawrence and one trooper were soon on their way to the place that Plaistow had described as being the scene of the hold-up that had unhinged him. There they found the Cape cart stuck in a dry spruit, the dead mule having securely anchored the rest of the team to their harness. A search revealed that all the gold bars had vanished but nothing else appeared to have been taken. Even the loaded rifle, securely tied to the side of a suitcase, was found at the scene.

There was no sign of the buggy's driver and it was only several days later that the terrified man arrived at the police camp. He had been hiding in the bush, without food or water, in the firm belief that the bandit was looking for him. He was certain that Plaistow had been shot and killed and that he was being hunted to destroy any remaining chance of the gunman being identified.

It was several more days before the driver was coherent enough to tell his story but when he did so it fully confirmed all that the mine secretary had said. The driver seemed to be almost as deranged as Plaistow had been and, by all accounts, was never quite the same man again.

The police had begun the formal investigation of the robbery immediately after Plaistow had made his report. Two important things had been noted. The first was that both the mine secretary and the driver had been sure that the bandit was European. The second was that Plaistow had noticed that the gunman had pronounced the word 'gold' as 'gould' and that he carried a Service rifle. These points were to have an important bearing both during the investigations and at the subsequent trial of the alleged criminal.

There were only a few Europeans living in the Filabusi area at that time and their movements were soon accounted for to the satisfaction of the police. So it appeared that the robber had come from outside. No strange white men had been seen in the district. The police were up against a dead end when a break came their way.

There was a small post office attached to the Filabusi camp, run by one of the police, a Trooper Page. At the time of the hold-up, he had been away in Bulawayo on official duties. He returned to Filabusi and, hearing the story of the robbery, at once told Corporal Lawrence that some time before the event one of the troopers stationed at Filabusi, an Irish-Australian named Joe Phelan, had asked him how he would like a holiday at the coast. Page had replied that on his salary such a thing was impossible. Phelan then came out with a startling suggestion. Page had regarded it as a joke at the time, coming as it did from a policeman who enjoyed the confidence of his superiors and had a very good record of service.

Phelan had asked Page to tell him when the next consignment of gold was to be sent from the Killarney Mine to Balla Balla and he, Phelan, would hold up the Cape cart and steal the gold. Phelan said he could easily dispose of the bullion through a friend who owned a small mine in the district. Page was promised three hundred pounds for this information, which was only known to the postmaster and the officials. Not being officially concerned in the transportation of gold, unless requested to provide an escort, the police would not know when the next transfer was to take place.

Page had laughingly refused the invitation, thinking that it was one of the Irish-Australian's well-known leg-pulls, but the incident now took on a more serious aspect. Trooper Phelan was away on leave, having been granted a few days to go shooting at a favourite spot called Whitestone Kopjes. Corporal Lawrence at once sent a native messenger to him ordering him to return at once to help in the investigation of a very important case, thereby lulling any fears that the trooper might have that his recall was due to being suspect in the hold-up.

As soon as Phelan arrived back in camp he was called into the charge office and closely questioned by Corporal Lawrence. The latter quickly noticed that Phelan pronounced 'gold' as 'gould'. This, Lawrence considered, was sufficient to arrest Phelan and charge him with the robbery. In spite of vigorous protests, Trooper Phelan was placed in one of the cells attached to the camp and a new line of investigation was started.

It had been noticed that there were tracks of booted feet leading from the scene of the hold-up in the direction of a small mine owned by a man named Jack Friend, who was a great pal of Phelan's and with whom he often stayed when on occasional leave. These tracks had been followed but had disappeared among some stones not far from the mine mill.

The police now visited the mine and made a thorough search, without finding any trace of the gold. Jack Friend was then called into his office and questioned. Not all of his answers were satisfactory, however, and Corporal Lawrence decided to arrest him on suspicion.

Phelan and Friend were placed in the same cell and a trooper was put into the cell next to them with instructions to listen very carefully to their conversation, which could easily be heard through the corrugated iron partition.

Phelan was far too experienced in the ways of the police to be caught out in such a simple manner, and all that the trooper heard was exactly what Phelan would do to certain people as soon as he was set free, as he was certain he would be in due course.

Corporal Lawrence had extracted one bullet from the carcass of the dead mule, and this he compared with bullets fired from Phelan's service rifle. All had the same distinctive markings on them, and a piece of black cloth was found in his trunk from which a portion had been cut off, sufficient to have made a mask. This cloth was found to have been purchased by Phelan from the local store, and when measured did not tally with the amount sold to him. The actual mask worn by the robber was never found, so an important piece of evidence was lost to the prosecution.

A small piece of 'sponge' gold had been picked up by the police when following the tracks of the booted feet, and the place had been marked, close to a wild creeper. A large number of natives were now called in from the kraals and an intensive search of the whole country surrounding the scene of the crime was begun.

One native noticed that the ground on which the wild creeper grew had been disturbed recently, and on digging down only a few inches below the surface one bar of gold was recovered.

Later on, another bar was found buried not far from the first. The remaining bars of gold were never recovered, however, although there was a rumour that they were circulating among the small mines in the Belingwe district some years later, but that the mine owners were afraid to buy them. This story was not confirmed, and their fate is still a mystery.

There was no plaster of paris available with which to make a cast of the boot tracks, but it was found that Phelan's police boots exactly fitted the impressions, and with all this evidence, admittedly circumstantial, it was decided to put Trooper Phelan on trial.

The first trial took place at Bulawayo before the High Court of Southern Rhodesia. The jury could not agree upon a verdict, so another trial was ordered. At the second trial, the same evidence was led, with Trooper Page telling his story and the Coloured driver giving his version of the hold-up. The mine secretary was unable to give evidence owing to his mental state, of course. The defence was a complete denial of the crime, and several natives were called who swore that Phelan had been in their company out shooting at the time of the hold-up and that he had shot a small buck many miles away about the time the robbery was committed.

This time the jury agreed, and Trooper Joe Phelan was found 'not guilty' and acquitted – a free man. Leaving the High Court after the trial, Phelan encountered Trooper Page near the entrance, and without a moment's hesitation, proceeded to give the smaller man an unmerciful thrashing before being again arrested by Corporal Lawrence, who had witnessed the attack.

Charged before the Magistrate with assault, Phelan was found guilty and fined. The Commissioner of Police took advantage of this conviction to discharge Phelan from the Corps, and he found employment as 'chucker-out' in a bar in Bulawayo, where he was looked upon as something of a hero by its hard-case patrons.

He did not stay long in this position, however, but was soon wandering from place to place in Rhodesia doing one thing after another, but not keeping his employment long after his reputation became known. Then, one day, he again fell foul of the law and a warrant for his arrest was issued. The trooper sent to bring Phelan into camp had been a friend as well as a comrade and, strangely enough, Phelan made no resistance at arrest. He even allowed handcuffs to be placed on his wrists without protest and, mounting his own mule, rode off beside the trooper towards camp.

The two men chatted in a friendly manner as they rode along until Phelan asked for the handcuffs to be removed after complaining that they were hurting him. At first the trooper refused to do this but when Phelan chided him on his lack of friendship for an old comrade, the foolish policeman agreed to take them off until they were within sight of camp. As the handcuffs were being removed, Phelan managed to snatch the trooper's revolver from its holster and, thrusting it into the policeman's stomach, threatened to pull the trigger if he so much as made the slightest move. Then, putting the cuffs on to the trooper's wrists and pocketing the key, Phelan mounted his own mule and, driving the policeman's animal before him, disappeared in the distance, bidding the unfortunate trooper an ironical farewell and wishing him joy at the unpleasant interview with his superior which would follow when he returned to camp alone.

Several years passed before Phelan was again heard of in the Caprivi Zipfel, a no-man's-land which before World War I was unclaimed by any country, had no administration and no police. At that time in the Caprivi Strip, as it is better known, there were several Europeans of doubtful character living safe from the law. Phelan joined forces with one of these men, Ben Johnstone. Not far from their camp lived Moodey, a reputed killer. Further on there was a Greek known simply as 'Billy the Greek' who ran a store of sorts and imported liquor which was much in demand by the outlaws.

Phelan, Ben Johnstone, Moodey and 'Billy the Greek' were drinking one night at Johnstone's place when a quarrel arose. Moodey shot Phelan, killing him instantly. Then Moodey disappeared, although there were rumours that he had merely gone to another country. Only Ben Johnstone and the Greek were left to keep each other company, but they had never been on the best of terms.

Drinking together one night at the Greek's store, another quarrel arose, and without warning Johnstone picked up his rifle and shot the Greek dead. Thus was enacted the final chapter of this tragedy.

Among the many short stories written by Mr Napier in retirement in Durban, this previously unpublished tale of the infamous gold robber, Trooper Joe Phelan, is one of several versions of the scandal, none of which explain satisfactorily how Phelan escaped the consequences of his crime.

KILLICK'S TALE

Robert Arthur Killick
Trooper (2385)
British South Africa Police

Sometime ago I was asked 'What did the Old Hands do for entertainment and to pass the time when they came to Town in the early days? You as a policeman must have known and had contact with many of them.' Indeed I did and have fond memories of many of them whom I met officially and otherwise over the years of service in Bulawayo.

There were two 'Bioscopes' in the Town but few of the Old Hands were interested in the 'Flicks'. They much preferred to go on a 'Pub Crawl' and meet old pals, talk of successes and failures in the prospecting fields, get news of old comrades not seen in recent years. Not infrequently they would meet up with old friends, members of the Force who were also on a 'pass time' tour of the bars, there were thirteen of them within a quarter of mile radius from the Town Station Charge Office.

Without doubt, the most popular meeting place was the Market Square on a Saturday morning when they could always find a pal for the weekend (or a week, according to how long his money would last). A number of hotels surrounding the Square (to be named later) had a row of rooms which, though not elaborate, suited the needs of the occupants who, in any case, did not spend much time in them, but as residents they could drink and entertain their guests on a Sunday. This was a difficult day on which to obtain a beer or a 'tot' unless one was a registered guest at the Hotel, or a 'bona fide traveller' having travelled at least 20 miles from the place at which one had spent the previous night.

Having worked up a thirst on the patrol of the various auctioneers stands on the square, the favourite spot from which to start the 'crawl' was the nearby Tattersals Hotel, the site of the present Selbourne Hotel. The row of rooms at the back were popular with the Old Hands as also was Mrs Humphries, the licensee. In those days the signing of cards for drinks 'on tick' was legal. I am afraid that when the estate of Mrs Humphries was wound up, one of the most valuable assets (on paper) for sale was 'unredeemed Bar Cards' which I subsequently heard was bought by an optimist for a few pounds. I wonder if he ever got his money back? From 'Tatts' the next call was the Market Bar, about 90 yards away (on the site of the present City Hall) next to Bridgemans & Hasletts sale rooms, taken over in 1921 by the popular Knight brothers. At their stand on Saturday mornings, the Old Hands would gather the latest news from 'Cocky' Standing or renew acquaintance with Mrs 'Baby' Edwards, whose house opposite the old Masonic Hotel, with her young ladies, was, in the old days, a haven of rest!!

The next stop was the Palmerston Hotel (later the Central and finally Le Chateau, pulled down in 1970) this was a stroll of about 80 yards from the Market Bar. This was one of the elite Hotels in the town where ladies could accompany their 'gentlemen friends' in the Saloon Bar lounge. Next on to the Savoy Hotel (about 100 yards) across the Square to Fife Street, now a row of shops opposite the Pioneers well, which was sunk during the Matabeleland Rebellion in 1896, when the Laager was established on the Square. Previously on this site was the Maxim Hotel where Dr Jameson made his famous speech on the 1st June, 1894, when declaring Bulawayo a Township. He said, in full: 'It is my object to declare the Town open. I don't think we want to talk about it. I make the declaration now. There is plenty of whiskey inside. Come in'.

The next move was around the corner to Abercorn Street, to the Avenue Hotel (now the Avenue Chemist ?). The last licensee was Mr Sid Dennett, (ex Cpl. No. 1116) who became a hotel keeper on discharge having served as Mess Sergeant in the Officer's Mess at Bulawayo Camp on return from service with the B.S.A. Police Column in the Boer War. He was a 'buddy' of Cpl. 'Hacker' Matthews, one time i/c Troops Mess in the same Camp. He later became owner and licensee of the Willsgrove Hotel on the old Essexvale Road, famous for its moonlight picnics and bathing parties. They were not too fussy about bathing costumes in those days! The next call, on the far corner of the same block, in Main Street, was the Empire Bar (now Southampton House), which was run in conjunction with the Empire Theatre, and in polite circles referred to as the 'Sods Opera' or the 'Bug Hut'. Sometimes used for visiting theatre shows or Boxing Contests. It was here that ex.Sgt. 'Pat' Kealy and Piet Steyn fought their 15 round contest, which ended in a draw. 'Pat' afterwards became well-known as a Boxing

Instructor at Bulawayo and Umtali schools, whilst still a member of the Force.

One night when making my 'point' at the Bar corner, a crowd milled out and crossed the street to the vacant stand on which the Mutual Buildings and Princes Theatre were later built. On enquiry, I ascertained that after an argument in the Bar over horse racing that afternoon, a well-known local character, a 'Brickie' called 'the Irish Giant' (Fitzgerald), he stood about 5 ft. 2 ins, was going to fight it out with Sgt. Major Looby, a member of the Drill Hall staff, i/c Stables.

The crowd, shouting their support for their respective favourite formed a ring. At this time my Section Sgt. (Joe Daly) arrived to pay me a visit on Beat. The natural question, 'What's going on here?' I reported the information gained, and asked what action we should take. He replied, 'You get on with your Beat, it's on private property.' So I missed the contest. I heard later it was a good scrap. I have an idea that Joe, an Irishman, favoured his countryman, 'The Giant.' Joe on retirement later became the Usher at High Court in Agency Chambers, burnt down a few years ago. One of the events, talked of for many years which originated at the Empire Bar, was Rhodesia's one and only 'Tar and Feather' case, when a well-known local character 'Monkey Nut' Jones was the victim.

Following a 'Master and Servants' case at Court in which the complainant was his wife and in which Jones gave evidence for the defence, 'Jimmy' Hooper, the Licensee and his wife Violet, gave vent to their feelings in the crowded bar. They say 'Vi loaded the gun and Jimmy fired it.' The result, the male clients in the Bar streamed out to look for Jones. They found him and tar and feathers were produced. Riotous behaviour – and Jones' complaint of Assault – resulted in a Court case (Details published in the *Chronicle*). The male accused was fined; the case against Vi was withdrawn 'owing to her condition!' A subscription list from sympathizers settled the payment of fines. Now back to the 'Pub crawl'. The next call was at the opposite corner in Main Street, then known as the Grand Hotel 'Corner Bar'. Here Bulawayo's most well-known barmaid, 'Greasy Kate', was respectfully greeted by the Old Hands. It was known far and wide that the prospectors and miners could come into Town and hand over their cash to Kate who would dole it out each day, as required. Until the request, 'Let me know when I am down to the last couple of pounds,' was complied with. They all swore by the honesty of Kate and so will those who still remember her. The arrangement was popular and necessary for it was not uncommon for one of the Old Hands to recover, after a session, on a vacant plot (of which there were many around Town) to find his pockets empty, with a vague memory of a rickshaw ride.

After a cheery 'So long' to Kate the next stop would be at the Charter Bar, on the Rhodes Statue corner in Main Street. For many years after known as George Cummings (shop) corner. Here in the old days, the Band Stand was erected on special occasions, in the centre of the street. The S.R.V. Band played there, for some years, on Public Holidays and Sundays. It was also the centre for revelling crowds on Christmas Eve when the Town centre was closed to traffic and the shops remained open until 10 p.m. The last occasion which I remember the Band Stand was used was for the public reception of Prince Arthur of Connaught, in 1921, when the escort was mounted on greys, a special tribute to the Prince who was an ex Officer of the Royal Scots Greys. A proud day for R.S.M. Jock Douglas, also an ex member of the Greys, when he was presented as such to the Prince in Salisbury. The Charter Bar was the nearest to the Police Camp and was popular with members. Amongst them in their time was ex Sgt. Major George Salt (of Wankie fame) and ex Farrier Cpl. 'Snitch' Hutchings, alias 'The Duke of Bermonsey'. George, now in his nineties is living in Sussex, but 'Snitch' his buddy up to the last War, has had his last 'Roll call'. 'Hops' Freeborn, now on a visit to U.K. hopes to look up George. He remembers George and 'Snitch' as members of the Home Guard on the outbreak of War when 'Hops' attested in M.I.S. Special Police. He tells of how George and Snitch when meeting on sentry duty on London Bridge, used to greet each other, 'All correct, Private Hutchings?' to which Snitch replied, 'Yes, all correct Private Salt'.

On we go again. The next call being at the Bodega Bar (now Cement House) on the corner of the same block. Not much time was spent in walking. This corner will be remembered by old residents as the strong hold of 'Daddy' Williams who used to guard the footpath from trespassers with his vintage walking stick. He fought the repeal of the Bye law, which barred natives from the Town pavements, to the bitter end. Actually, he was the cause of much amusement to the African population. One did not need to be very agile to dodge the swing of the old chap's stick and most knowing natives were ready for it or gave the corner a wide berth. Some would, however, stand by and watch some poor unsuspecting country cousin get 'clobbered'. Fortunately not severely. The Police and Native Commissioner were pleased when 'Daddy' through old age (in his 80s) and infirmity went off this beat.

The next move would be across the road, about 60 yards, to the Exchange Bar, still in existence. Mentioned a couple of times in your Sixtieth Anniversary Issue, in the *Police Review*, 1911, as 'the leading Bar in Bulawayo under the management of 'Jock Thompson, ex B.S.A.P.' Always on their best behaviour here, as it was often frequented by the Magistrate's Court Staff (Court close by). Here, on Racing week-ends, the Troops collected 'the tips' from Mr 'Jonah' White, the Court Interpreter (Owner/Trainer), and Sub. Inspector 'Jimmy' Skillen, the Public Prosecutor. They were seldom losers! Away again to the Comrades Club Bar just across the road, next to Mrs Shackleton's boarding house which still stands, one of the oldest buildings in Bulawayo. The Club stand was taken over by the B.E.S.L., now the Rhodesian Legion. After the Great War it was probably the most popular bar in Town. Headquarters of the 'Comrades of the Great War', there was always someone in the party who had the necessary membership. Many of the Old Hands were Boer War veterans, and I think 90% of the Force members were ex-servicemen. Roy de Bude, ex B.S.A.P. was the Club Manager. This was often a lengthy halt because the bar snacks supplied were exceptionally good and gave one the opportunity of 'stocking up' on some solid refreshment before continuing on the town.

The next walk took them to the Masonic Hotel in Rhodes Street, two blocks from the Club, now the Royal Hotel. On the opposite corner is the Fennela Redrup Hostel for young ladies. This was built on the site of Mrs 'Baby' Edwards' house previously mentioned. On her death she willed the property and money to Mrs Redrup and expressed the wish that a house for working girls would be built. Mrs Redrup was well-known to the Old Hands being a Pioneer Nursing Sister.

Her husband, Sidney Redrup, presented the first fire engines to the Municipality when he was the Mayor. The members of the Town Police became the Fire Brigade. Those in single quarters next to the Fire Station, were paid £2 a month, and what a blessing it was. Also another reason for remaining single when one had completed the qualifying period of service, ten years, before permission to marry could be claimed.

Back to the tour. The next stop was at the Park Hotel, 150 yards away in Grey Street (now Grey's Inn) opposite to which were the vacant stands where the Circus Tent and travelling 'Feast Shows' were pitched. One time licensee was ex Insp. Jack Bartter and in his day it was popular with the Troops. From here is was back to 'Tatts', 200 yards away, which completed the tour, where they would probably have a final yarn in a pal's bedroom. Not everyone's 'cup of tea', but it was one way for the Old Hands to spend their break from the bundu and to meet old pals. With beer at 6d and 9d a bottle, 'Dop' (Brandy) at 9d a tot, the cost of living was not high. The hard cases (drinkers) would today strongly object to the 'Tot measures' used in the bars. In those days the Barmaid (or man) passed the bottle and you helped yourself. Normally the tots got smaller as the evening went by.

Later as a Charge Office Sergeant, I knew most of the Old Hands by their Christian names or more often by their 'nicknames' and when, in the morning after a cup of tea, they were usually released on £2 Bail (which was invariably extracted in Drunk cases) they went their way after asking 'where did you pick me up?' There were no hard feelings. It was back to the mine or bundu, until the next visit to Town.

Contribution to *The Outpost* in May 1974 by a prominent Bulawayo ex-member but apparently never published.

POLES' TALE

William Eustace Poles
Trooper (2501)
British South Africa Police

The letter following was written by Bill Poles to Walter Hughes Halls (939).

January 1975

Dear Teddy,

I have very recently heard from our mutual friend George Style who tells me you are a bit 'under the weather'. He thinks it a good idea for me to write and cheer you up. I don't think I am particularly good at cheering anyone up from this distance. I'm sure a dissertation on the mad charade of our present Government, could only be depressing so I won't attempt it but leave you to enjoy your earlier memories of better days when traitors were (?), which certainly is not the case today. I dare say I might succeed in some measure were it possible to place a large scotch in your hand and let our thoughts wander along the pleasant paths of youthful days when we polished our buttons and strutted like fighting cocks.

Thinking such thoughts I wondered perhaps you might be amused with a story of a somewhat unconventional patrol.

An Unconventional Patrol

At the time – 1926 – I was stationed at Mount Darwin, having been transferred from Mazoe where I was sent after serving under you in 'B' Section (Salisbury Section). The happiest days of my 17 years service were the all too few years spent at Mount Darwin, first as a trooper under Cpl. 'Sandy' Fraser and, after a longish period in the civilised wilderness, again as N.C.O. i/c. However it is of my trooper days that I shall refer (I enjoyed more freedom and less responsibility). Sandy Fraser was my 'cross'. I suppose I must have been handy in the office for it was always a battle, not always successful, persuading him to send me on extended patrols into the district native reserves.

Wilfred Whittaker Cooper was my fellow trooper, an ex-public school boy who spent his earlier years as a 'Jackaroo' in South Australia. Perhaps it was the grinding routine of his recent past which made him so reluctant to sit in a saddle. I am sure no one took greater care of his horse nor did anyone ride him. He would leave camp on foot, his personal servant leading his grey horse – saddled and bridled of course and maybe a month later he would return, still on foot, and his boy still leading the horse. His dedication to physical fitness amounted to near mania. He systematically rationed himself to two tots of brandy each evening. Everyone, including the officers – most of which were martinets – were very tolerant towards Cooper. He died in the Seychelles very shortly after his retirement. I believe you once had him under command in B Troop and will perhaps recall to mind his closely trimmed moustache and dapper little form.

Mount Darwin! What adventure and sport I enjoyed there and what good life-long friends I made. If, as Mary Tudor pronounced, the name Calais would be found engraved upon her heart when she died, I likewise might maintain that Mount Darwin is engraved on mine. But I will do better than the queen, for another engraving will be entwined with it, 'Luangwe Valley' in which, for ten years prior to its spoliation, I roamed and reigned as king. Such wonderful and simple privileges seemingly have disappeared forever.

In my story, excluding myself, there were three principal characters of whom being by far the most important was a rogue bull elephant whose name I mis-remember (every notorious elephant is given a name by the indigenous Africans in whose territory he operates). This one might be said to own the natives' gardens along that part of the Rhodesia/Portuguese border in the vicinity of the river; he was responsible for prematurely sending several villagers to the spirit world with the result that he was black listed. Next, equal in importance, was D.M. Powley, Native Commissioner and 'Poo Bah' of the district. His files held the authority to eliminate the elephant. He had a brother-in-law who at the time managed the Shamva Mine, of whom more anon. The third personality was Native Constable Chaparisa.

A real 'jungle' African who, whenever possible, I arranged with 'Sandy' to be allowed to accompany me on my patrols. I feel sure we recognised in each other a dedicated hunter and so were drawn together through mutual respect. Even at that time, now so long ago, he was elderly, his hair was very grey and he was accepted everywhere as an elder. He was a good policeman

(I have a photograph of him with 36 prisoners, which on one of my patrols in the 'Dande', over several weeks, he shepherded to camp all safe and sound). Fingerprints confirmed that several were badly wanted for serious crime – and that with only two pairs of handcuffs; his and mine! Indeed, were not those times the days of our Empire's glory when the lone policeman represented the tip of the point of the spear? 'Gone are those days which are no more'.

Well, by now you have no doubt guessed the 'object of the exercise' as the military boys would have it.

Of course my ambition was to shoot this elephant and Chaparisa and I had given the matter a good deal of thought. In time it became such an obsession that I believe, given the opportunity, I would have shot it and got out of it afterwards as best I could, bearing in mind that much is possible on the border.

However it seemed both sensible and logical to do the thing legally and with this pious intention in view I approached Powley. I explained my intention and requested his authority to kill the elephant – he hummed and hawed a bit but realising perhaps that I was aware he held the elephant's death warrant, he gave his approval. I did not realise at the time that he had already earmarked the elephant for his brother-in-law who rather fancied himself as a bit of a nimrod (?) and had an eye to the nice parcel of ivory.

Chaparisa and I carried out several patrols into the Rukore but on each occasion we appeared to have narrowly missed the elephant's visits in border gardens. Finally, prior to yet another patrol into the area, Chaparisa and I held a council of war. Chaparisa was far more astute than I. He explained that directly Powley became aware that I was about to set out en route to the Rukore than he despatched a 'messenger' on a bicycle to get ahead of me, find out where the elephant was raiding and organise the local villagers to drive it out so that we shouldn't find it.

Chaparisa suggested that I should indicate to the Native Commissioner that we were bound for the Dande – part of the Zambezi Valley lying to the north westward of the Mvuradona escarpment and in a completely opposite direction to the Rukore. This I succeeded in doing in an ambiguous manner little short of a lie. To have perpetrated a downright falsehood would very likely have resulted in Powley doing likewise and denying having given verbal permission to slay the elephant.

Next morning off we went, taking a more or less westerly course towards Chitsi hill and spending the night at Chifumiras kraal. Long before dawn next morning we rose quietly and without alerting anyone in the village, doubled back eastward keeping to the unpopulated area which then existed along the southern foothills of the Mvuradona range.

We felt confident that the bush telegraph would confirm that Magocha and his 'black watch', were on the path towards the lowveld. I hoped my horse and pack donkeys wouldn't be mentioned because the Native Commissioner would hardly credit me mad enough to take riding and pack animals into tsetse country.

We travelled at our best pace with the minimum of rest and finally turned south into the Rukore travelling down the left bank of the Ruia river to Mukosa's kraal. The chief was a very old emaciated African, yet he exercised considerable authority. It appeared that our deception was so far successful; no native messengers had visited Mukosa's country for some weeks. I explained that I had come to destroy the marauding elephant and desired Mukosa to send word to all villages in the neighbourhood to despatch reconnaissance parties to locate the elephant's whereabouts.

I had already lion, rhino and buffalo, in addition to many of the larger antelope, to my credit and had established the reputation of a successful hunter, so there was no doubt in the natives' minds that Magocha membgue was up to the job. All local herdsmen set about looking for signs of the elephant with considerable enthusiasm.

The days passed and village after village reported no recent sign of the elephant; on the contrary, the most recent tracks were several days old and indicated that the old bull had trekked over the border into Portuguese territory. This disappointment, in the face of all the efforts we had undertaken, goaded me to desperation. I decided I would cross into Portuguese country and follow up the old spoor but realised that if I was to avoid a catastrophic termination of my career, the foray must needs be brief.

At my suggestion Mukosa sent to the neighbouring village instructing their herdsmen to bring in their heaviest axes. That evening a great concourse pitched up at the Chief's kraal and dozens of axes were laid out close to a bright fire at the 'dare' (council place) alongside a huge baobab. Beer had been brewed and all were in a merry mood. That was close on 50 years ago, yet today the scene remains clearly etched on my memory. I see the semi-circle of elders, their backs to the great tree, huge, majestic, its bark so suggestive of an elephant's hide but now silvery in the illumination of the flames and ebony where the shadows fell. So are the forms of the men, seemingly roughly sculpted by the play of light on the prevailing darkness. Mukosa, wearing the Charter Company's insignia of a Chief – a half moon shaped plaque of brass on which is depicted a lion grasping a perpendicular ivory tusk in its paw – reclines somewhat apart, on his side, his knees half drawn up towards his belly, his head supported in his left hand; on the edge of the firelight the people form a wide semicircle, the women apart from the men, the unmarried girls naked to the waist, their hair arranged in a variety of coiffures, ornaments in their pierced ears and lower lips.

Mukosa asks indirectly, through the medium of his senior elder, what do I intend to do with the axes? Without immediately replying, Chaparisa and I cross to where the axes are displayed and choose half a dozen having the heaviest blades and place them to one side. I then say 'Inform Mukosa that I intend to take these to cut out the tusks.' 'But it is said there is no elephant,' replies the elder.

Chaparisa then takes the axes away to my camp while their owners claim the remainder and the space is cleared for dancing. A young girl carries a small pot of beer to Mukosa, dropping to her knees and holding it towards him, lowering her head in deference. He touches it but remains silent. The girl rises, crosses the dare, again drops to her knees before me and in both hands proffers the pot. The drums have been throbbing away for some little while but suddenly they stop and for a moment all sound is hushed – the quietness breaks with several very loud drum beats which is the signal for all the drummers to play their part. Into the open space contained between the fire, the drummers and the baobab, steps the senior elder. He is old, hair iron grey, his face, strong and straight looking, is etched with heavy lines. He wears skins around his loins and ankles and wrists are bangled with massive ivory rings. Shuffling to the centre of the stage he faces me and, accompanied by the drums, commences to dance. It is the elephant dance which I had not hitherto seen and was never to see again. All the actions of the rogue elephant are mimed – his gestures and majestic movements: his raiding of crops, his overturning of grain bins and his ferocious anger and method of dealing death. How impressive it was, how descriptive and how well it was done. I have been greatly privileged.

Next day, August 7th, my party left the village shortly before dawn leaving my cook-cum-personal servant in charge of the horse and donkeys. My personal picannin carried the teapot and a bag containing tea, sugar, salt, mealie meal and biltong. Beside N./C. Chaparisa, my friend and right hand man, there were two experienced local African hunters together with another local to carry a pot and sufficient meal for his fellow Africans. Chaparisa was armed with a S.M.L.E. rifle (usually the 'black watch' of this period were armed with single shot .450 Martini Henry rifles firing a soft lead bullet propelled by black powder in a rolled brass case). I can't remember how I had succeeded in wangling a .303. As regard myself, I carried a Westley Richards .318 express – an accelerated express, I remember it called itself. It was a lovely rifle which I bought from Fereday in Manica Road in 1924. I believe it cost about £35 – a small fortune to a chap earning $13.16.2 a month which was a trooper's princely salary in those days. I might add that I had no income other than my pay. The weapon was single breech, Mauser action, magazine rifle, the best I could afford.

Well, away we went, visiting villagers' winter gardens strung along the winding riverine strip; oases of lush greenery in striking contrast to the surrounding desiccation.

We had not gone far – I remember the sun had not risen much above the eastern hills – when the leading hunter stopped and with his spear indicated the fresh footprint of an elephant. To my inexperienced eye it seemed immense – Chaparisa and the two hunters agreed that the elephant was an adult bull – they thought a big one – and agreed that it had passed at daybreak. We took up the spoor which at first was easy to follow and soon occasional piles of dung confirmed the animal's recent presence. It soon became evident that the elephant was alone and that it was on trek. Presently the last of the cultivations fell behind and we entered arid stony country, where tracking became more difficult and our progress correspondingly slower. On and on we went, our distance from the river increasing as time passed. I am unsure whether or not we crossed the Rhodesia /P.E.A. border but I confess to having felt some nervous twinges.

The wind was light and at first towards us but, as the heat increased in the broken hill country intersected by deep gullies, it blew fitfully, frequently changing its direction. It wasn't long before the spoor showed signs of the elephant's nervousness. He altered his course and made towards the Ruia which was reached early in the afternoon.

Hereabouts, even in the middle of the dry season, the river is fairly wide and, in places, deep. Unaware as to which way the elephant would turn on reaching the opposite bank, it was decided to follow him across. This presented a problem because, about halfway across, the main current poured between two groups of large rocks about 15 feet apart. And we soon discovered it was pretty deep. Chaparisa, the two hunters, the carrier and I formed a chain, our arms interlocked. The picannin, carrying the various bags containing our food and cooking gear and the rifles, made several crossings, his weight submerging in turn, each link of our human chain. I remember feeling distinctly queasy in the realisation that the river swarmed with crocodiles.

We were now in either Mrewa or Mtoko district and I realised I was getting very involved, though the risk of being found out seemed small and therefore acceptable. In any case no one gave a thought to giving up.

On reaching the other side we found the elephant had turned down wind, following the right bank of the river down stream. This, of course, was hazardous towards success and our spirits dipped. This action of the elephant was deliberate, intended to pick up our wind should we still be following and might have proved disastrous but for the long delay necessitated by our difficulty in crossing the river. In about half a mile the elephant turned away from the river and in a little while turned again into the wind and more or less parallel to the course of the river.

The afternoon was wearing on – so far the elephant had not stopped but now it was pausing from time to time to feed and signs indicated that we were catching up on him. The country through which he led us was dreadful; 'jesse bush' growing out of loose stony ground. The stuff was a jungle of dense giant pea sticks intermingled with particularly vicious thorn scrub. There were narrow game paths everywhere but whereas the growth yielded to the heavier animals and the smaller ones, such as bushbuck, crept beneath, their stems intruding across the paths made human progress difficult. We pushed ahead as quietly as possible and excitement mounted for all the signs showed we were now very close

Suddenly, not very far ahead, there was a loud swishing sound; something large and immensely powerful thrusting the bush aside. Being highly keyed up and desperate, having no first hand experience of the behaviour of elephants, I came to the conclusion, very mistakenly as it turned out, that our quarry had taken flight and was 'on his bicycle'. The bush immediately ahead had thinned out and I hurried forward, Chaparisa close behind. Just as we approached the edge of more dense thicket, the vegetation seemed suddenly to open and the great grey bulk of an elephant materialised, not in flight but bearing down like a ship under full sail. His trunk was curled under his chin and he let out a scream which cut the eardrums like a sword. I cannot recollect how close to us he was after this lapse of time but certainly much closer than I had bargained for, nor had I foreseen that the engagement would be end on, and the sharp end at that. I fired into its head, aligning the foresight on the place where the upper part of the trunk met the lower ridge of the frontal bone. The elephant was turning as N/C Chaparisa fired his .303. I noticed a puff of dust appear about a foot below its left eye which I feared (correctly as it turned out) had damaged the base of the tusk. I told him to fire into the chest of the elephant should it turn on us again.

The bush was too thick to enable us to move out to a flank for a broadside shot so we were obliged to follow. Twice more it turned with the idea of charging us but each time we turned him and continued after him, running close behind. It is said with truth that the Almighty looks after drunks and madmen and obviously he was on our side that day. As I may have stated already, this was my first experience with elephant. Subsequently, many years later, as a game ranger, I killed a great number of elephants in the line of duty and learnt to treat them with the greatest respect – in fact the elephants taught me to do so. Looking back over all those years I realise, in the light of later experience, the enormous risks I then so lightly undertook. It's extraordinary what the combination of youth and enthusiasm gets away with.

After some time we came into slightly more open thorn scrub which enabled me to run alongside the elephant. I was about 20 feet from it when it stopped. I killed it with a heart shot.

Although our small party set out alone and local information discounted the presence of elephant in the neighbourhood, the elephant was hardly on its side than Africans started to arrive and by nightfall there must have been well over a hundred. It was too late to start cutting up so we camped down where we were. We had no blankets. The night was typical of the season – chilly; the vault of the sky hung with stars whose brilliance diminished with the advent of a full moon.

What with the cold and the excitement, I slept fitfully. The moonlight and the flickering light of dozens of campfires provided an eerie illumination for the dead raider whose uppermost tusk gleamed whitely in contrast to the deepening shadows.

The following day was spent in an orgy of blood and gore. Those cutting out the flesh, frequently kneeling within the ribcage, were unrecognisable under an overall congealed cloak of blood and filth. Women, staggering under baskets containing enormous weights of meat and youths with loads scarcely less burdensome and tiny children clasping scraps, dispersed in various directions towards villages like streams of ants.

There was a great feast in Mukosa's Kraal that night. I was asked by the chief to name a price for my 'medicine'. It was explained that it was obvious I had a charm which enabled me to force success and to direct my quarry within gunshot. On asking the chief to explain why he considered me so gifted he replied: 'You chose axes to cut out the tusks, why should you do that if you did not know you would need them? Furthermore only medicine could be capable to materialising the elephant where there was no elephant.' I would have been foolish to make a denial and fraudulent had I attempted to capitalise on this superstitious belief.

Our journey homeward through the river villages became a triumphal procession – every man, woman and child turning out to see the tusks and forefoot of an animal all had learnt to fear. Incidentally this foot with a hinged leather seat now stands in front of my wife's dressing table. The tusks 52 and 48 lbs hung on a wall in my parents' house in Surrey for several years before I sold them.

On returning to Mount Darwin I did not receive a 'conquering hero' reception from Sandy Fraser. I had brought in sufficient cases to keep him busy in court for a day or two and in general my patrol report showed that I could not be fairly accused of wasting time on a hunting trip. All the same, Sandy was obviously worried and initiated defensive action in case any trouble I might get into could rub off on him.

Fortunately D.M. Powley confirmed my authority to kill the elephant though I had the impression he did so reluctantly. The authority was operative only in the Mount Darwin district while the elephant had departed this life in the Mrewa district; the Ruia river forming the mutual boundary of the two districts. N./C. Chaparisa and I finally solved this rather tricky problem and in due course Sandy Fraser received a detailed report which it was hoped would take care of the matter.

Sometime later a bolt from the blue descended in the form of a minute from the District Superintendent. It covered a complaint from a headman in the Mrewa district who alleged that a trooper from Mount Darwin had entered his tribal area and shot an elephant. 'Trooper Poles to submit a full report, etc. etc.' Concluding his letter the D.S.P. informed the N.C.O. i/c, Mount Darwin, that he was proceeding to Mrewa in the near future and would himself open an investigation. When, rather shaken by this heavy cloud on my horizon, I confided to N./C. Chaparisa the dangerous complications he advised me not to worry. 'Inkos,' he said, 'do you suppose that the Inkos, Capt. Phillips, with those shiny leggings and his beautiful clothes will ever go down into the jesse bush?' Apparently he didn't, for no more was heard of the matter.

An indispensable member of the Force. A B.S.A. Police Pack Mule on patrol in the pre-1920's days

Strangely there was a sequel to the incident. Several years later, after failing an appointment for a commission, Capt. Phillips, knowing my affection for my old station, sent me back to take charge at Mount Darwin. Shortly after I had taken over I went on patrol to the Rukose. An indaba was in progress at Mukosa's kraal at which was present the headman of the village across the river who had reported me with the intention of getting me into trouble. The reason he had done so was because he was dissatisfied with his share of the meat. As the elephant had fallen in his area he contended that by native custom all the meat on the side of the animal lying on the ground was his. This man had not seen me on the occasion of the hunt and therefore did not appreciate that it was I whom he had reported. He now complained that a herd of elephant had, for some years, taken up residence in the vicinity of his village and that their raiding had brought his people close to starvation. Dear old Chaparisa, who again was my companion, had tipped me off regarding the identity of the complaining headman. Being one of the hard, slow to forgive kind, I decided to hurt him a little through his superstitions. I reminded him that several years ago his jealousy and greed led him to make an accusation against a 'majoni' disregarding the fact that the majoni had rid the neighbourhood not only of a persistent garden raiding elephant but one which had killed several people including a member of his own village. I went on to explain that the spirits were angered and had sent a herd of elephants to punish him. This may sound childish but it would not be treated lightly by primitive rural Africans of that period. They would be sure that I had medicine which lent me occult powers. It could be possible that I had sent the elephants. The headman would now bear the responsibility for the people's misfortune. Only a 'nganga' could lift the curse and his fee would certainly not be small.

This, should you have followed me so far, is the end of a rather longwinded story of the adventurous days of long ago. If you disapprove of my conduct – which I freely admit is far from blameless, I think it only fair that you accept at least a minimal modicum of blame for, after all, yours was my first station. You my original instructor.

With every possible good wish for a happy Christmas and the future.

Stand to your horse. Prepare to mount!
Yours ever
Bill.

There is an epilogue to my story. During the war I met a fellow soldier named Giles whose father was a resident of Mount Darwin in my time and he, himself, then a schoolboy. Having introduced himself, he told me how fortuitous was our meeting because he had not thought of ever meeting me.

It appeared that several years previously he was travelling in the Mount Darwin district when he came to a village where he was directed to an old man who lay dying and who wished, urgently, to talk to a 'Musungu'. The old African was my friend, N./C. Chaparisa. He said, 'I want you to give a message to Magocha. Tell him that I am thinking of the days we shared together.'

Not previously published. The letter at the start of this tale was written by Bill Poles to the doyen of 'Old Comrades' Walter Hughes Halls (939) who appears in many stories of the B.S.A.P., in January 1975 when 'HH' was unwell (he died three years later). The correspondence had been encouraged by George Style (2696), one of the most prolific contributors to the magazine over several decades, and who drew attention Bill's 'elderly' service with the Chindits in WW2 Burma where he earned the Military Cross. Attempts by 'The Chronicler' to persuade Bill to write of his 'unconventional patrols' in Burma were unsuccessful.

MULLIN'S TALE

Dermott O'Carroll Mullin
Trooper (2744)
British South Africa Police

I joined the B.S.A. Police on January 1st, 1926, was given the Force Regimental Number 2744 and, after three months in Depot, was posted to Fort Victoria with three other recruits.

Our first assignment was the 1926 Census. I was allotted the Gutu South area where my last port of call was the Altteit (sic) Mission where the Reverend Olandini was in charge. I arrived at a scene of much excitement. A child had died a few minutes before having been bitten by a mamba. Olandini greeted me with great enthusiasm. Who better to destroy the snake than a policeman? The snake was waiting for me on an anthill about a quarter of a mile away.

Before reaching Rhodesia I had heard terrible tales of mambas. It could move faster than a racehorse; it could strike from as far away as ten or fifteen feet; its bite was deadly and escape was impossible once you were in its sights. I protested that my .303 rifle was hardly the weapon with which to challenge such a monster. To no avail. Olandini promptly produced a double-barrelled shotgun, handed it to me and clinched the matter. Escape was impossible. It was do or die so off I went.

I must have been about twenty yards from the anthill when the mamba reared some three or four feet from the ground, presenting an almost perfect target. I fired and did not miss. I walked back to the mission feeling much more confident than when I had set out. There was a noticeable improvement in the regard in which I was held by the Reverend Olandini and his congregation.

The census proceedings went off without a hitch and I returned to Fort Victoria. In July I was sent to Bikita to replace Trooper George Style who was required elsewhere. It was still the old Bikita camp consisting of separate brick-under-thatch huts with Corporal Busky Knight in charge. It was also still wild – leopard would come right on to the verandah at night after the chickens that roosted there. Busky was a great man for the poultry business and there must have been close on a hundred at any one time. At sixpence a time, they represented a useful augmentation of a policeman's salary.

Troopers Mullin (left) and Style with Native Constables at Bikita in 1929; N./C. Gondino is fourth from left.

The patrols from Bikita were almost continuous. The south patrol was the long one, taking a month to six weeks. The north patrol could be completed in a fortnight. As the role passed on to me by George was that of 'patrolling trooper', I saw very little of the local court proceedings – indictments, prosecuting and so forth. But in 1927 illness took Knight off to Salisbury and I was told to carry on alone despite my lack of knowledge of legal procedures. With the assistance of Mr Watters, Bikita's Native Commissioner and Magistrate, I managed to get into the hang of things and, after a couple of months, was confident enough to venture out into a Public Violence and/or Man Stealing case – and won a conviction. But the successful verdict only started another row in which an American missionary from Chipinge was the complainant.

I had sent one of the Black Watch out on the case to arrest the two suspects. The constable was a big, rather vicious-looking (or intimidating) African named Katokwe who was alleged to have man-handled both accused when arresting them. This was in the Sabi Valley where the two accused lived. I had little doubt that Katokwe had in fact been heavy-handed. He was quite capable of dishing out such treatment and might even have taken some pleasure in so doing. However, Katokwe had played a vital part in a successful prosecution (there was no doubt about the guilt of the accused) and had to be protected if possible.

By the time the police docket arrived at Bikita, it was about half-an-inch thick and seemed to have been all around the country, giving everyone a chance to make his mark – even if it was only 'FYI' and a signature before another sheet of foolscap was added.

I had the prisoners brought up and questioned each one separately. Katokwe, as the accused, was present. I asked the first prisoner:
'Look at this Black Watch. Do you know him?'
'Yes.'
'Did he arrest you on …?'
'Yes.'
'Did he assault you when effecting the arrest?'
'No.'

That the baleful look on Katokwe's face influenced the emphatic 'No' was quite evident. Two closely typed sheets of foolscap were added to the docket which was sent off and there the matter ended.

Came Christmas 1927 and I was still alone on the station but in the New Year Trooper Paddy Hodgins (Henry 2404?) was sent to take charge and I could make my escape and get back on patrol.

Two rather doubtful characters had been reported at R.F. Dott's Angus Ranch. They were believed to be a pair who had escaped from gaol in Port Elizabeth and, as far as the S.A. Police were concerned, had vanished into thin air. But Salisbury C.I.D. were quite sure that they were the escapees.

I was instructed to arm myself with rifle, revolver and leg irons and to take with me at least two Black Watch. Dick Dott was presumably unaware of the identity of his 'guests' so before reaching the house I sent my cook to Dott with a note explaining the position to avoid any confusion. He replied to the effect that he was surprised – they were very nice blokes who were just going round prospecting. However, they had since left his place and were on their way to Mkondo Mine which had been abandoned several years before. But the most disturbing news was that they were armed with a .303 rifle and that Dott had unwittingly sold them a hundred rounds of ammunition.

I knew the old mine quite well, having camped there several times. At night there was an eeriness about the old boilers which, with their long chimneys, stood out ghostlike in the moonlight and, because there was water in some of the troughs, lions abounded.

When I was about a mile from the mine I halted and briefed the two African policemen, Gondobondo and Nyenyesa. The latter was to remove his uniform and, wearing my cookboy's clothes, see if there was a job going with the two 'prospectors'. His real job was to reconnoitre and report back. By this time it was nearly dusk, but it promised to be a clear moonlit night.

By eight that evening Nyenyesa had not returned. I was getting uneasy and so was the overdue constable's partner, Gondobondo. The two of us set out on foot over the kopje (on which the club is now situated) and crept very cautiously from cover to cover down towards the mine. The boilers some eighty yards away looked even more ominous than on my previous visits. Then I heard a low moan and a cry for help. 'Mambo!' ... 'Ishe!'

I could see nothing and had no idea what had gone wrong but Nyenyesa was obviously in serious trouble. In the eerie half-light, my hair was standing on end and I'm sure even Gondobondo's fez was inches higher than it had been. And then we almost stumbled over Nyenyesa's body.

Instead of being tied and tortured as we half expected, he had accidentally stepped on a lion trap – the Jane type with double springs. We managed to release him but he was not far from passing out so we let him rest and recover a bit before asking what he had discovered. The simple answer was that the birds had flown – several days previously judging from their campfire.

I bathed Nyenyesa's wounds with permanganate and next morning gathered six locals to make a stretcher before sending them off to Angus Ranch with a note to Mrs Dott. She was a trained nurse and I asked her to treat Nyenyesa and send him to Bikita if an opportunity occurred. I set out after my quarry with Gondobondo, getting information from the locals as I went to confirm that I was on the right track. With one casualty already, my force had been reduced by half – or rather two-thirds – and we were at a considerable disadvantage unless by some luck we came upon the escapees by surprise. However, whilst passing through the Mtsai Reserve and still hot on their spoor, I met two Africans who freely admitted that they had been carriers for the fugitives who had been arrested at Zaka. A great weight was lifted from my shoulders.

Later I learned that Sgt. Collings, assisted by – or rather with the cooperation of – Native Commissioner Morkel, had effected a very clever arrest in the Morkel's house after having previously gained possession of the .303. They were handed over to the S.A.P. at Mafeking but escaped again only a week or two later. They were at large for six months until they were eventually found living in luxury in one of Pretoria's posh hotels. They had evidently decided not to come within reach of the B.S.A. Police again.

I had several 'prohibited immigrant' cases. The Bikita District, for some reason, was a favourite destination for runaways. Most of these cases were straightforward except for the one related above and another which involved a Bloemfontein bank robbery.

Once again it was Salisbury C.I.D. who told us what was happening in our own back yard and we never learned how they got their information. Von Richie was the name of the accused in this case and he was also reported to have ended up at Angus Ranch. Again, I set out armed to the teeth – leg irons, rifle, revolver and two trusty Black Watch. On the way to Angus I came across an ox wagon by the roadside with a European on it. I hadn't been seen – or so I hoped – and I turned my horse off into the bush. The rest of my entourage, including the pack mule, was still about half-a-mile behind.

I managed to get right up to the wagon and, as I suddenly appeared from behind a convenient anthill, the man on it made a dive for his kit. I was already pointing my .45 revolver at him. Having never seen him before, I was fairly sure he was my man. I told him not to move but to put up his hands. I challenged him as being Von Richie which he rather reluctantly admitted. I told him to get off the wagon – on my side – and stand there until my reinforcements arrived. Once he was handcuffed, I searched the wagon to find a .22 rifle with a full magazine and a round in the breech. I decided to leave the wagon where it was and walk my prisoner back to Bikita.

Our first night stop was at Huze Store, owned by Gordon Hughes who was away at the time. I commandeered a vacant hut and put my prisoner inside, handcuffed to the pack saddle. Taking the first watch, I laid down across the doorway – and promptly fell asleep, quite unpardonable in the circumstances.

Waking with a start, just as my prisoner was in the act of stepping over me, I leapt to my feet and landed the poor devil a hefty smack between the eyes. Then I literally woke up to what I was doing as I looked down on my victim, flat on his back under the pack saddle to which he was still safely secured. When he recovered, he protested that he had only been answering the call of nature.

Unsurprisingly, Von Richie was quite docile for the rest of the way to Bikita and subsequently gave us no trouble in the weeks that we had to keep him there. His stay with us was prolonged simply because we could not decide how to get him to Fort Victoria. I certainly did not feel like escorting him the sixty-odd miles on foot. There would have been more overnight halts!

Trooper Frank Blake was Bikita's Member-in-Charge by this time, Paddy Hodgins having taken his discharge from the Force to become dip supervisor at Bikita. To celebrate his new career, Paddy had suddenly invested in a motor car – an old Ford Tin Lizzie – which was duly delivered to Paddy at Bikita. He invited us to borrow the car to deliver Von Richie to Fort Victoria. This was a generous offer but there was a snag. No one at Bikita could drive except the Native Commissioner and we could hardly ask him to run our prisoner to town. While we were pondering over this difficulty, Von Richie rather hesitantly informed us that he could drive. We concluded that this was the only way out – literally. But first our prisoner had to pass his test. Frank Blake with drawn revolver got in the back seat with the intimidating Katokwe next to the driver in the front. There was no doubt that Von Richie knew all about driving a car, or at least enough to get us safely to Fort Victoria.

We set off early the next morning. This time I was in the back seat with the .45 and Katokwe again in the front. We reached Fort Victoria mid-afternoon by which time I had decided that we could hardly arrive at the camp with our prisoner driving. The car was parked – or rather hidden – in the bush where the present camping site is located and the three of us walked into the camp.

Then the trouble started. Sergeant Major Hewlett wanted to know how we had got there. I said that Mr Watters had given us a lift. Who drove the car? Mr Watters drove. Was he a licensed driver? I thought so. Hewlett wasn't satisfied until he had phoned the Native Commissioner who very decently confirmed my story. (Everyone in Bikita had been aware of our strange departure.) Much later I took Mr Watters a bottle of whisky which in those days cost eleven shillings as thanks for standing by my version.

How Paddy's car got back to Bikita I can't remember. I had to carry on to Mafeking by rail with Von Ritchie and hand him over to the South African Police. Well, the story is getting rather long so I will leave other tales to a later date if they are wanted. And so bring we the curtain down for the time being and trust that there are those who will find these memories of mine as a member of the old B.S.A.P. convivial reading. All the best to a great Force.

This is an edited transcript of a letter written on 1 October 1972 by Mr Mullin of Box 110, Triangle, to George Style, alias 'Nimrod' of Buffalo Range. At this time Nimrod had written his 'Reminiscences of Bikita', published in the November and December 1972 issues of *The Outpost*. In Nimrod's story he had recorded handing over at Bikita in 1926 to Trooper 'Mac' Mullin, this name being inadvertently published as 'MacMullen' in both the main text and in the caption to a photograph of Troopers Style and Mullin with native constables at Bikita. Mr Mullin's response to Nimrod's subsequent request for his input on police life in the 1920s is this Tale and has not been published anywhere as far as is known. Mr Mullin's letter was rediscovered among Nimrod's letters to 'The Chronicler' early in 2006 when Mr Mullin's grandson, Ian Robas, also a former B.S.A.P. member, was researching family history on the B.S.A.P. History website.

GRIESBACH'S TALE

Ronald Charles Griesbach
Trooper (2031)
British South Africa Police

WHEN the first war ended, the B.S.A. Police consisted of scattered military detachments doing civil police duty, which ensured a good deal of variety in their work. At an inspection the N.C.O. in charge and his party perhaps captured a mountain; on the following day he might be reading Tredgold's *Handbook of Colonial Criminal Law* before framing an indictment for perjury. The passage of time has put an end to this system. It would now be unusual to consult K.G. VI about the admissibility of a dying declaration.

Inspections were serious undertakings, during which police work closed down for the time being. If Mr Hickory King turned up on some unimportant business, his reception was not cordial. A serious offence was to produce a horse with a sore back, because the detachment, if not mobile, was useless. F.H. Addison, of Salisbury District, often began his inspection with the stables. If the animals were in good order, the atmosphere became more serene. Pitt-Schenkel at Hartley enjoyed the bayonet exercises, then a part of the routine, but they were not so popular with the troops.

An inspector not easily bluffed was the late Colonel Capell, who believed in hard living and would have enjoyed the Tom Brown period at Rugby. He used buckboard and mules until driven to the motor car by force of circumstances. As he could still shoot big game at 73, there was much to be said for his creed. One remembers his misgivings when it was proposed to lay on hot water in the Depot bath house.

Colonel Capell had led a roving life. In his youth he went to sea; then followed nine years in the Cape Mounted Rifles, a D.S.O. in the South African War, Staff Officer in the South African Constabulary and service in Kenya and the West Indies until 1913, when he came to this country, Rhodesia, as Assistant Commissioner. He commanded the 2nd Rhodesia Regiment in East Africa and wrote their history in that campaign. When General Edwards departed after the war, Capell became Commissioner and Commandant-General, retiring in 1926. A.E. Capell could do many things well, including painting. His mournful sarcasm on inspections is not forgotten. He had had a full life when he died in 1952 aged 83.

A foundation member was Major G.J. Thornton, who joined in 1896, served in the South African War and was commissioned in 1904. He was with the Rhodesia Native Regiment in East Africa. In 1907, when the western boundary of Southern Rhodesia along the Pandamatenka Road became overgrown and in places diverted, Thornton, then a lieutenant, was responsible with Lieut. H.V. Eason, of the B.S.A. Police, for examining the position and beaconing the agreed line.

Lt.-Colonel Henry Bugler, who retired in 1945 as Assistant Commissioner and Officer Commanding Bulawayo District, was another who inspired confidence. With a good-natured disposition he combined a practical and commonsense approach to police work that caused many to regret his death in 1949 at the age of 59.

There was no military band in 1919, the Police and S.R.V. bands both being no more. For the Prince of Wales's visit in 1925, the N.R. Police Band was, I think, sent from Livingstone, then capital of Northern Rhodesia, Lusaka not being established until 1935.

Our own melody was provided by the portable gramophone, of which three kinds were to be had: H.M.V., Columbia and Decca. My machine was a low-brow affair that only played such compositions as 'Dardanella,' 'Chu Chin Chow' and 'Kitten on the Keys,' also that heartrending masterpiece, 'You Made Me Love You,' which I remember hearing at the Palace in Shaftesbury Avenue about 1913. The dance bands of 1920 were fair to medium, but people were not so fussy then. The thumps on the drum helped to cover up the shortcomings of the other musicians. Who now remembers Paul Whiteman or The Revellers or Jack Smith? All gone and forgotten; but to-day's lot are no – perhaps not as good.

Referendum Day in 1922 was 27th October, when the late Frank Collington and I were on duty at the Umsweswe Hotel polling station in Hartley district. There was much debate, and Charley Finder's contribution of secret and confidential information caused some surprise. General Smuts opened the Salisbury Show shortly before this, using his eloquence in vain to persuade Rhodesians to declare for Union. On 1st October, 1923, the title British South Africa Police became obsolete and misleading, as the B.S.A. Company was no longer in control. If the name had to be changed, this was the proper occasion, when the Corps was barely 30 years old and about 85 per cent of its members had less than four years' service.

Hartley in 1922 was a fairly large district, mainly given over to gold mining. It gets its name from Henry Hartley, the hunter, who penetrated to the Umfuli in 1865, when he also noticed indications of gold. There were five stations. The D.S.P. presided at Hartley, which also had a Town policeman or two. At Gatooma was the A.D.S.P. with five District police, five Town and two C.I.D. – Riddell and Bond. Collington and Austin were District and Town Sergeants respectively. Makwiro and Battlefields were run by Corporals, and Shagari (later Chakari) by two Troopers.

At Battlefields the squire was I.J. Minnaar (1894), who lived on the Washington Mine across the railway from the camp, where also were the Trafalgar, Inkerman and Tel-el-Kebir, apparently the origin of the name. The Battlefields Mine began crushing in 1905 and the Kanyemba in 1911. In May, 1923, the price of gold was 85s. plus 4s. 1fd. premium (Ifd is one and three-quarters pence) per fine ounce, the leading producers being the What Cheer, Kanyemba, Cricket and Trafalgar. East of the camp was the Elephant Hill section of Rhodesdale Ranch, a property of over half a million acres belonging to the B.S.A. Company. The police strength was a Corporal, two Troopers and four African Police.

In the twenties it was thought in Salisbury that a monthly examination paper for all ranks would fill a long-felt want and lead to a higher standard of efficiency. The scheme did not receive a rousing welcome and perhaps failed to achieve anything of note, as you could copy the answers from the textbooks provided the paper was endorsed to this effect. One organiser, who kindly typed his paper with four copies for his comrades, did not amuse the authorities. How long this ordeal lasted is forgotten.

It has been suggested that horses should be used more often for patrolling the remote areas. Whether this would be an advantage is hard to say. The horse certainly makes less noise than a motorbike, but bush country often looks uninhabited because kraals cannot be seen by the horseman, who may think he is giving one and all a big surprise. The horse also leaves its tracks behind it, nor can it carry a second passenger unless the pillion comes back into use. Moreover, its food has to be carried. In lowveld droughts a horse can be more of a liability than an asset. In actual fact the most effective way to patrol the backveld is on push bikes, but it has little appeal in this nuclear age.

It is probable that a good many policemen have been lost in the bush, which does not mean arriving an hour late for supper, but wandering about for days without food and in a state of general dilapidation.

In 1913 the late C.E. Pitt-Schenkel, the Lieutenant at Gwanda, was well and truly bushed near Elephant's Pits on the old Gwanda coach road 30 miles north of Tuli camp, when he was on his way to inspect. He had outspanned in thick and uninhabited country and gone to shoot birds. After four days without food or water he was found alive, but very weak.

One of the classic cases, and a grim one, was that of an ex-B.B.P. Trooper named van der Riet, who as hospital orderly accompanied the Dominican nursing sisters on their way to Salisbury in June, 1891. On the Pioneer Road a few miles northeast of the Umzingwane drift, he left the wagon to shoot for the pot and did not return. After a week's search, the party moved on. He was found 40 days later by a family trekking up the Bubye River, quite daft, partly naked, with his teeth blunt and broken from eating hard stuff and with fingernails worn away with digging for roots and water. He was living in an antbear's hole and could not speak. After careful treatment by his rescuers he made a good recovery, was hospital orderly for some years in Salisbury and did good work with the troops in 1893. The Bubye at its nearest point being 20 miles east of where he was lost, some idea of his misery can perhaps be imagined.

Many of the roads 35 years ago were so old-fashioned that the trooper on his horse was more comfortable than the man with cart and horses or in a primitive motor car. Those early four-cylinder cars did wonderful work, but ended their lives rather the worse for wear. Some of them are no longer seen. Essex, Hupmobile, Overland, Terraplane, Reo and Graham Paige – all from the U.S.A. – have vanished. English makers had nothing to offer fit for use in the outside districts. Indian and Harley Davidson motorbikes were popular, being heavy and powerful. There were some useful crashes.

A fair number of deaths took place in the wet season at the river crossings, or drifts as they were called. J.I. Cowgill, Native Commissioner, Gwanda, and two messengers were drowned in the Umzingwane at West Nicholson in February, 1946. The car stalled with the water less than knee deep, but the river rose nine feet in 20 minutes until it was 13 feet over the low-level bridge, by which time it was 200 yards wide, with waves three feet high. Cowgill swam well for a quarter of a mile, but could not get out of the main stream. He then began to go under for short periods until he went under for good. The messengers were drowned within three minutes. Joining the B.S.A.P. soon after the war, in which he won an M.C. and reached the rank of Major, he left for the Native Department in 1925.

These low-level bridges, begun in the early thirties, were a boon to the traveller, who had hitherto bounced over the drifts hoping for the best. The trouble was that the bottom washed away in places, becoming deadly to the under part of the vehicle. Some of the larger rivers had a cage or skip running on a wire rope between posts where the banks were high, for use in heavy floods. This went at a good pace until halfway, the passenger then hauling himself uphill to his destination, taking care not to get his fingers crushed.

Soon after the Limpopo Bridge was opened in 1929, the road became congested with Cape to Cairo expeditions of various kinds. Some ran out of funds; others battled gamely through Congo swamps until they faded from view. All had their destination painted clearly on their vehicles. One gentleman wished for some reason to drive from Cape Town to Stockholm and I believe actually got there. A road race was organised from Nairobi to Johannesburg, which was won by a Terraplane. Special arrangements were made to enable the competitors to go through the border formalities at Beitbridge in a few seconds.

The more remote parts of the Gwanda district held a certain fascination as a place where it was always afternoon, where elephant, lion and antelope went freely about their business, and where in November, 1912, 115 degrees in the shade was recorded at Tuli Camp. When the tenants were evicted in 1936 from the company blocks west of Umzingwane, this area also became a game park with a large variety of species, including ostrich, so that a journey from Mtetengwe to Tuli could at times be full of interest. An excellent photograph of 35 elephant, including calves, crossing the Shashi in line ahead, was taken by Hornsby when he was in charge in 1937. There was no record of rhino in these parts for many years, the only reference to these creatures being a rock painting near the Umzingwane River, seven miles west of Mtetengwe.

There was in most seasons a fairly large pool at Tuli Camp which induced

Horace Evans in 1926 to make a boat of two sheets of corrugated iron. As an engineer he was in advance of his time, fitting a stabiliser consisting of paraffin tins attached to an outrigger. He could also dismantle his motorbike down to the last nut and re-assemble it without any trouble, which made the less handy types gape with astonishment. He died in 1958.

The telephone line to Palapye via Semalali and Macloutsie (about 135 miles) enabled police to talk to Bulawayo and Gwanda if conditions were favourable, but elephant and giraffe often put it out of action. The Pioneer telegraph line crossed the Shashi, presumably at the fort, in a span of 518 yards from pole to pole, the wire weighing about 130 lbs.

One would think that these figures might also apply more or less to the telephone line crossing the river at the autographed baobab near the present camp. Many of these initials belong to policemen stationed there during the last 50 years.

Although Tuli spent much time dreaming in the sun, contact was sometimes made with the outside world. A private aircraft from Johannesburg made a landing in the bed of the Shashi in 1932 owing to engine trouble. After repairs, Dashwood, then at the camp, and Francis were given a joyride before it continued its journey, thus becoming pioneer aviators of the Shashi valley. About this time the landing ground was constructed, the Commissioner, I believe, using it in later years to inspect the camp.

On the west bank of the Tuli River, at its junction with the Sabi, was a marble tablet weighing about 55 lbs, set in a big tree in 1919. It read:

'As I walked through the wilderness of this world'
In memory of Arthur de M.W. Vickers, killed in the Galway Castle
disaster, Sept. 12th, 1918.
Erected by his brother.

The deceased had prospected in this area, which appealed to him strongly. He and his partner pegged the Farvic Mine near Colleen Bawn. The *Galway Castle* was torpedoed in the Channel with the loss of 154 lives. Vickers was not a trooper, as has been stated.

During the last war, a tragic accident occurred when a plane with a team of R.A.F. boxers from Rhodesia to Johannesburg crashed in the bush. There were no survivors. The exact spot is forgotten, but was somewhere between

Tuli Camp and the Limpopo. The Transvaal authorities provided the rescue team, which had to make its own road and only reached the scene after much hard slogging.

Nearly a hundred years ago Captain J.F. Elton explored the course of the Limpopo from its junction with the Shashi to the Olifants confluence. Leaving Tati in July, 1870, he carried a 13-foot flat-bottomed sailing boat called 'Freeman' on a wagon to Madume's, who then lived on an isolated hill halfway between the Tuli and Shashi Rivers, 25 miles north of Shashi. Obtaining carriers there – it eventually took 23 to carry the boat – they marched to the Tuli River somewhere near Sengazani, but found it unsuitable for boating. They therefore lugged it down the Tuli to the Shashi River, where there was a marsh full of buffalo. The Shashi was no good either, which meant a 30-mile tramp to the Limpopo, not without labour troubles. The crew embarked on 31st July, a shore party driving some pack oxen along the bank. Five days later 'Freeman' was smashed at the Tola Azime rapids in the gorge (Chituriradzimu), between Beitbridge and the Umzingwane River. Hippo were plentiful above and below the rapids, with a few buffalo on the north bank. Elton and four servants continued on foot to the Olifants junction, then went across country, reaching Lourenco Marques in September. The yacht seems to have done about ten miles a day. In places they found the river a broad channel from four to ten feet deep. Tsetse were seen near the Nuanetsi confluence. Nowadays, in an average August, broad channels ten feet deep must be extremely rare, if not unknown. At the Umzingwane junction, Elton reported the Limpopo as more than a mile wide, which, though it takes some believing, is impossible to dispute.

Sengazani brings to mind O.J. Isherwood, who once ran the store there and is believed to have been in the B.S.A. Police in the early days. He died in 1938.

The combined Tuli and Shashi enter the lowveld about 12 miles above the camp, both being more remarkable for sand than water in most years. Some of the early fathers in 1890 became lyrical about the beauty of the Shashi River. One reports 'a broad and beautiful channel of bright yellow sand, with tiny threads of glistening water near the far side,' but returns to earth with 'for ten months in the year there is more sand than water.'

On a remote and sparsely inhabited border, practical jokes are bound to occur, especially with firearms. Not all these weapons were of the type used at Agincourt; a Westley Richards or Mannlicher was also captured occasionally. The native sportsman with dog and gun was probably not unknown when Tuli closed down from 1941 to 1955. Many will remember the spacious days of the twenties when rifles lay about on farmhouse verandahs in complete security. A disarmament was taken in hand in 1904 in Gwanda-Tuli, whether to trace military weapons stolen or bought in the Transvaal during the war or the museum pieces used for hunting is not known. Tuli, like some other things, is not what it was. Although the wind of change has not blown half a gale here as elsewhere, its breezes have been felt. Wide roads have been made, boreholes sunk, an irrigation scheme is in preparation in the native area. On the Limpopo are three large ranches from the Umzingwane River to within 20 miles of the camp. The fascination has gone with the wind.

When Police and Native Department moved from Mtetengwe to Beitbridge in 1930, they continued to operate the Mtetengwe sub-district, then the south-eastern half of the old Gwanda district. About ten years ago Beitbridge became a district in its own right, including Tuli camp and half the ten-mile radius. More than half the district is lowveld (i.e., under 2,000 feet), which the motorist going south strikes three miles south of Mazunga; but if he turns left at Beitbridge for Salisbury he will not leave it until after the Lundi River. Beitbridge is given as 1,500 feet and Messina 1,948. The lowest point in Southern Rhodesia, where the Limpopo leaves the country, is said to be 660 feet.

Borders sometimes provide comedy. Before the Union went off the gold standard in December, 1932, the smuggling of currency across the Limpopo caused some amusement at Beitbridge. Some concealed it in the spare wheel, others in the sump. Others went to remote spots to make contact with desperadoes on the south bank. At one period African passengers from Johannesburg, booking a seat on the R.M.S. to West Nicholson, gave the driver a Union pound note, were handed a Rhodesian note in exchange, and they had paid their fares. In the thirties, for some reason I cannot remember, but possibly to do with foot and mouth, a great demand arose in the Transvaal for donkeys. These creatures, hitherto sold on the pound sale for 2s. 6d., now fetched £3 f.o.b. (Free Over the Border).

The underworld took full advantage of this, donkeys being scooped up regardless of ownership and hustled across.

The Limpopo was a temperamental stream – occasionally a raging flood, but more often a beautiful channel with tiny threads, etc., or a sandy waste with no threads at all. There were 30 feet of sand on some of the bridge foundations. The best flood of recent years was in February, 1929, during the building of the bridge by Dorman Long. The water encroached on their buildings on the south bank, a large quantity of cement being spoiled. This was used to make a crossing for motors at Liebig's Drift until the bridge was finished five months later. In heavy flood the river is a sight, big trees and other debris going along at a respectable pace. At half flood it was possible to row up to the rapids, about one and a half miles, and come back with the tide.

The river was at its driest in 1935, when a bad drought caused disaster over a large area. There were 5¼ inches of rain from April, 1934, to November, 1935. Crops were nil, stock losses heavy, both on the ranches and in the kraals. Beitbridge water supply was cut off for several hours daily. It was estimated that the native losses from drought were 15,000 head in what is now Beitbridge district. The price of cattle fell to 15s. 9d. instead of the £3 to £4 then usual for oxen, the buyers gambling on getting them away or leaving them with the owner until such time as rain came. Throughout the district dead cattle were scattered about in many places. Zebra lay dead round dry waterholes; koodoo, so thin that they could hardly walk, could be seen being chased around by kraal dogs until they collapsed; dead donkeys were also seen. The glorious sunshine hardly let up at all, nor was there any grass, the whole area looking like a parade ground. Fortunately December, 1935, to April, 1936, produced nine inches which, owing to the recuperative powers of the low country, restored the situation.

The lower course of the Limpopo was a mystery for many years. Robert Moffat in 1842 thought it joined the Sabi, as did many early hunters. Erskine first traced its course in 1868 from the Olifants to the sea after a rough and unpleasant journey. At the sea it was known as Inhampura; further into P.E.A. as Miti or Bembe, the latter extending above Beitbridge. The Zulu name was said to be Gulugudela which, owing to its similarity to the Afrikaans Krokodil, became the origin of Crocodile River. Bembe dates from 1727.

Donovan went fishing in 1893 at the Umzingwane-Limpopo junction. Using a 16-foot green-heart rod, 200 yards of line and a bright spoon bait, he caught 22 tiger fish weighing 76 lbs., the largest being 8½ lbs. He found them keeping together in shoals and biting most freely when a breeze ruffled the water. He also mentions a spinner with a red and white worsted tag.

Two adventurous spirits on the Messina Mine prepared to reach the sea in a canoe about 1926. Fifty miles below Beitbridge they struck the rock barrage which is said to last on and off for 20 miles, where the boat had to be carried. One was reported to have injured his hand severely, which led to acute poisoning and the amputation of one or more fingers. How far they managed to get is not known.

The crocodile population was considerable. It was not uncommon to see three lying on the same rock. Their size is usually exaggerated, only that of measured kills being trustworthy. Whether the Limpopo crocodiles exceed 12 feet may be doubted.

The Limpopo appears to have been regularly patrolled for some years since 1891, when Police from Tuli were sent to garrison the hunting drifts: Masebe's, Middle and Main. Masebe's, marked 'Bad' on the 1893 map, was four miles east of Ipayi River. The troopers lived in reed huts, as they did in those posts occupied in 1923. Chief Masebe was on a ridge to the north of the horseshoe-shaped earthwork which was about 1,000 yards from the drift.

Middle Drift, five miles west of Umzingwane River, was a broad crossing in 1893 with a sharp pull-up on the north bank. Apparently also known as Lower or Waterfall Drift, it was used by the Posselts in 1889 and by Millais and Donovan in 1893, when Sgt. Chawner was in charge.

He advised Millais to go back to the Transvaal, as the Matabele were beginning to boil over. He went on, however, to shoot on the Nuanetsi, returning in good order in spite of one or two alarming incidents.

Liebig's Drift, about 600 yards above the bridge, dates from 1910, when Liebig's Extract of Meat Co. Ltd (LEMCO) bought over one million acres 20 miles north of the river, importing stores over the drift which were carried to Mazunga by donkey wagons. Their cattle also used it on their way to Messina station and Johannesburg. The old Limpopo camp overlooked the drift from a ridge half a mile to the north.

About Dicky Dick's Drift, 1½ miles below the bridge, nothing is known. Main or Fleures Drift, 10 miles below the bridge and five miles north-east of Messina, was used by the Posselts in 1888 and by motor traffic to Fort Victoria and Bulawayo until 1928. There were no police or immigration officers, the only symbol of officialdom being a notice board directing the traveller where to report himself. Cars were pulled across by a span of donkeys and it was unwise to tackle the river with any depth of water. On a rock in mid-river is a brass plate in cement recording the death of J.D. Percy-Roberts, drowned while helping to get a car across in January, 1928. Above the drift the P.W.D. erected a substantial pontoon for motors which was not a great success owing to sandbanks. The fort was on a hill with small earthworks commanding the drift, which hunters used for many years before 1890 – possibly the road referred to by Selous as made by Boer hunters from Zoutpansberg between Matibi's and Chibi's, passing to the south of Sitoutsi's (in 1890 three miles west of the Bubye River on the Pioneer Road). Here also the Nuanetsi Ranch cattle were put across for Messina station and Johannesburg in pre-bridge days. Another visitor in August, 1903, was John Buchan, who reported the river about a quarter of a mile wide with a bed of bullrushes in the centre. Seventeen miles east of Main was Scrutton's or Sterkstroom Drift on the farm Scrutton (south bank), Sterkstroom and Tave being alternative names of the Nzhelele River in the Transvaal a short distance east of the drift. Malala Drift was 14 miles below Sterkstroom, near the Nwanedzi River, in the Transvaal. A road to Fort Victoria crossed here in 1915, possibly from Louis Trichardt.

Eighteen miles east of Malala was Kaffir Crossing, at or near which the Germans Mauch and Jebe are supposed to have crossed from Lydenburg in 1868, travelling on foot up the Bubye River. They were held near Inyati because of their entry dismounted and by an unauthorised road.

Another drift, name unknown, about two miles east of Bubye River, carried a hunting road from the North-Eastern Transvaal, while yet another crossed five miles west of the P.E.A. border, following up the Nuanetsi valley. It will be seen that in the 1956 map these drifts are transformed into 'fords' — a somewhat belated triumph of tribalism. These old landmarks have played their part in history as drifts and are now on pension. Little is gained by giving them new passports at this stage.

Immigration was free and easy in 1907 when Yank Allen drove his pack donkeys from Pietersburg via Messina, entering Rhodesia at Makakabula's. Proceeding north, he met a trader who advised him to report to Fort Tuli, which he did. After telephoning Gwanda, the Corporal in Charge authorised him to carry on. The Sergeant at Gwanda relieved him of his rifles, handed him a summons and had his donkeys inoculated by the farrier. After fining him one shilling for importing firearms without a permit, the magistrate suggested they both write to the Attorney-General in Salisbury applying for the return of the rifles, which were restored a fortnight later. For the last 35 years Makakabula's has been on the east bank of Umzingwane, 1½ miles north of the Limpopo. The late Captain V.A. New, who died in 1955, was O.C. border guard and immigration officer on the Limpopo in 1908. Mr Lownds, who was on the border guard in 1912, reports one trooper near Tuli camp, two at Masebe's, an officer and two men at Makakabula's and three troopers at posts further east – whether Main, Sterkstroom or Malala is not stated.

The cordon was for seven months annually, but immigration duties are not mentioned. 'Mabutshani,' at Tuli, 1914-15, makes no reference to a cordon, which may have been withdrawn owing to the establishment of the Limpopo camp in 1914, where immigration would be dealt with. In 1923, to the best of my knowledge, it was in operation to Plumtree from Ipayi junction only, being disbanded a few years later. In the early thirties it rose again as a foot and mouth cordon from Beitbridge to the Shashani, I think. The late Rex Borland was at Umzingwane Limpopo junction; further west were Long, Holman, Mason and Winter.

The outback did not suit everybody. In some remote places the public refused to commit enough crime to keep even a one-man station humming with maximum activity. There were no Europeans in some of these sections except perhaps an occasional storekeeper or prospector. A man had to know how to provide his own amusement and organise his interests off duty. I remember meeting an urban type in charge of a foot and mouth cordon well in the long grass 30 years ago. On being asked how he liked it, he replied in three words, 'I loathe it.'

He may have done, but he was doing the job and had learned to shoot guinea fowl with a rifle, which would have been helpful had he wished to join a circus. It was an experience for a city boy when he first lived in the bush, where he might perhaps not speak his own tongue for months at a time. Some hermits were known to run for cover when strangers approached. If, however, the wild places capture a man properly, he will stay there until the end, far from the jabber of T.V. and radio.

And now to end the news, here are the headlines of an old but appropriate song:

> Show me the way to go home,
> I'm tired and I want to go to bed.

An earlier series of R.C.G.'s reminiscences with the title 'My Old Shako' had been published in *The Outpost* magazine and republished in the book *Outpost: Stories of the Rhodesian Police*. This sequel appeared in the magazine in May and July 1962.

A Note on H.G. Seward, 1899–1999

By his son, Richard Seward

Henry George Seward (known by everyone as 'H.G.') was born in London on the 29th September, 1899. He was the second eldest of six children and the older of twins.

He left school at the age of 14, and worked in the Post Office, firstly as a postman and afterwards in the telegraph section. While with the Post Office he studied and passed local Oxford examinations.

He joined the armed forces in 1917 and was posted to the Royal Flying Corps (the forerunner to the R.A.F.), but was only there for a short time when it was revealed that he had had rheumatic fever as a small child, regarded in those days as an impediment to a flying career. Because of his experience in the telegraph section of the Post Office he was then enlisted into the Signals Branch of a Cavalry Division and was posted to the Middle East where he served for the remainder of World War 1, mainly in Syria.

His enlistment into the B.S.A.P. is covered in his memoirs, but unfortunately does not cover his entire service with the Force. His postings during his 28 years service covered the entire country and he rose through the ranks to Lt. Colonel, retiring in 1948 (at the age of 48). At the time of his retirement, the B.S.A.P. hierarchy comprised the Commissioner, the Deputy Commissioner and two Assistant Commissioners, of which he was one. Some of the highlights of his career in the B.S.A.P. included perhaps the largest recruiting exercise undertaken by the Force, when in 1946, he spent several months in the U.K. recruiting personnel who were being demobbed from the armed forces at the end of World War 11. Many of these recruits subsequently rose to high rank within the Force, whose reputation extended beyond our borders. As Officer Commanding Matabeleland, he was responsible for all the security arrangements in the Province during the Royal Visit to this country in 1947.

On his retirement from the B.S.A.P. he went farming in what was then known as Melsetter (now Chimanimani) before moving to Mutare in 1948 and then to the Vumba in 1960, where he and his wife spent the next 21 years of his life.

Notwithstanding the paucity of police pensions, an issue he was to pursue over the years, he was both mentally and physically active, resulting in his being employed by the British Motor Corporation (B.M.C.) as Personnel Manager from 1960 to 1965 when the advent of U.D.I. made him redundant. He then took up part-time employment as Secretary to the Forestry and Wattle Growers Association, which later became the Timber Growers Association, right up to 1981 (at the age of 81) when he and his wife moved to Bulawayo. The move to Bulawayo was largely necessitated by his wife's poor health and the lack of specialist treatment in Mutare. His wife died in 1983 and he continued to live in his cottage at the Garden Park Trust until 1997 when he was moved to the Athol Evans Hospital in Harare.

He enjoyed exceptionally good health right up to the age of 95 when he was admitted to the Mater Die Hospital in Bulawayo for a week with very low blood pressure and other minor problems. Shortly after this he started to become frail and began losing some of his mental faculties. He was, however, determined to retain his independence and remain in his cottage at the Garden Park Trust, albeit with some nursing care, and it was not until 1997 that he was persuaded to move to the Athol Evans Hospital in Harare, where he passed away on the 12th March, 1999, aged 99 and a half.

Prior to his health problems in 1995, he retained all his mental faculties and had an exceptionally good memory for names, places and events. He never kept a diary and his memoirs, which he started to write in 1974 and sadly never finished, were written entirely from memory.

He led a full and interesting life, which spanned the greatest changes in our times. Some of the first motor cars were starting to appear on the streets of London when he was a small boy and he remembers seeing people running in front of them waving a red flag. His father was a journalist in Fleet Street and as such was allocated seats in a press box from which he saw the Coronation of King George V. At the time of his death, computers, facsimiles, e-mail and internet were all part and parcel of modern day life.

H.G. was married in 1928 and had two children. Richard was born in an old house, since renovated and still standing, at the corner of 10th Street and Fife Avenue in the Police Depot, Harare, in 1932. June was born in Gwanda in 1934 at a time when all the water for the Police Camp houses was carried up from the river in buckets on the heads of convicts. Both still live in Zimbabwe. At the time of his death, H.G. was survived by his two children, five grandchildren and fourteen great grandchildren.

SEWARD'S TALE

Henry George Seward
Trooper (2324)
British South Africa Police

It all started with a chance meeting in London Wall on an overcast May morning in 1920 and hurrying along London Wall I caught sight of a figure I had last seen in Allepo some months before. It was my former troop leader and we were soon engrossed in swopping notes on all that had happened since the days when we had both served in the Fifth Cavalry Division. He told me he was thinking of going to a place which he called 'Rhoadesia', which I gathered was somewhere in the middle of Africa.

Having been persuaded by my father on demobilisation to try my luck in Fleet Street where he had spent the greater part of his lifetime, I was finding the hectic world of advertising hardly my cup of tea. With my war gratuity rapidly disappearing, I was intrigued to hear more about Africa and, in particular, 'Rhoadesia'.

We thereupon adjourned to the nearest bar and, over a Bass, I heard for the first time something about the British South Africa Police. Up to that time my knowledge of Africa — apart from short sessions in Alexandria and Cairo towards the end of World War 1 — was confined to browsing over old copies of a weekly illustrated paper called 'Black & White', the predecessor of the now defunct 'Sphere'. My father had bound volumes of this paper covering the period of the South African (Boer) War, and I had become familiar with pictures of Generals Gatacre, Buller, Kitchener and Roberts as well as pictures of the battles of Colenso and Magersfontein and vivid accounts of the sieges of Ladysmith and Mafeking. South Africa appeared to be a land of vast open spaces peopled by various 'Native Tribes', 'Tommies' and some rather rough looking characters called Boers, who, I gathered, had the temerity to challenge the might of the British Empire. But, with the thought of those wide open spaces, the idea of spending a life-time in Fleet Street soon became more and more unpleasant and I decided it was not for me.

And so it was, a couple of days later, I went along to the offices of the

British South Africa (B.S.A.) Company in London Wall looking for a General Bodle who, I was advised, was the recruiting officer for the B.S.A.P.

I eventually ran him to ground – underground, in fact, as his office was in the basement of the building. Although I did not know it at the time, 'Billy' Bodle had established a tremendous reputation in Rhodesia – a short squat figure of humorous eye and a somewhat staccato manner of speech. He told me at once that he was only interested in getting men for the Town Police Branch. Would I like to be considered for that?

'Not on your life!' I thought – the idea of wandering around some small frontier town on foot was just what I didn't want. But after I had explained that I had served in a Cavalry Division during the war, he said he might be able to find a place for me in the mounted branch provided I passed the medical examination and could produce satisfactory references. The references presented no problem and, having emerged from the medical 100 per cent fit, came the time for a final decision.

I would have to serve for three years, pay for a trooper was £185 a year plus a curious ration allowance of 6d a day. From the other conditions of service, I learnt that if I ever rose to the dizzy heights of Corporal, the pay would rise to £225 a year and, away in the distance, a Sergeant-Major's pay was £320 p.a. Uniform, saddlery and horses were on the house!

Later, browsing around a Smith's bookstall, I came across a book called 'The Rhodesian' by Gertrude Page. The hero was a Rhodesian police officer, and life in Rhodesia as portrayed by Gertrude Page resolved any doubts – Rhodesia was the place for me. I pictured myself riding on horseback through the African bush – a guardian and administrator of the law, free, untrammelled and far from the noisy smelly streets of London. However blessed the uses of advertisements might be, they were OUT as far as I was concerned. A couple of weeks later, with all my worldly goods in a cabin trunk, I found my way to the barrier of the boat train at Waterloo.

Waterloo Station

Waterloo looked much as usual, the suburban trains disgorging their thousands of office workers rushing to their offices – the girls in summer frocks, men in straw boaters and grey suits, all hurrying, scurrying, jostling and chattering and anxious to get to the office before their masters.

Time, which I was later to learn in Africa is valueless and given to all men to enjoy, seemed all important to this bustling crowd. They had to get somewhere quickly; to the office where they would remain poring over typewriters, ledgers, shipping documents and all the paraphernalia of business until five in the evening. This daily tedium relieved only by office scandal, whispering over tea, window shopping after a hurried lunch, plans for the coming weekend or the annual few days holiday by the sea. Thank God that life was, for me, to become a thing of the past.

As I stood watching the crowd – trundling porters; passengers studying timetables; friends meeting friends and saying good-byes to friends; sightseers; idlers – in fact all the conglomeration of humanity inseparable from any large London terminus, a small gathering of youngsters about my own age near the boat train barrier seemed to indicate they might be my fellow recruits.

They were indeed and, with the arrival of one of the Company's staff, we introduced ourselves. I remember Heriot-Hill, a gaunt, pallid ex-subaltern of the Machine Gun Corp, later to meet his death in Rhodesia in a petrol fire; Grimmett, young, fair-haired and whose parents were there and who, at the last minute, decided to accompany us to Southampton where they gave us a rousing lunch before sailing. Ruffel, ex R.A.F.; Catchpole, lately a gunner and Ward, soon to be known as 'Fluffy' because of his huge mop of unruly hair were among others that I recall. There were twelve of us in this recruit draft, but with the exception of Killick who later became responsible for the first Radio Communications Branch, I cannot remember the names of the remainder. Only Heriot-Hill, Grimmett and myself were destined for the Mounted Branch and we soon realised that there was not much, shall we say, community of interest between the two Branches and already we three started considering ourselves as 'superior' to the 'beatpounders'.

Southampton to Capetown

Following lunch with Grimmett's parents at Southampton, we boarded the R.M.S. *Armadale Castle* and found ourselves six to a cabin in the blunt end. By present day standards the accommodation would be regarded as pretty austere, but to those of us who had experienced the 'joys' of troopships, it represented a reasonable standard of comfort.

We had not been long on board when we discovered there was a B.S.A.P. Corporal among the passengers who were returning from leave – one Mark

Cook who had joined in 1910 and, in our eyes, a very old hand indeed. He regaled us with stories of shooting trips in the Sabi valley – wherever that might be and places with such romantic names as Msikavana, Mutema and Chimanimani, which left all of us to conjure up pictures in our own minds of exciting patrols in store. He told us of the idiosyncrasies of those 'powerful beings' – Native Commissioners, and of weird African customs. In spite of the tranquillity of the voyage, which in those days took seventeen days, we couldn't get to Africa quick enough.

Came Madeira – in a matter of moments the *Armadale Castle* was surrounded by small boats filled with gesticulating traders and small boys shouting, 'Tickey, I dive, tickey I dive', and it was not long before the water teemed with these lads diving for these coins. It was the first time we heard the word 'tickey', soon to become so familiar in Southern Africa. At the same time, the decks were soon covered with lace work, the famous Madeira cane chairs, baskets and fruit of all descriptions.

Most of us decided to have a look-see at Funchal and we went ashore in one of the many small boats and launches that had surrounded the ship. Surrounded by touts, we decided to do the usual trip up the mountains, returning by the ever popular sleighs over the cobbled streets.

Our first glimpse of Cape Town was in the early morning, with Table Mountain shrouded in cloud and mist – unbelievably beautiful. At that time there was none of the huge buildings in the dock and lower town area, which now seem to detract from the mountain panorama as we saw it then.

Going through customs, there was an amusing incident. Like most of us, Heriot-Hill reported 'nothing to declare' and, passing through the exit door of the customs shed, he dropped his British Warm and out of the pocket fell two .45 revolvers with a resounding plonk. Resourcefully, he quickly covered the guns with the coat and scooped them up without any further ado. And got away with it. It seemed to me to be a good start for an embryo law enforcement officer in a new country!

An official from the B.S.A. Company's Cape Town Office came to meet us with the information that we would have to wait over in Cape Town for a couple of days, as it was necessary for us to be attested there. We learnt later that a previous draft had refused to attest on arrival in Salisbury, alleging that conditions there were not as represented in London, so that the powers that be were not taking any chances as far as we were concerned.

In my particular case, the attestation in Cape Town was a blessing in disguise. Before leaving London, I had accumulated £15, being the balance of my war gratuity and savings from my meagre Fleet Street earnings. My father had been at pains to warn me about how easily money could be stolen, particularly on board a ship, unless you had it with you all the time. To this end he had bought me a money belt and shortly before we arrived in Cape Town, I had taken it off and inadvertently left it in a toilet – never to be seen again. I arrived in Cape Town penniless, but after being attested we were all given an allowance to see us through to Salisbury. Cape Town in 1920, apart from the dock area, seemed to be something of a sleepy hollow – Adderley Street almost devoid of traffic save for the trams, a few horse drawn drays and, wonder of wonders, hansom cabs of Victorian vintage.

Accommodation had been arranged for us at the Cardarga Hotel in the Gardens, afterwards known as the Hotel Edward. It may still be in existence under yet another name.

Cape Town to Bulawayo

Two days later, we climbed aboard the mail train for Bulawayo – six in a second class compartment. We passed through the Hex River valley in the evening and next morning woke to find ourselves in the Karoo.

Reminders of the Boer War could be seen in the shape of derelict blockhouses. For the remainder, isolated homesteads surrounded by the inevitable pepper trees; hungry looking donkeys; an occasional African huddled in a blanket; a few sheep grazing off the most unappetising grey scrub and, away in the distance, the odd dust cloud usually associated with ox-drawn wagons. What kind of country was this, I wondered? But, with three meals a day for 7/6 (this was the price in those days when one bought meal tickets for the day from the Chief Steward in the morning), beer at 9d and a half bottle of South African red wine – Heritage, I think it was called, for 1/-, there were compensations.

Came Mafeking and, looking out at the motley collection of corrugated iron buildings and dusty, untidy streets, one wondered where all the glamour of this name came about and why was it ever relieved?

We arrived at Plumtree, the Rhodesian border village, in the small hours on a Saturday morning and, on our way to the dining saloon, passed an imposing figure in uniform. Khaki drill breeches, polished leggings, spurs and wearing, on the right sleeve, the Royal Coat of Arms. The shoulder titles – B.S.A.P. Ah, we thought, this could be none other than the R.S.M. Later we discovered this to be Inspector Tom Goddard, then in charge of the Bulalima-Mangwe sub-district, of whom I was to see a great deal more in the not too distant future.

Bulawayo came into view shortly after breakfast and the station seemed to be one tremendously long platform, as indeed it was in those days. We soon discovered that we would have to spend the whole day in town, as the mail train for Salisbury would not be leaving until eleven that evening. Bulawayo in those days looked rather like a bigger version of Mafeking – the same corrugated iron buildings, the same dusty roads and the same stunted pepper trees. With the exception of the Grand and Palace Hotels, all buildings were single-storied ones. Africans were only allowed to walk in the roadway – apparently there was a bye-law which prohibited them from walking on the side-walks.

According to Corporal Cook, the 'in thing' on a Saturday morning in Bulawayo was to amble round the Market Square where almost everything one could think of was auctioned. In due course we arrived there – the auctioneer was quite a figure resplendent in immaculate white breeches, gleaming leggings, wearing a double terai hat, was tall and slim and with a seeming wealth of anecdote. 'Listen to Tottie', I heard someone in the crowd say, and there was Tottie Hay, the auctioneer, in full splendour. One of Bulawayo's famous characters who had forsaken pub-keeping at the old Maxim Hotel in Market Square, and who was now in full cry auctioneering a bunch of rather scruffy looking horses. Apparently someone in the crowd had suggested the animal being sold had bog spavin. Off went Tottie, 'Some of you buggers don't know the difference between bog spavin and bog seat. Who'll offer me a fiver?'

I began to think there really is something about Rhodesia. To the best of my recollection, no one on the Market Square was wearing anything resembling a suit – most were in khaki slacks and shirt with a bag of 'Boer' tobacco hanging from the belt. This seemed to be the accepted dress – everything free and easy. Someone else nearby said 'Look, there's Tom Meikle – he's always around looking for a bargain'. 'Who is Tom Meikle?' we asked. 'You'll soon know,' was the reply. 'He and the white ants own just about everything in the country.'

From the Market Square we drifted to the Charter Bar, which stood at the corner of Eight Avenue and Main Street. The Charter was presided over by a Mrs Williams whose husband, we were soon to find out, had been in the B.S.A.P. When she heard we were recruits on our way to Salisbury she said, 'You poor so and so's – you should have been here in Jimmy Blatherwick's days, he turned out real men, I tell you.' We gathered that Jimmy Blatherwick had been R.S.M. in Depot, but now replaced, Mrs Williams informed us, by one Jock Douglas, also something of a legend in his time. In the afternoon, Cpl. Cook suggested we might like to have a look see at the Bulawayo Police Camp. It was not impressive. The troops lived in a rather drab wood and iron barrack room, seemingly very crowded. There we met Trooper Bill Hakeman, lately a subaltern in the 10th Hussars, who seemed to be on first rate terms with 'Snitch' Hutchings the farrier, lately of the 4th Hussars. The latter was a real character and I shall have much to tell about him later.

Because the mail train to Salisbury did not leave Bulawayo until 11 p.m., we made our way in rickshaws to the Great Northern Hotel, situated conveniently close to the station, before boarding the train well before its departure.

We arrived at Gwelo at breakfast the next morning, where the station platform was crowded. It seemed as if the entire population of the town was there, and we wondered what it was all about, but soon learned that it was the thing to do. The arrival of the mail train on Sunday mornings was one of the events of the week. In the absence of anything resembling roads between the main centres, everyone travelled by train and people took advantage of the opportunity of meeting friends and relations to hear what was going on in other parts of the country. Very much a social occasion. From then on, all the way to Salisbury, every station and siding where the train stopped, there were little gatherings of people exchanging gossip with those travelling.

Salisbury

By the time we reached Salisbury, it had already started to get dark – the dimly lit station, a rambling wood and iron building, looked pretty unprepossessing for a Capital City. We were met by a mule wagon, which was to take us to Depot. We climbed aboard with our possessions and started up a red, dusty track lined with dimly lit corrugated iron stores, when suddenly, we came upon a 'modern', well lit, two storeyed building. 'That's Meikle's Hotel,' Mark Cook told us, 'it's the only place you'll get a hot bath in Salisbury.'

It was a cold July evening and quite dark by the time we arrived in Depot. We were ushered into a wood and iron barrack room, dimly lit by two low powered naked electric light bulbs. The only furniture comprised twelve iron beds of Victorian barrack room pattern, each with three coir biscuit mattresses supplied for our creature comforts. A long, lean individual in mufti, whom we afterwards learned was Sgt. Hughes-Halls, suggested that we get over to 'skoff', otherwise there might be nothing left. 'The skoff kia is over there,' he said, vaguely pointing away to the east, so off we went and had our introduction to messing facilities as they existed at that time. A long, low wood and iron building with a brick floor was crowded with youngsters, more or less our own age. Shouts of 'futi' (which we were later to learn meant more) and 'who the hell's got the salt' were the sounds we heard on entering. Being a Sunday there was a variety of dress – uniform, tennis kit, football jerseys and khaki slacks, but one thing seemed clear, there was no shortage of 'skoff' and 'futi' seemed to be the order of the day. We did notice that one table in the corner seemed to be getting a lot more attention from the African waiters. 'Ah, yes,' we were told, 'that's the Corporals' table – they do themselves well.' It certainly looked like it.

Our meal over we went back to the barrack room to find a pile of blankets in the middle of the floor. A Corporal came along and told us to help ourselves to three each. Our bedding for the night. 'Pillows,' we asked. 'Not on your bloody life,' said the Corporal. 'If you want a pillow you'll have to get one at the Canteen.' We wandered off in the dark to find the Canteen, which in those days consisted of a large bar on one side, and a small dry canteen known as 'the rat pit' at the back. The bar was crowded and a piano on a platform in the corner was being thumped to some purpose churning out the popular songs of the day – 'How you gonna keep them down on the farm after they've seen Paree' and 'Where do all the flies go in the Winter time?' Shouts of 'Chad, buck up with my beers,' 'Three dop and gingers, Chad.' Chad the barman, we discovered later, had been the Battery Sgt. Major in the Police and what a battery! Guns brought to the country before the Boer War, 8-pounders, muzzle loaders – far more dangerous to those behind than those in front! The 'rat pit' round at the back got its name from the surreptitious drinking that went on there after hours, which put most of its patrons well into the red by the end of the month. Anyway, into the rat pit we went in search of pillows.

It was presided over by Bill Over, who had a contract for running the canteens and messing in Depot. 'Yes, of course, you could have pillows,' said Bill, 'but you can only pay in Canteen coupons.' 'Sign the book and I'll give you each a £1 book of tickets.' Thus was our introduction to the incredible system of credit which existed in Rhodesia at that time, of which I'll have more to say later. A quick nightcap in the bar before making our way back to the barrack room just as the last post was sounding, which brought to an end our arrival in Depot.

Cavalry reveille the next morning woke us on a clear frosty morning. Shortly afterwards we heard a stentorian voice, with a distinctly Scottish accent, call out 'File on Parade'. This then was none other than the voice of the R.S.M., Jock Douglas, a character if ever there was one, of whom more anon. It was over to the ablution block to get ready for our first day as policemen. The temperature was well under 40 degrees F – there were baths, cold forbidding cement tubs and the temperature of the water not much above freezing. Now we could appreciate Mark Cook's remarks about hot baths at Meikle's.

Over to breakfast and, as the latest recruits, we were allocated the last table at the bottom end of the skoff kia. We were making progress, however, having learnt that skoff meant food of any kind and kia a room or house. Almost immediately, Heriot-Hill's prowess as a trencherman became apparent. He had four helpings of porridge and whatever else followed – eventually to become known as the human boa-constrictor, but, strangely enough, never seemed to put on weight. 'Futi' (more) was the first and most important local word he learned and he certainly made the most of it.

Breakfast over, we had time to look around us. The Depot buildings surrounded a grass square, to the north the Officers' Mess, the Guard Room and Depot offices. Beyond the offices were a collection of rather ramshackle buildings which included the Sergeants' Mess, Canteen, tailors, saddlers and the armourers' shops.

African Police buglers sounded 'Stables', almost immediately followed by the order once again, 'File on Parade'.

There for the first time we saw Jock Douglas, the R.S.M., ruddy of countenance, of medium height, leggings and Sam Browne belt polished like glass, Boer War ribbons together with Mutt and Jeff of our war, he was an imposing figure. 'Now,' he said, 'I want each and all to pay attention', and proceeded on a homily on the shortcomings of recruits in general.

There appeared to be between 70 and 80 recruits on parade, all in khaki shirts, slacks and felt stable hats, the hats being shaped rather after the fashion of those worn by Boy Scouts. The homily over, the parade was marched off to stables whilst we were instructed to report to the Depot office, where we were shortly joined by the R.S.M. himself who then proceeded to give us the usual pep talk, given, I presume, to all new recruits – we had responsibilities as policemen; we were not to spend all our money in the Canteen; not to get into debt (credit, he told us, was all too easy in Rhodesia and a policeman in debt was a liability); give the bars in town a wide berth and, finally, he advised us against what he called 'fishing in dirty water', which we took to mean 'leave African women alone'. Jock had a fatherly way of putting this over and impressed upon us that if we were ever in trouble, we should get in touch with him.

All of us having served in one or other of the services during the war, thought that this was quite a new brand of R.S.M. In the event, Jock was a firm disciplinarian, but always tempered with understanding. 'Jock' gave us our Regimental numbers and I found myself No. 2324, Trooper Seward, then off to the Ordnance Store to collect kit, saddlery and equipment. Under this not inconsiderable burden, we staggered back to the barrack room to start sorting it all out. We, that is to say Heriot-Hill, Grimmett and myself, had been placed in the same squad with those who had arrived in Depot a week before and the squad now consisted of Munn Lace, lately a subaltern in the Scots Greys; Tufty Arnott, M.C. of the Machine Gun Corps; Blake, an ex-London Territorial Officer; Meridith, an Old Harrovian (too young to have served in the war); Turner-Dauncy, ex-King Edward's Horse; and Fish and Barthorp, ex R.N.

The emphasis in those days seemed to concentrate on military training, much of it in our opinion rather antiquated. A routine of early morning rides, stables twice a day, foot drill, arms drill, lectures on animal and basic veterinary management, mounted rifleman training, musketry instruction – which included Vickers and Lewis guns, Stokes mortars – were the order of the day. However, one hour a day was devoted to what was called 'Law and

Police Instruction'. This, under Sgt. King, consisted of each recruit reading out a passage in what was called the *Police Code Book*. This book contained a kind of precis of the Statute Law and definition of common law crimes. Little or no attempt was made to give any actual instruction in police duties as such and it was left to the individual to study the Code Book in his spare time – this being a rare commodity as most of one's 'spare time' seemed to be spent on cleaning equipment and saddlery, although, let's be honest, some did find not inconsiderable spare time to frequent the Canteen.

Depot staff in 1920 consisted of; Major G. Stops, Commandant; Lieuts. Culver and Parr; the R.S.M. Jock Douglas; Sgt. Major Hampton, Chief Equitation Instructor (late of the Dragoon Guards); Sgt. Simpson, D.C.M.; Sgt. Page, the Provost Sgt.; Sub Insp. Walker and Cpl. Graham, Musketry Instructors; Sgt. Major Ashwin, the Farrier; Sgt. Major Shettle, i/c Pioneers; Sgt. Hughes-Halls and Saville; and one or two Corporals who were in charge of the various recruit squads.

Morning rides were the event of the day – there was no enclosed riding school and recruits were taken out into what are now the sports grounds – at that time just bundu, where we trotted or cantered in circles. Our mounts in a number of cases were only recently broken remounts – not well broken at that and many were the involuntary dismountings and runaway horses!

Later we were initiated into the mysteries of what were called 'Basi Bazooks' – charging towards Gun Kopje and, at a given signal, hastily dismounting and going through the motions of firing at distant targets – a manoeuvre developed during the Boer War.

To those of us who had had war service, it seemed a complete anachronism, as it undoubtedly was, but training was based on the Manual of Mounted Riflemen – training which first saw the light of day during the South African War. It was amusing but, as we saw it, of little practical value.

After a couple of weeks in Depot, a few of us decided to 'explore' Salisbury, to see what the town had to offer by way of entertainment. There was a fairly well beaten track running S.W. towards the town over more or less open veldt. Except for a few isolated houses, there was nothing between Depot and the present day intersection of Samora Machel Avenue and Fourth Street. Manica Road was the main shopping centre – First Street was mainly vacant stands except for the Palace Theatre, presided over by Joe Wheeler. The Salisbury Beer Hall and Skittle Alley, the Commercial Hotel (later to become the Grand Hotel), Lennons and Henwoods chemist shops, completed the picture. In spite of the efforts of the municipal water carts, the place looked pretty dusty and we decided that the first thing we would do was to go for a hot bath at Meikle's Hotel. I've forgotten what it cost – about two shillings I think, but the joy of being able to wallow in hot water was quite something and worth every penny of it.

There were a few taxis in those days, all driven by Europeans and damned expensive. Rickshaws were the alternative and most people patronised them in spite of the 'odour d'Afrique' associated with those pulling them.

Our 'recce' by rickshaws disclosed that, apart from the various bars Salisbury had not much to offer by way of diversion or amusement. Many of these bars have disappeared over the years – the Empire, diagonally opposite Meikle's Hotel where Kingstons now stands, was well patronised by the troops as was the old Posada Bar in Manica Road, where Jeff Clinton was ever ready to entertain. The Langham, Masonic, Castle and Market Bars were for the more adventurous. Each had its bevy of barmaids whose repartee was of pretty high – or low – order, depending on the circumstances. There were no tot measures – if one ordered a whiskey, brandy or gin, the bottle was handed over and one helped oneself.

Moreover, if you were in good standing no cash was passed – one merely signed a card to be settled at the end of the month. Save by a few, this was rarely abused and in fact as the evening progressed, smaller and smaller tots became the order of the day. The Palace Theatre was dowdy, the red plush seats had certainly seen better days and the old silent films pretty ghastly. Except for Wednesday and Saturday nights, Fred Hooper provided the music, thumping away on what appeared to be a fairly ancient piano. But Wednesday and Saturday nights were gala nights, when Fred's efforts were augmented by Sgt. Major Shettle of the Police Pioneers on the double bass, a couple of fiddlers and a drummer – those were the days, or rather nights. What intrigued us, as newcomers on the scene, were the large numbers of men in dinner jackets and women in long evening frocks on those nights – dressing up to go to the pictures was something quite new in our experience.

With so little in the way of entertainment in town, we created our own amusements in Depot and these mostly centred around the Canteen where the usual sing-song went on night after night. On morning rides, we would occasionally be visited by the Commissioner, Major General A.H.M.

Edwards, an ex-Dragoon Guards officer, resplendent in red and gold tabs and usually followed by his groom, Trooper Montague.

The arrival of a batch of remounts from Kimberley caused some excitement as they were only halter broken and pretty wild. Volunteers were called for to break in these shaggy looking brutes at an extra shilling a day. I volunteered but was not selected, but I did have one experience which I thought at the time was worth considerably more than a shilling a day. In those days, there were no electric lights in the stables and the night stable picquet had to feed the horses at 9 p.m. by the light of a candle lamp. This presented no great difficulty as far as the troop horses were concerned, who were housed in stalls – apart from the usual kicking that went on when the food was being thrown into the mangers – but feeding the remounts which were in the open part of the stable was quite another kettle of fish. As soon as the wheelbarrow containing the feeds was brought into the stable, they started snorting and kicking and generally playing up. On this particular night I went in with the candle lamp, pushed my way towards the manger, when the lamp was promptly kicked out of my hand and I landed in the straw. Apart from the danger of fire, I was now in complete darkness among a kicking, snorting collection of rather frightened horses who were obviously pulling back on their reins. There was only one thing for it. I climbed up on the manger and, steadying myself by pushing my hands against the corrugated iron roof, I crept along the manger until I could reach the nearest troop horse stall. Fortunately this particular animal was a docile one and I was able to get away with what could have been a pretty nasty experience. I found myself in complete agreement with a wit who had once observed of the horse, that it is 'dangerous at both ends and uncomfortable in the middle'.

This was not the opinion of one Sgt. Major Ashwin, the Farrier Sgt. Major who took us for lectures on Animal and Veterinary Management. He was constantly reminding us that the horse was a noble creature – our only means of getting around the country and should be given constant care and attention. Henry Ashwin treated his 'h's in a cavalier fashion and one day, when lecturing us on the ills we might encounter in the animal entrusted to us, said, 'Now when this 'appens, you puts a little hoil of h'acifacitate on the wound.' When one of the squad piped up, 'How do you spell hacifacitate, Sgt. Major?' Henry replied 'H a c – aint you never been to school?' Needless to say, the squad collapsed. But Henry was a dear old man, kindly, extremely knowledgeable and beloved by all. Only a couple of months ago I received a photograph taken in Depot in 1920 of Henry sitting among a group of recruits – appropriately enough, I was at his feet.

Training went on, the only diversions, if they can be called that, being funerals. For some reason which we never fathomed, any ex-serviceman who died in Salisbury at this time, was considered worthy of a military funeral and we spent a lot of time marching down to the hospital or cemetery for this purpose. The only other departure from normal routine was a parade on what was called 'Occupation Day', the first we had heard of the public holiday. Fifty of us in the so-called full dress – khaki drill tunics, breeches, leggings, spurs, bandoliers and helmets, marched from Depot to what is now called Cecil Square. In 1920, this was seemingly a piece of waste land with not a tree on it as far as I can remember. There, together with a small group of Boy Scouts and Girl Guides, we were inspected by the Administrator, Sir Drummond Chaplin, a handsome figure of sartorial excellence, in striped trousers, morning coat and grey pith helmet, the latter being much favoured by all the local V.I.P.s. The B.S.A. Company's flag, the Union Jack on which was superimposed the Company's crest of the Lion and Elephant Tusk (known to us irreverently as the Lion and Toothpick), was hoisted on a temporary flagstaff in the middle of the Square while we stood at the 'Present Arms' position. A group of what appeared to be old hands, in a queer variety of clothing, stood by – these we were told were some of the Pioneers. They certainly looked the part which reminds me of a story I heard at a much later date of the late W.T. Smith, a well-known magistrate. The story goes that an elderly gentleman once stormed into his office, labouring under some real or imagined grievance, shouting, 'I'll have you know, Sir, I am a pioneer of this country,' to which W.T., with his caustic sense of humour, replied, 'In that case, you have my sincere sympathy.'

Came November (1920) and our 'passing out' parade, when we paraded mounted, and, under the eagle eye of Major Stops, were meticulously inspected – and, miraculously, survived. It was customary then for each squad to arrange a 'passing out' dinner at one of the local hotels, to which the various instructors were invited as guests. Our dinner was at the old Queens Hotel at the top of Manica Road and, on the night in question, we duly repaired there. Well fortified in the bar before dinner, the evening developed into the usual hilarious occasion, when the opportunity was taken to indulge in insincere flattery of the instruction staff. In strange contrast to the qualities normally attributed to them on more formal occasions, suggestions were made that, in some cases, it could have been possible that their fathers might not have married their mothers!

Someone proposed that we should have a rickshaw race down Manica Road to the Langham Hotel, the last arrivals there to pay for the drinks. After several false starts, mostly due to arguments over the respective merits, including the 'horse power' capacities of the rickshaw boys as everyone was out to get the strongest pullers, we were flagged away. The losers eventually turned out to be those who, finding themselves getting left behind, swopped over and putting the African in the rickshaw, took over the role of pushing and pulling themselves! And so home, via the Empire and Posada bars, with 'bonsellas' for the rickshaw boys after their long pull back to Depot. Most of us were asleep long before we got there. The next morning is best forgotten!

Given the opportunity of electing as to which district we would like to be posted, most of us opted for Gwanda (which seemed to be as far away from Salisbury as possible), or, failing that, Bulawayo. In the event, Grimmett, Fish, Blake and myself found ourselves destined for Gwanda. Before leaving Depot, most of us had stocked ourselves up from the Canteen – dry, not wet this time, with the result that when our cheques arrived at the end of the month there was only a matter of a few shillings left. One, I've forgotten who, received a cheque for twopence which he promptly had framed, only to be pursued for months afterward by constant reminder that it hadn't been presented for payment. On the way to Gwanda we had to spend a couple of nights in Bulawayo Camp – sleeping on the floor; there were no spare beds in the antiquated old wood and iron barrack room.

On the 11th November (Armistice Day) we climbed aboard the Gwanda Express, a mixed goods and passenger train which left Bulawayo at 8 a.m. and was scheduled to reach Gwanda, 90 miles away, at 4 p.m. – an average speed of a little over 10 miles an hour – things were certainly moving!

Soon after the train started we were joined in our compartment by a rather diminutive figure who introduced himself as Max Maisel – he had quite a lot to say for himself about his war service with the Rhodesian platoon in the

60th Rifles in France. He then went into some detail about some of the various characters in the Gwanda district, where he himself was running a store near the Antenor mine. It was not long before he went off to his compartment and came back with a bottle of 'dop', a water bag and a couple of mugs, suggesting that we should celebrate Armistice Day in the proper way. The day was hot with a thunderstorm in the offing and we were soon down to the last dregs. Max became quite garrulous, full of reminiscences of his days in France. At one of the stops he insisted on going along to the engine driver and instructed him that the train must stop at 11 o'clock, which the driver duly did. Max and ourselves disembarked and stood rigidly to attention at the side of the track somewhere near Balla Balla.

At about midday the train stopped at Balla Balla where all the passengers alighted for lunch at Sanderson's Hotel; I don't remember much about the lunch, but the beer was cold, even before the days of refrigerators, being kept in wet sacks hanging at the back of the bar. In due course the train conductor looked at his watch and shouted to the driver, 'Tom, it's time we were off,' so we trooped back to the compartment and resumed our leisurely way towards Gwanda, arriving there, curiously enough, on time at 4 p.m. 'Tufty' Arnott, who had passed out of Depot a week or two before us was on the platform to meet us and give us some information on Gwanda and what we might expect.

Gwanda
Gwanda in 1920 certainly had all the appearance of a pioneer village; facing the station were a row of corrugated iron stores and a wood and iron hotel; dust everywhere; a collection of 'buggies' of various types and a few saddled horses tied up to a hitching rail outside the pub.

A mule cart with a Coloured driver rejoicing in the name of Christian, collected our kit and saddlery – we followed on foot up the hill and, at the crest, looked down on the Umshabezi Valley and the Police Camp. What did the Police Camp look like? Well, there was a wood and iron office on stilts at the entrance on the left, further to the left a stone barrack room enclosed on two sides with a dirt verandah and below that, another wood and iron building – the skoff kia, obviously sadly in need of a coat of paint. On the far side of the square, a long, low, corrugated iron stable and, facing the barrack room, another rather tumble-down building which, we were told, wonder of wonders, was the billiard room. In the centre of the square were the cells. The square itself, hard schist and rock – not a blade of grass in sight.

The barrack room itself, with its immensely thick stone walls was, we were told, built at the time of the Boer War. Looking at it, it appeared more like a relic of the Crimea War! Already occupied by about a dozen men, we nevertheless crowded in and found ourselves beds. As yet we had no servants, but the troops already there each had a servant. These piled in and made our beds and fixed up the mosquito net under which everyone had to sleep at this time. 'Tufty' told us that there was to be a dance in the Court Room that evening to celebrate Armistice Day. 'What about going?' he asked, but added, 'there are only two unmarried girls in the place and you new blokes will have little chance of getting even a single dance.' On this encouraging note, we decided to call it a day – candles, the only form of lighting provided were lit and 'old' hands gathered round to give us some insight as to what we might expect of Gwanda District. The stories lost nothing in the telling.

We were joined by a short stocky figure in shorts and singlet who introduced himself as Corporal Giddings, the District Clerk and who was running the mess. He suggested that if we wanted to get anything to eat, we should get cracking. We did. The skoff kia was generously provided with tables, soldiers 4ft, and forms of the same pattern; candles stuck in bottles provided the illumination. The food, stews or roasts with potatoes and rice only – green vegetables were at a premium. Long after midnight we were woken up by the revellers returning from the Gwanda Armistice Ball! From the racket which went on, it was pretty obvious that, while there might have been a shortage of partners, there had certainly been no shortage of liquid refreshments.

The following morning, roused by the clanging of a gong indicating reveille, we reported to the office while the rest of the troops were marched off to stable parade. Having had all our particulars entered into that mine of information, the General Record Book, we adjourned to clean ourselves up – no bathroom in those days, only an old iron shed with a few galvanised basins on a bench and a water cart that stood outside. That was it. Water was brought up from the Umshabezi River; it looked, and was, pretty foul. A bath? – yes if you were lucky enough to find any water left in the cart and were content to sit in two or three inches of water in the dilapidated, galvanised flat bath which stood in the corner. We found out later that most of the troops went down to the river in the evening and cleaned themselves up in the railway dam, a tiny affair shared with cattle, donkeys and umfazies washing clothes. Bilharzia? – no one had ever heard of it.

There was quite an impressive detachment in Gwanda at this time, headed by Major G. Thornton, a Boer War veteran, as District Superintendent of Police (always referred to as D.S.P.). Lieut. J.S. Bridger, Asst. Supt.; Sgt. Major Sima, a kind of Troop H.Q. general dogs-body; Cpl. Giddings, an ex-regular of the Black Watch as District Clerk; and Farrier Tpr. Jacobs, Sgt. Carey and Cpl. Nyman, together with six Troopers, constituted Gwanda Police Section.

The remainder of the troops formed a kind of District Reserve – these varied in numbers according to the exigencies of the moment. In due course we were allocated mounts and I was fortunate in getting a dun with black points – Troop Horse No. 1242, Khaki, who was destined to carry me many hundreds of miles before I parted with him some six years later. I had always had a predilection for duns as being hardy and good-doers; Khaki certainly justified my faith in him and a couple of years later during a bad horse-sickness season, he was the sole survivor of four horses at Figtree Camp where I was stationed at the time.

In the early twenties, horse sickness was rife. Animals were inoculated against this disease before leaving Depot, but had to be temperatured every morning and evening and laid off work against any appreciable rise in temperature. Temperature charts were kept for every animal and these were sent to District H.Q. at the end of every month, together with a report on the animal showing the mileage covered each month. In spite of all the precautions taken, there were some years when mortality was extremely high.

There was not a great deal of crime in the Gwanda area; periodically a couple of troopers would leave on patrol, accompanied by African Police and pack animals. These would last two or three weeks, depending on the area and on return to camp, the result of the patrol would be written up in what was known as the Patrol Area Book. To help newcomers on patrol, maps were provided showing details of paths and information regarding the few European homesteads. Experience was to show that such maps were often misleading and inaccurate, much depending on the ability of the Gwanda individual compiling them.

Some of the pack animals, either donkeys or mules, were pretty long in the tooth and the story was told of one Trooper who was sent on patrol with an aged pack mule who, on return to camp, recorded something like this in the Patrol Area Book:

'5 p.m. Arrived at Mr X's homestead. Decided to await the arrival of my pack animal.
6 p.m. Still waiting.
7 p.m. Still waiting.
8 p.m. Still waiting.
9 p.m. Still waiting.
10 p.m. Still waiting.
11 p.m. Still waiting.
12 m.n. Still waiting. It may be for years or it may be forever.'

The D.S.P., perusing through the reports, took a pretty dim view of this entry and recorded: 'Trooper... is not to give vent to his warped sense of humour in the Patrol Area Book.' The story has it that the Trooper's wit was in fact rewarded, as the ancient animal was boarded shortly thereafter.

Gwanda was a mining area and contained a large number of small mines working small stamping mills ranging from one stamp up to five stamps. Some that I remember were: Abercorn, Antenor, Champion, Tuli, Sabiwa and Big Ben. Farming was confined to cattle ranching and few, if any, crops were grown on any scale. In any case, mealies were five bob a bag and there couldn't be much profit in that. I was struck by the optimism of the miners – always hoping there was a possibility that they'd strike it rich. Farmers on the other hand were generally pessimistic – cattle prices were poor to say nothing of droughts and diseases.

After a few short patrols I was detailed to work in the Gwanda Section office and there, under the guidance of Sgt. Carey and Cpl. Nyman, I started to learn something of Police work, taking statements from African complainants with the assistance of one Asangana, the interpreter. Asangana, who was from Nyasaland, had received his education at a Scottish Mission and his English was tinged with a strong Scots accent which I found most amusing – especially some of his Scottish colloquialisms. One day, while sorting out the mail, I found a letter addressed to Alexander Gibson-Hall, Esq. Not knowing anyone of this name in camp, I enquired of Asangana. 'Oh,' was his reply, 'That's for me. Sah.' It turned out that this was the name of the headmaster of the mission where he was educated and he had adopted it as his own.

Temperatures in the Charge Office during the months of October through to February were usually around 100 degrees F. In order, as he thought, to cool things down a bit, Sgt. Carey conceived the idea of hanging sacks on the windows doused in water and, at the same time, have the wooden floor treated in the same manner. It turned the office into a veritable Turkish bath and only needed a little 'odour d'Afrique' and copious Boer tobacco smoke to provide the ideal environment for tempers to occasionally flare up. At the end of the day there were two alternatives – one could either go down to the river or dam for a bath, or to the pub. On really hot days, the pub won every time, although there were those who managed both. The Gwanda Hotel was owned by Messrs Levine and Cohen, while the bar was presided over by one 'Doughy' Sutton, so called because he was also the local baker.

One evening, there came into the bar one of the local farmers, a veteran of the '96 Rebellion. As frequently happened, the talk got round to experiences during the last war. Up got the farmer and said, 'What do you so-and-so's know about war? You should have been here in '96 – then you would have known what war was all about.' This was a little too much for Jock Nicol, one of our party from Camp who had served four years in France. Turning to the '96 Rebellion 'hero', he replied, 'Yes, you must have had a terrible time. There were all these Africans with their spears and knob kerries and all you had were machine guns and rifles.' – Point of view is everything.

Occasionally 'Yank' Allen, the well-known hunter who originally hailed from America and who was employed by Liebigs to shoot lions on their Mazunga Ranch, would turn up at the pub and regale us with stories of the big 'cats' as he called them. A dry, usually taciturn character who had a dry sense of humour, he would sometimes keep us amused with his tales of adventures round the world.

At the beginning of December, 1920, it was decided to hold a Christmas season dance in Camp and invitations were sent to all and sundry throughout the district. The only place where it would be possible to dance was the barrack room and two days before the dance was to take place we had to move all our beds and kit out and sleep wherever we could – some on the open verandah, some in the old billiard room, some even in the old wagon shed. As usually happens on these occasions it rained: beds got wet and tempers frayed, but it all worked out well in the end. The barrack room was festooned with paper chains, the floor dry scrubbed and liberally sprinkled with mealie meal, a bar set up in one corner of the verandah and all was set for the celebrations.

There were no motor cars in the district – for that matter there were no roads on which they could have been used. People trekked into camp in all kinds of utility carts, Cape carts, buggies, buckboards and one family, I remember them telling me, had been three days on the road in an ox wagon.

The dance itself was a tremendous success; Mrs Bridger, wife of the Asst. D.S.P. played the piano and I, having imprudently mentioned that I had some rudimentary knowledge of the violin, was loaned an ancient instrument and managed to keep up with Mrs Bridger for most of the evening. The 'piece de resistance' however, was provided by an old Afrikaans farmer who produced a concertina and played music which, I was told, was called 'tickey drei.' It certainly went with a swing but recovering from this frolic was anything but a 'dry' business.

About this time, a notice appeared in Regimental Orders inviting applications to sit for promotion exams for Trooper to Corporal and for Corporal to Sergeant, to be held in Depot in January, 1921. Having less than six months service, I thought there would be little object in submitting such an application but, on the off-chance, I decided to apply for permission to sit. To my surprise the application was approved and my good fortune held for, at the end of a week's grilling in Depot, I found myself the proud possessor of two gold stripes, the youngest Corporal in the Corps.

Returning to Gwanda, I found myself under orders for transfer to Bulawayo District by road. Perhaps the term 'by road' was something of a misnomer because at that time there was no actual road from Gwanda to Bulawayo, besides a track running through the Matopo Hills. District transfers in those days also involved taking the mounts allocated to you as well.

Riding Khaki and accompanied by my African servant and an African constable leading a pack donkey, I set out for Bulawayo under a lowering sky – it was hot and humid even before we left. The Umshabezi River was in flood and, arriving at the drift, the pack donkey was offloaded. My servant, together with the pack bags and my small fox terrier, climbed into the 'skip' (a small metal box-like affair slung on cables across the river which, before the days of low-level bridges, provided the only means of crossing rivers in flood), and were hauled across. Khaki didn't take kindly to the idea of plunging into the fast running water, but after a certain amount of persuasion, we managed to get over with the water well above my stirrups. Then the damned donkey wouldn't face the water, so eventually I had to return and lead it over – it was quite happy following Khaki. By this time, the African constable had crossed in the skip and we were on our way.

By midday, we reached the old Sabiwa Mine where I decided to outspan for a couple of hours. To the north I could see heavy clouds, accompanied by thunder, gathering over the Matopo Hills. With the promise of a storm, I decided to push on in the hope of getting somewhere under cover before darkness set in. My terrier had by this time decided she had enough, so I took her and put her on top of my cavalry cloak which was strapped on the pommel of my saddle. She settled down quickly and looked at me as much as to say 'Why the heck didn't you think of this before?' A flash of lighting, followed almost simultaneously by a crack of thunder and the storm was upon us and it came down in buckets. Raincoats were not an issue in those days, instead we were provided with what was called a cloak, cavalry. A long heavy khaki serge affair, reaching down to the ankles, with a bright scarlet lining.

It rained and rained, my cloak was getting heavier every moment, with 'Pups', the terrier, wriggling and whimpering beneath it. About five in the late afternoon, I arrived at an African village and decided to wait for the others with my pack whom I hadn't seen for the last couple of hours. The Kraal head suggested that I should spend the night there and there seemed nothing else for it. Off-saddling Khaki, I tied him to a tree and waited. Half an hour later, the constable, my servant and pack arrived, all thoroughly soaked – including my blankets, food, animal rations, the lot. This was 'sunny' Africa with a vengeance. The language difficulties now overcome with the arrival of the African constable, I was kindly offered a vacant hut into which I moved all my kit and saddlery, by which time it was dark and still raining steadily. The only light was from flickering fires in some of the other huts. Presently, a young 'umfaan' arrived at the hut with a lamp of sorts – a small bottle filled with paraffin, a metal top with a hole from which protruded a bit of 'limbo' forming a wick. Tickey, my servant, came along with some tea and with supper off a tin of bully beef, life began to look a little rosier. I had a final look at Khaki to see that he'd been fed and so to bed in wet blankets on a hard floor and odd 'things' that fell from the thatch during the night.

As soon as it was light, I went to see how Khaki had fared. He was not to be seen. I thought at first the African constable had moved him to a better spot, but was soon disillusioned on that score as he emerged from another hut, having just woken up. Light rain was still falling, but we could see Khaki's spoor leading off on the path back to Gwanda – he evidently had quite enough of this caper. So, there we were, stuck in the Matopo Hills with no mount. I was just about to send the African constable off to follow the spoor and try and find the animal, when along the path came an African leading the missing horse. The story had already got round that a 'Majohnny' was spending the night in this village and Khaki was back before we even started looking for him.

The weather looked anything but propitious and, after a scratch meal and 'bonsellas' to the Village head for his hospitality and the horse retriever, we were once more on our way. Down came the rain again and by the time we reached the Matopos Mission, our little cavalcade was completely waterlogged. When I took off my coat, I found that the red dye from the lining had run and my shirt and breeches were a bright scarlet, helmet more or less reduced to pulp and leggings which could be rolled up in a ball. The American missionaries were kindness itself, loaning me dry clothes while my own were put to dry. Cleaned and refreshed after being cared for by the missionaries and a good night's rest, we set off the next morning for Fort Usher. The rain had stopped, the sun shone, the going good and we reached Fort Usher by late afternoon to be accommodated and Lieutenant H.G. Seward, B.S.A. Police entertained by Cpl. Lea and Tpr. Young. A couple of sundowners, a hot meal and so to bed. The last thirty miles to Bulawayo the next day was completed in good time and we arrived in Depot in the afternoon, where I reported to Sgt. Major Salt.

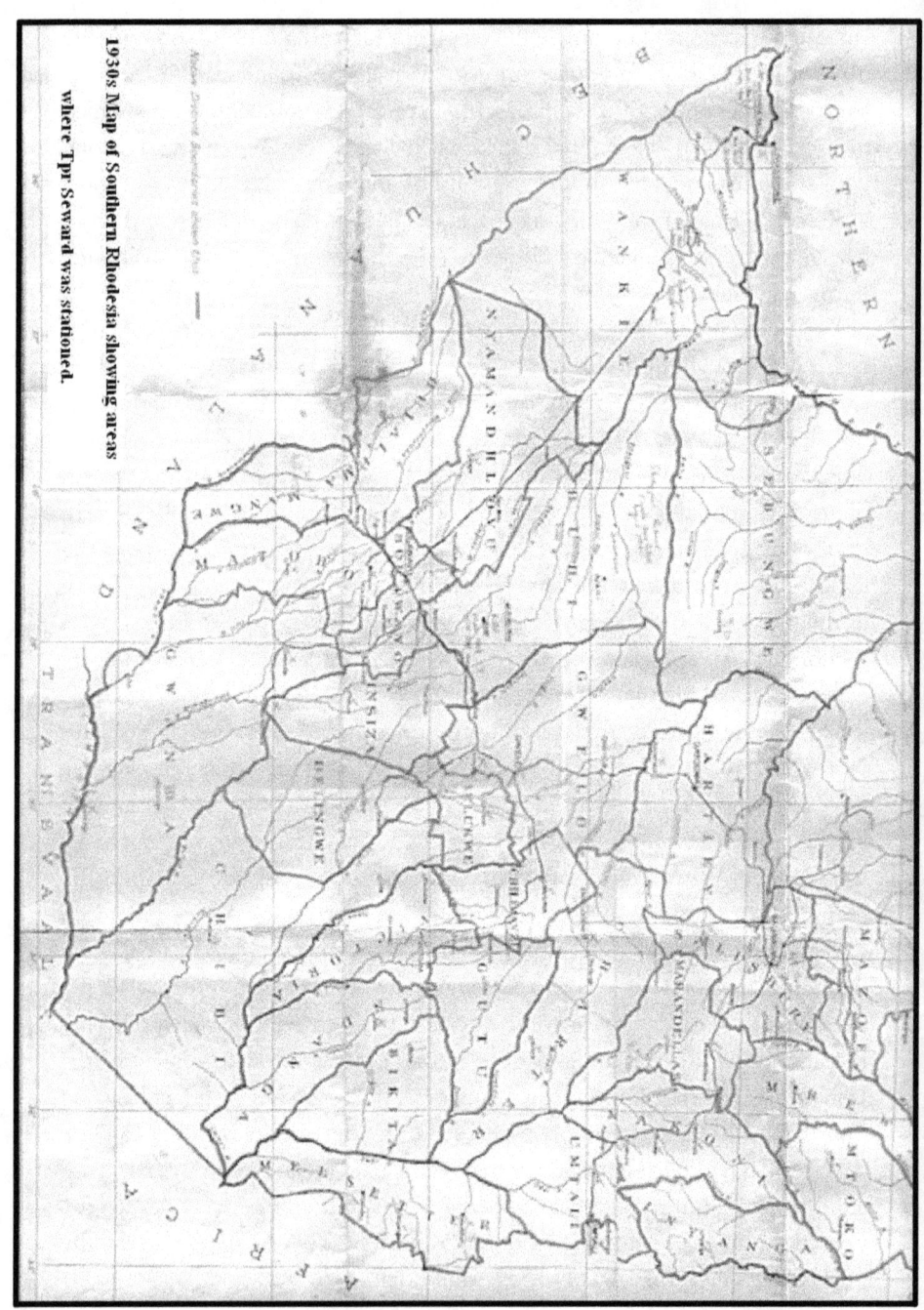

1930s Map of Southern Rhodesia showing areas where Tpr Seward was stationed.

Lieutenant H.G. Seward, B.S.A. Police

Bulawayo

Bulawayo Camp in January 1921 seemed to be a collection of nondescript, ramshackle, ant-ridden buildings – the only attempt at improving the surroundings being windswept, stunted pepper trees which surrounded a sparsely grassed square.

In the days before centralisation in Salisbury, Bulawayo had been the headquarters of the Matabeleland Division and there remained an Ordnance Store, Tailors, Saddlers and Armoury shops, together with an African Police Training School. And, there were certainly characters in Camp. One who remains in my memory even to this day was Farrier Corporal Hutchings, known to everyone as 'Snitch'. A cockney who had served many years in one of the Hussar regiments in India, who had a tremendous sense of humour and a fund of stories which earned him many a free drink in Bulawayo bars.

He lived in a pokey little room next to the stables and farriers shop which he always referred to as 'me virtuous bug-walk'. Only the very privileged were permitted entry to that holy of holies to inspect the walls which were plastered with photographs of groups of his old comrades, superb in shell jackets and pill box hats worn at incredible angles.

Snitch was a regular attendant at the Bulawayo racecourse and one day a rather supercilious young trooper, who had taken his girl friend to the races, ignored – or pretended not to know – Snitch. Rather nonplussed at first, Snitch soon recovered and turning back, went up to the young trooper and said, 'Hi, h'aint yer going to h'introduce me to your donah. I h'aint a bleeden burglar, h'am I?' I believe the girl, daughter of a well-known Bulawayo resident, was secretly delighted, for the story went the rounds for many a long day.

In matters of the turf, Snitch had a boon companion in the shape of Rodney Stone, the District Clerk. Together they were always devising schemes to beat the books, which usually ended in disaster. Rodney even had a brief career as an owner and put into practice all kinds of unorthodox training methods – even, I suspect, a little doping. He and Snitch finally gave up the ghost after a meeting during which the well-known local owner Dan

Vincent won all six races on the card, following which Snitch sagely observed very little purpose could be served by 'making rude noises' against thunder. Incidentally, I believe Dan Vincent's record of winning all the races at one meeting has never been equalled in Rhodesia or, for that matter, in South Africa.

The Troopers' Mess was run by one Jim Hannifan, an Irish ex regular soldier and a light weight boxer of no mean skill. He was at one time light weight champion of the Army in India. Somewhat irascible, he had an Irish liking for pigs and kept a little nondescript sow which used to run in and out of the mess room and woe betide anyone who dared criticise this creature's habit of pushing its way under the table during meals.

As for criticising the food, the dissatisfied one might well find himself lying on his back wondering what hit him. The poor standard of messing at this time was a frequent source of complaint. It was cheap, about three shillings a day, and nasty. The culinary art was conspicuous only by its entire absence. In the case of the town police in Bulawayo, this led to an unfortunate contretemps. One night, the night shift on returning to the main station for their midnight meal, found themselves faced with food which they considered, not without cause, quite inedible. This was the culmination of dissatisfaction which had been brewing up for some time and to a man, the five constables refused to continue their duty that night.

This dereliction of duty severely jolted Headquarters and, within hours, a Board of Officers was convened to try the offenders under the Police Ordinance and Col. Capell, the Assistant Commissioner, came down from Salisbury to act as President. Notwithstanding an able defence put up by Advocate 'Bob' Hudson (later to be a Minister in Sir Charles Coghlan's first cabinet), the five were sentenced to two months imprisonment with hard labour, Col. Capell remarking that the conduct of those concerned was tantamount to mutiny.

The sentences were served in Depot, Salisbury, but immediately after the trial the five were taken to Bulawayo prison pending their removal to Salisbury. I came into all this because the following day I was ordered to take charge of the escort to Salisbury. On arrival at the prison I was utterly confounded to find the five men had had their hair completely shaved and dressed in prison clothing. No transport was provided and I had, perforce, to march these unfortunates through the streets to the Police Station. To them it must have been a most humiliating experience and, I must confess, all my sympathies were with them. But, other times, other manners – it would be difficult to imagine members of the Police Force being treated in this manner today. The interesting thing about this episode is that one of the men concerned later became General Manager of the Rhodesia Railways. Had he stayed in the Police, he might well have ended up as Commissioner, for he was a man of many parts. Shortly after this, I was transferred to take charge of Figtree, which was to be my first posting as N.C.O. i/c.

Figtree

Figtree Village consisted of a hotel-cum-store and the railway station – the population comprising the storekeeper and his wife and the stationmaster and his wife who was also the local postmistress. The Police Camp some six miles away had originally been established as one of the forts on the Mangwe Road during the 1896 Rebellion; it was certainly picturesque, being built around the base of some huge boulders on a kopje. From the top, where one got a magnificent view of the Matopo Hills, there flew the B.S.A. Company's flag. With the exception of the office and stable, which were of Kimberley brick and iron the rest of the buildings, were pole and dagga huts, badly in need of re-thatching. There was nevertheless, plenty of elbowroom for the Outspan on which the camp was sited, being some 3,000 acres in extent – a relic of the days when this route was used by ox-wagons travelling down the Mangwe Pass Road.

Having taken over from Corporal Currie, I found that I was not only N.C.O. i/c but also had other responsibilities such as Issuer of Process, Issuer of Cattle Permits and Prosecutor. These carried in those days what was known as Extra Duty Pay (E.D.P.). It was rather a pernicious system as it often happened that at an isolated post where there were no other officials and where there was very little police work proper, the Member i/c by reason of the E.D.P. was better off than others of higher rank at much busier Police Posts. This led to people being reluctant to take leave for fear of losing a quiet station which carried substantial E.D.P. Some years later, when I was at Police Headquarters, this whole system was abolished. Almost my first patrol at Figtree was as a census enumerator in the 1921 census. I had a large area to cover, which took me towards Nyamandhlovu in one direction, down to Syringa in the other, but it was a most useful exercise, enabling me to get to know the people and the district.

One of the difficulties I encountered, however, was getting away from many of the homesteads visited. There were no telephones or radios in those days – some people relied on their news of the outside world from the weekly *Bulawayo Chronicle*, but for most the arrival of a policeman therefore was an event, he was regarded as the harbinger of news. Over the inevitable cup of tea he was expected to bring farmers up to date as to what was happening in the outside world. Getting away was always a bit of a problem and if one arrived fairly late in the afternoon there was always the pressing invitation to stay the night. Acceptance meant a squawking in the back yard of yet another chicken being sacrificed to Rhodesian hospitality.

One of the problems I had to face for the first time on this patrol was the number of men living with African women, they varied in character and habits. A number kept their women, and offspring, in the background and maintained a good standard of living. Others had obviously degenerated and lived in apparent squalor. Bulalima-Mangwe District was perhaps exceptional in this regard. But the early settlers in that part of Rhodesia found themselves in a country where there were scarcely any white women and the pattern followed that of the Cape, where, in the early days of white settlement, 75 percent of the children born to slave women in the first 20 years of Dutch occupation, were half-white. There was, about this time, a great deal of agitation in Bulawayo, led by a Mrs McKeurton, wife of the local undertaker, against miscegenation, but, listening to the men concerned, I had some sympathy with their viewpoint. Most were determined to do the best for their Coloured children, many of whom were sent to schools in South Africa for their education. And, I must add, that I admired those who accepted their responsibilities in this regard as against those who indulged in promiscuous relations with African women, regardless of the consequences. The situation too had other aspects, for I remember going to a homestead of a man who, incidentally, had been brought to the country by Rhodes as one of his bright young men. On enquiring how he was off for labour, he replied, 'Labour, I have no problems, I breed my own.' He certainly did – all Coloured.

But one sometimes wonders what all this fuss is about – after all one of the greatest governors of the Cape, Simon van der Stel, was a Coloured man. Unfortunately, skin pigmentation, then as now, is all too often the criterion applied, as against brains and the ability to use them. I do not for one moment suggest that I was able to take such a rational view in my initial contact with the problem of race as it existed then and which has been further exacerbated over the years, but it has always seemed to me that pride in the colour of one's skin over which we can exercise no volition, is not necessarily based on sound premises. But, enough of this digression and back to the patrol.

One night I had pitched my camp and over a sundowner, was watching Maleme, my servant, cooking the evening meal when along came an African with a note, yes, in a forked stick. It was from a European about two miles distant. I had purposely avoided pitching up at his homestead in the late afternoon as I'd heard he was eccentric to a degree, and hadn't much time for the police. This note, however, indicated he wanted to see me on urgent business and so off I went. It was after dark when I arrived at the pole and dagga homestead, numerous African men and women outside the door. The light of a candle revealed a bearded figure sitting on a couple of bags of mealies at a table covered in a mess of dirty plates and dishes. 'Sit down,' he said, 'I wanted to see you badly – you know the world's coming to an end,' and with that, he pulled towards him a huge Bible and started to read from the Old Testament in support of his views of the impending holocaust. Poor 'Stefan' (as he was known to the Africans) had been living with an African woman for years, completely isolated from the European community, in any case his nearest neighbour was some 15 miles away and, quite obviously, he was under some severe mental strain.

I sat with him for a couple of hours saying 'yes' or 'no' occasionally, but his hallucinations had got the better of him and it was quite impossible to hold any kind of rational conversation. His condition deteriorated fairly rapidly and within a few weeks of my visiting him he was admitted to Ingutsheni where he eventually died.

My next day's trek took me to three Europeans who were all living with African women on the borders of the Nata Reserve. One begged me to stay the night, but I couldn't as I'd left my pack some 12 miles back. He later committed suicide by taking, of all things, strychnine, a most ghastly death. In retrospect, I always regretted that I had not stayed the night with him to help with his obvious loneliness, if only for a few hours. Often these people were cut off from any form of communication during the wet season – no roads, merely meandering tracks, no bridges, no telephones and seeing no other European for weeks on end. Small wonder that some of their lives ended in tragedy.

Census over, and it's interesting to recall that the figures revealed that the total European population of Rhodesia at that time was just under 30,000, over 80 percent of whom were living in either Salisbury, Bulawayo or one of the smaller towns. I was now able to settle down to ordinary police duties.

Apart from the occasional stock theft, there was little, if any serious crime. A periodical Court was held once a month to deal with these few petty cases. It was fortunate that this was so, for the first time I ever went to Court was to prosecute. There being no other place available, the Periodical Court was held, of all places, in the dining room of the Figtree Hotel. This had its drawbacks – and advantages. The magistrate sat at a table at the end of the dining room with a door opening into the bar on his left. There were occasions when the noise from the bar tended to interrupt the proceedings and I had to go and ask the people to please be quiet and, sad to say, refuse the drinks offered me. One farmer on one occasion suggested I should go back and tells the 'beak' that the Prosecutor had been formally 'Called to the Bar'!

There was another occasion when the holding of the Periodical Court more or less coincided with my birthday and that of Tpr 'Teddy' MacPherson, who had joined me at Figtree a few months before. The court proceedings being over by midday, we adjourned to the bar together with the Magistrate and one or two others who had been witnesses in the cases before the Court. The Magistrate had to wait for the evening mail train to take him back to Plumtree and while a gin or two before lunch can be fairly innocuous, too many thereafter can be quite disastrous. To cut a long story short, the birthday celebrations got just a little out of hand and by the time the train was due to arrive, there appeared to be some doubt as to whether the 'beak' would make it. Eventually, he was wheeled to the train on the station luggage trolley and handed over to the conductor for 'safe keeping', complete with a label attached to his lapel which read: 'Extremely Fragile – Handle with Care'!

These Periodical Courts in the rural areas often had their humorous angle.

There was for instance, one 'Tiddley' Woods, who, as his name indicated, had a weakness for the bottle. At one time a fairly prosperous businessman in Bulawayo, he had fallen by the wayside and was living in somewhat strained circumstances on a small farm in the Matopos. He conceived the idea of getting a little ready cash by preferring charges of petty theft against Africans and they really were petty. This involved his appearance at the Periodical Court for the hearing and getting his witness expenses. On one occasion, in dismissing the charge, the Magistrate remarked that he thought the case a most frivolous one to have been brought before the Court. Up jumped Tiddley, 'I call that a most impertinent remark from the Bench.' Instead of fining him a fiver for contempt of Court, the Magistrate, knowing Tiddley's circumstances, observed he had had a lot to put up with from Mr Wood in the past and he hoped he'd heard the last of these ridiculous cases. Meeting a friend afterwards, Tiddley complained that there was no such thing as justice in this country, saying, 'How would you like to see your own property handed back to the thief. On enquiring as to the nature of the stolen property handed back to the thief, the friend was informed, 'A piece of soap and a box of matches!'

Some time later, Tiddley made another appearance in Court – this time as the accused. He had been indicted for the High Court sitting in Bulawayo on a charge of attempted murder, it being alleged he had fired a shotgun at an African with intent to murder. The case turned on certain remarks made in the local African language and when Tiddley went into the witness box to give evidence on his own behalf, he was questioned by Mr Justice Russell as to his knowledge of this Native language. Leaning nonchalantly over the edge of the box, Tiddley replied, 'My Lord, I have a language of my own of which all natives entering my employ have to learn,' 'My vocabulary consists of a few words such as "bonele" and "aswele".' This was in the days before assessors and Tiddley had the jury tittering and eventually they brought in a verdict of 'not guilty'. It is perhaps a good thing that trial by jury has largely disappeared in favour of experienced assessors.

Shortly after my arrival at Figtree I was approached by an old hand, Ben Morrison, who was running cattle somewhere in the Semokwe River area, to buy some 30 odd head of cattle. Owing to an outbreak of African Coast Fever, they had been stopped on their way into Bulawayo and were grazing on the government Outspan. They could not be moved until such time as the restrictions were lifted. It was necessary for any civil servant or policeman to obtain the permission of the Administrator before they could acquire livestock. I thought about it and eventually having obtained the required permission, I bought the lot for £7.10/- a head. It was a bad business deal, for shortly afterwards the bottom fell out of the cattle market and young steers were almost unsaleable in Bulawayo. On one occasion, turkey toms fetched better prices. To some extent, the uncertainty as to the political future of the country was to blame, as, in 1922, the country had to choose between continuing under the B.S.A. Company, becoming a self governing colony or joining the Union of South Africa as a fifth province. Feelings ran high – no one seemed to want to stay under the Chartered Company and protagonists of Responsible Government or incorporation into the Union stomped the countryside for some weeks before the referendum. I remember Jock Brebner and Harry Huntley from Matopos coming into camp one day and urging us to vote for going into the Union, declaring that the B.S.A.P. would have marvellous opportunities for accelerated promotion in the South African Police. But we remained unimpressed.

General Smuts visited Rhodesia during the campaign to lend his powers of persuasion in favour of joining the Union, but to no avail. Nearly fifty years later, it is interesting to recall, in view of all that has happened since, there was a very real possibility of what was then Northern Rhodesia being included in the deal for Responsible Government, but at that time no one wanted anything to do with what was called the Black North. On Referendum Day, I presided at the local Polling Station when, for the first time in the history of Figtree, there were actually three cars outside the hotel. Such a thing had never been known before – things were really moving – not to the extent of having a traffic problem though! At that stage roads in the rural areas were such that it was much safer and more reliable to stick to the old horse or mule cart. Roads meandered all over the place, as a track became unusable, a detour was made, so it was not long before some roads became over 100 yards wide and, in sand veldt, very heavy going.

It was about this time that it was decided to try and organise race meetings at Figtree, and Wally White who was breeding horses and mules, was the moving spirit in getting the Figtree Sporting Club going. I become Hon. Secretary, and several successful meetings were held on Wally White's farm where he had laid out a race track. We relied on Bulawayo owners and public for support and arranged with the railways for a special train to bring people down from Bulawayo on race days. A special train was quite an innovation and as far as my memory serves me no other race specials had ever been run before or for that matter, since. A feature at one meeting was a match between Major Gordon, a well-known Bulawayo character always known as 'Boomerang', riding his horse called Monk against Cliff Little on a horse whose name I've forgotten. A tremendous amount of interest was centred on this match which was at catch weights. In the event, Cliff Little won – he was a much younger and lighter man but old Boomerang certainly gave him a run for his money and was cheered all the way to the finish. Major Gordon, D.S.O. endeared himself to everyone in Bulawayo. He was a bachelor, had a fund of dry humour, loved entertaining and will always be remembered for his exploits with snakes which he would seize by the tail and, using them as a kind of stock-whip, crack their heads off in an exploit he had learned in his early days in Australia. He was also quite an expert at throwing the boomerang, hence his nickname.

Time passed, interrupted only by monthly inspections by Inspector Tom Goddard who was in charge of the Bulalima-Mangwe Sub-District stationed at Plumtree. We, fortunately, always knew when he was coming as he had to travel by rail to Leighwoods siding, some six miles away and a message sent through the railways that a horse would be required at the siding, gave ample warning of an impending inspection. Occasionally we would be visited by the District Superintendent, Major Tomlinson, in an old Hupmobile car – a relic of the war in East Africa. It had a top speed of 25 miles per hour. Major Tomlinson, a Jameson Raider, was usually content to go through our outstanding dockets and accept my advice as to the manner in which they should be closed. The result was that the number closed as 'False on Enquiry' far exceeded those closed as 'Undetected'. Consequently, the number of cases that remained undetected at the end of the year was relatively small, for which, perhaps, we collected undeserved kudos!

There was really no Defence Force as such at this time – the Police in fact were the first line of defence. There were what were called 'Ride Companies' in most of the rural areas. The activities of these bodies were supervised by officers seconded from the Police, known as District Staff Officers. Monthly shoots were held and rallying points selected to which district residents were supposed to foregather in the event of trouble. Basically, it was a scheme for distributing arms and ammunition round the countryside and ensuring people knew how to use them.

As Police, therefore, we were interested in defence and to test our ideas on the subject, Major Tomlinson usually used to leave us with a problem like this: 'You are in Camp with two Troopers and six African Police when you receive a report that a farm house thirty miles away has been burnt and an impi of some 150 Matabele warriors armed with assegais and knobkerries is marching from the direction of Nyamandhlovu towards Figtree. State what action you would take.' With no communication with the outside world, save through the railway telegraph, this presented quite a problem. Trooper Grosse, a bit of a wit and who was stationed with me at the time, provided an immediate solution – catch the first train to Cape Town! We did eventually submit our ideas of how this situation might be met in theory. Fortunately they were never put to the test for apart from one old Gambo, one of Lobengula's ex lieutenants living in the Nata Reserve, the local tribesmen were a pretty docile lot.

Then someone in Headquarters conceived the idea of writing Monthly Examination Papers. Some twenty questions were set each month on police and military subjects. The object was not so much to find out what we knew, but to make people look up the book and keep themselves up to date. Some of the questions lent themselves to rather facetious replies and I had to blue pencil one of the trooper's efforts who, in reply to the question – 'How would you deceive the enemy as to your strength?' replied, 'Stuff a pillow in my chest and pad out my calves,' from which it will be gathered that life was not taken too seriously in those days.

As I mentioned earlier, the first time I ever went to Court was to prosecute, but close study of Gardiner and Lansdown did not altogether substitute for lack of experience. I was happy therefore when the summons to attend a prosecutors' course in Bulawayo arrived. This involved daily attendance at the Magistrate's Court in Bulawayo where, under the guidance of Sub Inspector Jimmy Skillen, then the Prosecutor, I began to learn something of the rudiments of the proper presentation of evidence. Jimmy Skillen dominated the Court, enjoyed nothing more than defended cases and took liberties which would never have been tolerated in these more staid days. If a solicitor asked what Jimmy thought was a ridiculous question, he would murmur in a loud stage whisper 'Bloody fool', and get away with it. Jonah White was the interpreter and, having grown up in Natal, spoke fluent Zulu, very similar to Sindebele. Very few police posts had interpreters in those days and I had been trying to master the language with the aid of Elliot's Sindebele dictionary, but found it much easier to learn listening to Jonah White. One particular phrase he used struck me as being rather crude. He would say to the delinquent in dock after sentence, 'You are fined (what sounded to me like 'fukeyrown') or seven days imprisonment'. On enquiring the meaning of this somewhat lewd term from Jonah, he explained that all it meant was half-a-crown, a curious colloquialism, which might easily be misunderstood. All languages have pitfalls, as I learned taking statements from Africans when I first arrived at Figtree. I would ask about the name of a kraal to be met with the reply 'it was the village of Nasinga'. This name 'Nasinga' kept cropping up and I remember asking the African Corporal why so many Africans in the district were named Nasinga. It transpired that this was the Sindebele equivalent of 'what's his name'. Thereafter I insisted on the proper name of the kraal head – Nasinga was out.

Whilst on this course I was instructed by Major Tomlinson to make some enquiries in town as to the affairs of a certain Corporal, whom rumour had it had got himself involved financially. He had the reputation of haunting bars in town amongst other things. I proceeded on what in other circumstances, might be called a 'pub crawl'. When I totted up the results of my visits to the various bars, the total of this gentleman's cards amounted to well over £100 – none of the bar owners seemed unduly worried and there was, apparently, no thought of restricting credit. Although the bar owners were not unduly worried, Major Tomlinson certainly was and, ere long, the Corporal concerned was on his way out.

With little control of credit in bars and the fact that there were few forms of entertainment in Rhodesian towns at night, men tended to drift into bars looking for company, which was always there, and credit, which more often than not, was freely available. To some extent, all this was changed in the early '30s when the then Minister of Internal Affairs introduced a new Liquor Bill providing for the abolition of all credit for liquor on licensed premises, save for bona-fide residents on the premises, the introduction of proper tot measures and prohibiting the employment of bar-maids. The Minister at that time was one William Muter Leggate, a dour taciturn teetotaller with very little sense of humour, a bit of an anachronism in those free and easy days and many were the stories going the rounds about this particular piece of legislation. The only printable one I can recall went something like this: 'Why is Leggate like a stork?', the answer, 'Because he can stick his bill up his backside!' Looking back, however, the abolition of credit in bars was one of the best things that ever happened.

But away from this digression – I returned to Figtree knowing a little more about criminal procedure and law, not to mention the local language, to be faced with what seemed to be a spate of sudden deaths. Three herd boys sheltering under a tree during a severe storm were killed by lightning and within a week, three others reported dead on an adjoining farm. These latter were not the victims of lightning however, for I found on arrival at the farm, that they had all bought 'muti' from an African herbalist to make them 'strong'. I found what I suspected to be the remains of an aphrodisiac in the pocket of one of the deceased. Later enquiries confirmed this and revealed that two of them had paid half-a-crown for their potions, while the third had bought five bob's worth. He died within an hour or two, while the other two lingered for some hours afterwards. We collected the herbalist, together with his store of so-called remedies and aphrodisiacs, which were later taken to Bulawayo with the stomach contents of the three deceased, for analysis. Unfortunately there were no government analysts at this time and the work had to be undertaken by a private analytical chemist whose real work was in the mining field rather than forensic chemistry. Also, there were no known reagents for testing many of these local poisonous substances. The analyst's report was somewhat inconclusive and a preliminary examination resulted in the Attorney General 'declining to prosecute'.

The next death in this 'black week' could scarcely be described as sudden death. An African road worker arrived in camp shortly after dark reporting that his 'boss', an Italian road overseer, had been ill in his tent for the past three days, during which time he had not eaten. I climbed on Khaki and reached the road camp only to find that the overseer had already passed away. I got in touch with Plumtree through the railway phone and asked for a doctor to be sent up for a post mortem. It was during the rains and unfortunately the doctor was not available for a couple of days. The weather was hot and humid and by the time the doctor did arrive, the corpse was in a pretty bad state. I took Tpr Grosse with me to help at the P.M. and burial, but as soon as the doctor started his grisly work, Tpr Grosse disappeared. The P.M. disclosed that pneumonia was the cause of death. In the meantime we found some planks at the road camp, knocked up some kind of rough coffin, had a grave dug by the road gang and I read the burial service from the *Field Service Pocket Book* over the graveside. Another 'Isolated Grave' was recorded in the *General Record Book* and a week or so later, we erected a small cross over the grave and fenced it in.

Life went on with the occasional visitor. One I particularly remember was Drummond-Forbes who lived in Bulawayo, but had a ranch at Sandown in partnership with a well-known Bulawayo dentist, Dr Freeze. He usually arrived at night when we had all gone to bed, his car full of all sorts of liquor. The parties that followed are best forgotten. Drummond-Forbes had some very fine shorthorn cattle and, if my memory serves correctly, one of his bulls, 'Lomond', won the thousand-guinea trophy at the Bulawayo Agricultural Show. Another Figtree district resident at that time was David Schwartz who died some years ago in Salisbury. He and his wife struggled with the native language without a great deal of success. At one time he was buying chickens from African hawkers at sixpence a time, fattening them up for two or three weeks before having them killed, dressed and despatched to a Bulawayo Hotel. One morning when their servant brought in their morning tea, David told him to tell the African responsible for poultry to kill a turkey hen. This for a specific order from one of his Bulawayo customers. A short time later, on hearing lots of squawking going on in the yard, he went out to investigate and found that 30 of his prize hens had been slaughtered. It transpired that the message to kill a turkey hen had been construed as 30 hens. The upshot of this was a shortage of eggs at the pub for some weeks afterwards!

Mrs Schwartz was always in trouble with African servants and one day I nearly collapsed when 1 heard her talking her inimitable chilapa-lapa to a poor, unfortunate houseboy. 'Now,' she was saying, 'if I engage wena, wena must subenza mushi, ikona fana-ko-lo first time. Now, tata lo bicycle round the back but ikona ride it.' Yet somehow they got by.

Getting back to visitors. One evening just as it was getting dark, a utility cart arrived in camp pulled by a couple of horses, one of which was obviously lame. The driver, a dear old gentleman on his way to Syringa, asked if we could put him up for the night. He seemed a pleasant old chap, full of reminiscences of the early days. There was nothing much to eat in camp, so we decided to break into our reserve of tinned stuff and give the old boy a slap-up meal with all the trimmings we could muster. When he got up from the table after what we considered was the best meal we had had for many a long day, he delivered himself of this prize gaffe. 'It has,' he said, 'given me the greatest pleasure to share your frugal meal.' Once he was out of earshot Teddy McPherson turned to me and said, 'Well I'll be buggered, he should have been here last night when we had those terrible rissoles.'

A more frequent visitor was Klingenstein, the Cattle Inspector from Fort Usher and ex member of the Police. A tall, spare New Zealand bachelor whose predilections for Picardy brandy frequently landed him in trouble. He drove round the countryside in a cart drawn by a couple of mules and always with a generous supply of what he called 'medical comforts'. Punctilious in carrying out his job during the day he was apt to resort to the joys of Picardy at night and occasionally became quite obstreperous. Keen on horses, he was a great follower of the English Turf and usually had pretty hefty bets on the Classics. He turned up in camp one evening after losing heavily on a horse ridden by Gardner, Lord Derby's jockey. Now Gardner's brother was stationed with me at Figtree at the time and 'Klinkie' started on him. 'I read in the paper the other day that your brother is a quiet and gentlemanly young man. So quiet and gentlemanly in fact, that he didn't like to push his way to the front and lost me all my damn money.' There was nearly a fight over this, but we managed to calm him down eventually and his next visit was on a much happier note. Gardner won the Derby for Lord Derby on a horse called 'Papyrus' – Klinkie won a packet, sold his cart and mules and bought himself a second hand Dodge car.

Another character, son of a well-known publisher in London, had a habit of pitching up in camp on foot. He scorned Picardy brandy, preferring gin and was never without a flask in his hip pocket. He tried to deceive others, and himself, that it only contained water for the road, but the aroma of London Dry never left him and he finally ended up in a road gang for destitute Europeans at five bob a day putting down some of the original strip roads. Like a number of others of his ilk, he was never without his old school tie round his waist in place of a belt.

Talking of old school ties reminds me of one, Tustin, a recruit in Depot with me in 1920. He had very little in the way of kit and was constantly borrowing clothes for his trips into town. Approaching one of the lads one evening to borrow a tie, the young lad told him that the only one he had was his old school tie. 'That doesn't matter two hoots,' replied Tustin, 'any good school will do.' Tustin didn't last very long in the Police, but many years later when I was running the C.I.D. and Immigration in Salisbury, who should be ushered into my office but Tustin, wearing, believe it or not, an Old Etonian tie. He obviously hadn't changed, any good school will do!

With the assistance of an infatuated woman, who had fallen for his glib talk about all his ranches in Rhodesia and who had paid all their expenses to get back here, it transpired later that he had just managed to leave England in time where things were getting a little too hot for him. On instructions from Joe Brundell, the Chief Immigration Officer in Bulawayo, I had to tell Tustin that he'd been declared a Prohibited Immigrant and would have to leave the country within three days. 'But my dear old boy, you can't do that to me,' Tustin protested. But the dear old boy could and did and Tustin duly departed for pastures new in which to ply his wits. His stock in trade: a plausible tongue, a vivid imagination plus a personality that had an attraction to women. The troops have a word for his ilk – the byproduct of a bull.

But to get back to Figtree days, it was about this time I came a cropper off Khaki. Cantering along a path some ten miles from Camp, we stumbled into a mass of spring hare holes and, in trying to avoid one, Khaki put his foot into another and we turned a complete somersault. I landed on my back on a rock which knocked me out for a few minutes, but eventually I was able to remount and get to a nearby farm where I was taken into Bulawayo Hospital where I remained for nearly a month.

Grey Ward in the old Memorial Hospital in Fort Street brings back memories of Doctors Eaton, Forrester, Standish-White, Strachan and Vigne, all practising in Bulawayo at that time. Our nights were often disturbed by yells and shouting from a small annex to the ward which housed the alcoholics, many of them with the D.T.s. There was no other place in which these men could be accommodated at this time and our sympathies went out to the nurses and probationers who had to cope with these people, screeching about all kinds of animals, dominated by elephants crawling up the wall. Knowing I was in the Police, Matron came to me in high dudgeon one morning saying, 'An awful thing has happened – a policeman was found with a probationer in the linen room last night – a simply dreadful business.' Poor Miss Pettigrew: she was, however, more upset with Dr Eaton, the Medical Superintendent, than with anyone else, because when she reported the matter to him, his rather dry observation was, 'Do you think they intended to steal the linen?' She was furious, but old Dr Eaton remained unperturbed – he had a sense of humour which Matron sadly lacked.

Soon after my return from hospital, Lieut. H.M. (Monty) Surgey took over the Bulalima-Mangwe Sub-District from Inspector Goddard. His inspection visits were a joy. Blessed with a refreshingly bright outlook on life in general, he was completely unconventional and had a marvellous sense of humour. He took a poor view of the conditions under which we were living and certainly the old pole and dagga buildings were in a pretty ropey state. Yet they were typical of the times and we had become attached to them. Bending almost double to get into the 'skoff kia' scarcely seemed to bother us, nor the borer dust which frequently descended from the ancient thatched roof poles into the soup. Monty wasn't happy and eventually managed to get a whole fiver (£5) out of the B.S.A. Company to re-thatch the worst huts. No more borer dust in the soup!

It was not, however, until Responsible Government took over in 1923 that things began to happen and it was decided to move the Camp from the old Outspan to its present site adjacent to the village. Brick buildings, a real bathroom with running water, was something completely new in our experience. It seemed the lap of luxury and as far as we were concerned, the white ants could have what was left of the old Camp, which they proceeded to do in remarkably short time. In the matter of a few short months, the whole place was completely overgrown and all that remained of some 25 years of occupation was the lone, isolated grave of Trooper Egan, who died there in 1908. Gone now were the old six mile treks to the station in the old springless scotch cart for tennis on a Saturday afternoon, gone were the evening rides to the station on Station Duty (at this time, it was usual to send a man to the station to meet every mail train, no one knew why, except perhaps to 'show the flag'); gone too were the periodical courts in the pub; and, gone also were the days when one could take a gun and a dog out in the evening in search of an elusive guinea fowl or the odd duiker. We were now confined to the five acres of the new camp site. No telephone yet, but we did get a typewriter, modernising the Corps was really on its way. Until now, all correspondence had to be hand written and copied in an old-fashioned letter book, using wet rags and the letterpress. I sometimes wonder what happened to all these old letterpresses, some of which it was rumoured had been used as 'thumb screws' to produce 'voluntary' statements.

Major John Ingham had taken over the Bulawayo District from Major Tomlinson and at one of his first inspections, he suggested that I apply to sit for the forthcoming examination for promotion to commissioned rank. Should I? I was not long in making a decision and in April of 1924, proceeded to Salisbury to sit the exam together with Jerry Watson, who later became O.C. Military Forces; Cowgill, who later became a Native Commissioner and who, during the Second World War years, met his death, trying to cross the Umzingwane River in flood at West Nicholson; Jim Appleby, who later became Commissioner of Police; Stanley Adams, a pre-war policeman who had rejoined in the early twenties and three others, whose names I can't recall. As far as I can remember, four of the eight who sat the examination, qualified, all of whom were subsequently promoted, although I had to wait until early 1927 until my turn came. Looking back, it was interesting to recollect that there were at that stage, only some twenty officers in the Force. Immediately after the examination, I proceeded on my first leave to England.

Reflecting on the past some fifty years later, what were my most important memories and impressions of those first four years? First and foremost was the marvellous climate. Memories of those crystal clear sunlight days on patrol with not a care in the world will always remain with me. I remember that I sometimes found myself singing at the top of my voice on horseback, just for the joy of living.

The friendliness of the people both in towns and in the country, everyone seemed to know everyone else and were happy to meet. The simple, unsophisticated African tribesman, still living much as he did before the arrival of the European, especially in the Matopo Hills, where, amongst the men, the 'mootji' was more often than not, the only article of clothing (if a 'mootji' could be called clothing) and many of the elder headmen still wore the Zulu head-ring.

The soft sibilant Sindebele language with its sharply contrasting 'clicks'.

Nights around the camp fire with the local tribesmen gossiping with the African constables. Wood smoke and the beauty of the star-studded canopy of the African night. Nothing quite like it anywhere in the world. The early morning flush of dawn and the soft lowing of cattle in the kraal, the beginning of another day.

The animals groomed, watered and fed, breakfast cooked on a campfire, saddle up and away without rush or stress. Time – does it really matter? Not at all – 'tis given to all men to enjoy. In any case, Africans did not have watches. If one wanted to know when a certain event look place, the position of the sun provided the answer – over here, overhead, over there, delightfully simple.

The women working in the lands with seldom a break in their gossip, the shrill whistle of the picannins driving the cattle and the old men squatting in the shade, moving only as the sun mounted to keep in the shade, beer pot close at hand.

All those wonderful memories of my early impressions that will be etched in my mind forever.

Other memories of getting back to civilisation – a couple of days' leave occasionally in Bulawayo where one could stay at the Grand Hotel, the leading hotel at the time, for 17/6d a day, all in. Old McMurray, the manager, greeting one with a Mr Errrr (he liked to think he remembered everyone's name, which he couldn't, and when told would say, 'Yes, of course'); Solomon the famous Head Porter who did know everyone – he was a kind of general factotum, handled all the baggage, booked seats on the train, supervised the African Porters and was a mine of information. He and Pat Fallon of the Meikle's Hotel in Salisbury were two of the best-known characters in the country and both retired wealthy men.

The Grand Hotel at this time had its little coterie of permanent residents – Sir Charles Coghlan, his wife and daughter, Petal; 'Kapata' Mitchel, the auctioneer and his daughter; old Blackler, the jeweller; Fingleson, the local bookmaker and his wife and last, but not least Miss Huntley, sister of Harry Huntley. She wore the most incredible hats, festooned with what appeared to be bunches of artificial cherries and other fruit. They were enormous creations and how she ever managed to balance them on her head as she swept into the dining room every lunchtime remains a mystery. But the balancing effort must have been quite a strain for I never remember seeing her smile or relax in any way.

These weekend trips into town usually meant racing in the afternoon –

Dick Kelly's Dunhaven was always good for a bet, trained by Jonah White, it always looked in the pink of condition. Among the other owners and trainers, Frankie Hams, Bernard Myhill, Miles Capstick, Dan Vincent and, not forgetting 'Atti' Atkinson, for many years the Secretary of the Bulawayo Club. Dan Vincent owned the famous Black Sambo, a hollow back black gelding who looked as if he might easily break in half when the jockey mounted. Jack Cohlan was the Judge, Major Tomlinson of the Police the Official Starter and uncle 'Alf' Brewer from Westacre the Handicapper. Stakes in those days were minute compared to present-day standards: £20 for the winner of minor races and occasionally as much as £50 for the feature race of the day. With the exception of one Belstead, all the jockeys were Africans, whose riding ability and tactics made the selection of winners an interesting if not a dicey business.

Major Tomlinson was a good starter of horses but there were times when he was not so good at getting his old Hupmobile car going or started. One day, this made him late for the race and I recall seeing his old car stationary in Selbourne Avenue in charge of his batman. I stopped and enquired what had happened, but all the batman knew was that the engine had 'gone to sleep' as he put it. I left the races early that day and on the way back to town noticed that the car had obviously been moved and was no longer there. The amusing thing about all this was that although the batman had eventually been able to get the thing started, he couldn't stop it and the car finished up in the Police Camp halfway into the dining room of Major Tomlinson's quarters, knocking down a wall in the process. Up to this time, no one had ever heard of an African driving a car, certainly there were no African drivers in Bulawayo – there were only a few cars anyway and the idea of Africans ever driving was looked upon as unlikely.

Nyamandhlovu
On my return from leave in the September of 1924, I was posted to Nyamandhlovu to replace Corporal Grantham who had died there shortly before.

Nyamandhlovu (translated literally the meat of the elephant) gave rise to some argument as to how the place got its name. Some believed that at one time it had been the happy hunting ground of elephant hunters, others that it was so named because it was the much favoured grazing ground for the

King's (Lobengula's) cattle. Sometime later, I was able to talk to two of Lobengula's sons, Nyamanda and Madholi Khumalo, who were still alive and living in the district. They both confirmed that the latter explanation was the right one.

But whatever might have been the state of the veld in Lobengula's day. Nyamandhlovu was a depressing sight when the Victoria Falls train dumped me off there late one afternoon. The 1923/24 season had been a disastrous one – the rains had failed, the whole countryside was dry and arid and livestock losses had been exceptionally heavy.

Troopers Spencer and Watts met me at the station with a couple of 'bandits' to carry my kit and saddlery. A hasty look round the collection of dreary looking, corrugated iron buildings that constituted Nyamandhlovu and we were on our way to the Camp, a few hundred yards away.

My quarters – a thatched kaytor hut in one corner of the square, looked reasonably comfortable. The troopers were accommodated in a wood and iron building in the centre of the square, a building which, apart from being in an advanced stage of succumbing to dry-rot, was the happy hunting ground of white ants. Progress across the floor was an adventurous business, as the white ant incursions had been repaired by bits of old petrol cases and blue mottled soap boxes. 'Careful how you go,' murmured Spencer, 'the floor's a bit uneven' – a masterpiece of understatement.

The following day I went the rounds meeting the local officials. S.W. Greer was the Native Commissioner – a short tubby figure who hailed from Natal and a first-rate linguist from whom I was to learn a great deal about African language and customs.

He had no use for anything approaching what might he called protocol, never stood on his dignity and went out of his way to help young policemen. I never saw him wear anything other than white slacks, white shirt and a white bow tie. He was never without a huge pipe, even in Court, from which he produced clouds of 'Magaliesberg' tobacco smoke. His native name 'M'nyeli nyeli', (a short stubby indigenous tree), suited him down to the ground. He was held in the utmost respect by the local tribesmen. The only other member of the Native Department (as it was then known) was H.F. Bawden, the clerk. He was a former member of the Indian Police whose career in India had been cut short by some unfortunate contretemps of which he rarely spoke.

He had later joined the B.S.A. Police and later still, having passed the Civil Service Law Examinations, the Language and African Customs Examinations, had transferred to the Native Department. Poor old Bawden. While he could pass any examination with ease, the practical application of the knowledge he had acquired seemed to be quite beyond him. He had an incredibly pedantic approach to everyday problems affecting administration procedures, which contrasted sharply with the quick wit and pragmatic approach of 'M'nyeli nyeli', his chief, and it was for this reason they did not make a very good team.

The only other Government official was 'Jock' Paxton, the Cattle Inspector. He and his wife lived in a couple of kaytor huts between the Police Camp and the railway station. What a couple! Jock, short and squat and very Scotch, his wife tall and angular with a complexion which defies description – a result of many years spent on the West African Coast combined with an incredible thirst for Johnny Walker and kindred spirits.

They were never able to keep an African servant for more than a few days. Almost every other week, a sad-looking African would turn up in camp complaining that 'the missus has chayered me'. I would duly send one of the troopers along to find out what it was all about, never, I'm afraid, with any satisfactory result. All he got was a tirade on the short-comings of every official in the country from the Governor downwards and a masterly description, in detail, of the inability of the local native Commissioner and Member i/c the Police to control the local population. This together with dire forebodings as to the future of the country if left in the hands of people like ourselves!

Poor Jock certainly had a cross to bear, but with the aid of Johnny Walker he managed to keep going, whilst the mountain of empty bottles behind the kaytor huts grew to enormous proportions. Great was our relief when they were transferred and replaced by Reynards. Reynards, a Jameson raider, was quite a different kettle of fish who afterwards became Warden at Victoria Falls where his repertoire and anecdotes of the early days in Rhodesia earned him quite a reputation.

Nyamandhlovu District covered a huge area bounded by the Gwaai River in the north, Bubi district to the east, Bulawayo and Bulalima-Mangwe District in the south and Bechuanaland in the west. The nearest Police Post to the north was Wankie, some 200 miles away. The intervening country (including what is now the Wankie Game Reserve) was largely uninhabited save for a few Bushmen, although the newly established timber concessions in the vicinity of Umgusa Spur on the line of rail, were just starting up. Patrols in that part of the country were quite an adventure and mostly undertaken by a mounted native constable. Nyamandhlovu being one of the two Stations in the country that had mounted native constables on strength – the mounts by the way being mules. The lack of any means of communication, other than by runner, created many problems, as did also the complete absence of roads.

On one occasion a murder was reported from a remote corner of what is now the Gwaai Reserve and I asked for a doctor to be sent out from Bulawayo to conduct a post-mortem. In due course, Dr Vigne arrived in a taxi driven by one Dick Farrell, a well-known Bulawayo taxi driver. I gave them a guide and after spending the night in camp, they set off at sun-up the next morning, only to return long after dark, reporting that it was quite impossible to get within about sixty miles of the spot where the alleged murder had taken place. There was nothing for it but to send Trooper Spencer out with instructions to try and reach the spot and if practical, to have the body carried in.

Spencer was away a week and came back to Camp with the head of the deceased in a nose-bag, reporting that the body was in such a state of decomposition that it was impossible to bring it back. However, as the injuries which allegedly caused the death were head ones, he thought the next best thing was to bring the head back for the necessary post-mortem examination. This grisly object hung in a tree overnight and the next morning Spencer took it into Bulawayo by train for examination. A little unorthodox perhaps, but the best that could be done under the circumstances. Such were the conditions under which the Police had to work at the time.

To digress, I thought the time had now come when I should make some enquiries regarding the cattle I had left behind at Figtree when I went on leave. They had been left with a farmer who had undertaken to look after them in return for a percentage of the calf crop. In reply to my letter, I was told that, owing to the drought, I had lost the bull, four cows and nearly all the new calves, who had died of stiff sickness. 'What did I want to do now?' he asked. My brief essay into the cattle business seemed doomed to disaster, as there was nowhere to keep the beasts at Nyamandhlovu. The silent rancher business was obviously out for me. I wrote to a dealer who offered me about a third of what I had paid but deciding to cut my losses, I accepted.

With the proceeds, I bought my first motor car, a second-hand Dodge two-seater from a firm in Bulawayo. The salesman was none other than 'Bunny' Cairns, the founder of a well-known firm now bearing his name in Salisbury. Running a car in those days was quite a tricky business – there were, for instance, no petrol pumps anywhere in the country. Petrol was only supplied in cases – two, four gallon tins in each case and running out of petrol could be quite a problem, so one never ventured too far without a spare case in the boot. A shovel and an axe also formed an essential part of one's motoring equipment.

It is interesting to recall that, at this time, drivers in rural areas did not require a driving licence and, save in the Municipal areas, there was no such thing as car registration or number plates. All we had to pay was a wheel tax of ten shillings a wheel per annum for which a small metal disc was issued to be attached to the car in whatever manner the owner cared to choose. Let it be said that it was just as well that car owners were not milked in respect of tax, for the roads were still pretty primitive and journeys of any length, quite adventurous. Digging out of sand in the dry weather, fixing chains and digging out of mud in the wet, only to find in the end that the only way of getting out was to be hauled out by oxen.

The big motoring adventure, however, was the arrival in Nyamandhlovu, a few days after Christmas 1924, of the Court-Treatt Cape to Cairo Expedition, the first of its kind ever to be undertaken. The car, a Crossley Tender of the type used by the Royal Flying Corps and the Royal Air Force during the 1914-18 War, rolled into camp late one afternoon and from it descended a tall burly figure who introduced himself as Major Court-Treatt! He was accompanied by his wife Stella, a very attractive, petite brunette and a youngster of about my age who turned out to be Stella's brother.

This was the first I'd heard of such an expedition and I got quite a start when, in reply to my question as to where they were off to, Court-Treatt mentioned, quite casually, Cairo. Good God, I thought, what the hell are they doing in Nyamandhlovu – the only road north from here peters out less than twenty miles away and Cairo is quite a bit further on! Still, better hold my horses for the moment until such time as we can get down to tintacks tomorrow.

So, having turned out the 'bandits' to help them pitch their camp on the edge of the square, I invited the party along for a sundowner and whatever dinner we could muster. The following morning I had a chat to Court-Treatt as to what route they intended to follow and he proceeded to produce a map showing the old Pandamatenga Road to the Falls! This did, many moons ago, provide a route for the pre-pioneers and missionaries from Bechuanaland along the border, but as far as my limited knowledge went, it hadn't been used for over thirty years and had probably disappeared altogether under bush encroachment.

How incredible I thought, that such an expedition should have started off without any reliable information as to roads or even tracks, theirs was certainly going to be a tough assignment. 'Time spent on reconnaissance,' says the book, 'is seldom wasted' but it appeared as if there had been very little, certainly on this section of their route.

All I could tell Court-Treatt was the nearest point to the old Pandamatenga Road was the Native Department sub-station on the west bank of the Gwaai River. If he cared to try that, we would send a runner to Tjolotjo and advise the people there to expect them and to assist in any way possible. Although he seemed to be perfectly happy with this, I was beginning to have second thoughts about it, with visions of possibly having to send out a patrol to rescue a stranded party.

I enquired about how they were equipped – petrol, oil, spares, food, medical supplies, water, etc., as there was literally no hope of them obtaining supplies of any kind on the route they proposed taking until they reached the Falls. The extra forty-four gallon drum of petrol was not likely to take them very far, given that part of the route would be heavy going through Kalahari sand. I managed to persuade them to leave some of their huge stock of spares with me and take an extra drum of fuel instead. As it was, the Crossley was carrying an enormous load of camping equipment, food, clothing, photographic material, apart from spare wheels and tyres and unless they could work out some kind of drill, the making and breaking of camp every day was going to be a laborious business for all concerned. Up until now, all had gone reasonably well as they had more or less been in touch with civilisation since leaving the Cape, but they scarcely seemed to realise that, from now on, the going was going to be, to put it mildly, tough with a capital 'T'.

Court-Treatt thought it would be a good idea to start off from Nyamandhlovu on New Year's Day (1 January 1925) so with this in mind the troops and I put our heads together with the idea of giving the expedition a good send-off. The chickens were duly slaughtered; we got the only two bottles of 'bubbly' from Iky Meltzer's pub and managed to lay our hands on a tinned Christmas pudding.

Sundowners put us in good form for the dinner, which incidentally, put quite a strain on our cutlery and crockery resources, not to mention the shortage of glasses.

None the less, in the frame of mind in which we found ourselves, the 'bubbly' tasted just as good in enamel mugs! Save that the chicken was as tough as hell and Charlie, my servant and cook, had rather overdone the Worcester sauce, the dinner all passed off well to the strains of de Groot and the Piccadilly Orchestra on my old gramophone.

We then took turns in dancing with Stella – this time by favour of Carol Gibbons and the Savoy Orpheans – nostalgic memories indeed. Rain was pelting down outside, but nothing mattered. Come midnight, we gave of our best over 'Auld Lang Syne', toasted the expedition and so to bed.

At daybreak the following morning, I sent my old horse 'Khaki' along the Tjolotjo Road in charge of a Native Constable, as I had promised to accompany the party in the Crossley for the first five miles. The village of Nyamandhlovu turned out to bid the party 'bon voyage' and off we set. Fortunately the rain had stopped and the sun was shining, but we had to go through a small muddy spruit which seemed to be a problem for the Crossley and I couldn't help wondering how the expedition was going to fare when they got into real mud, as inevitably they were destined to do.

By now, Khaki was in sight and it was time to say good bye. They left me saying that by this time next year they would be in Cairo. I couldn't help wondering if they would make it at all! In the event it took them two years after many trials and tribulations and as far as I can remember, it took them two months to get from Nyamandhlovu to Wankie. The only contact I had after that was a belated message from Kapiri Mposhi in what was then Northern Rhodesia, asking me to forward the spares they had left with me over nine months previously. My only memento of this visitation was a copy of Bernard Shaw's *Pygmalion*, given to me by Stella's brother and some snaps of Stella in camp at Nyamandhlovu, looking remarkably 'soignée' in her beautifully cut khaki suit. I often wondered what she must have looked like after weeks in the Ngamo Flats during the wet weather! I got the impression she had great courage, she certainly needed every ounce of it on what must have been an incredibly difficult trip. Curiously enough I happened to be in London during my leave in 1928 and there in the Stoll Theatre in Kingsway, the film of the Court-Treatt Cape to Cairo Expedition was being shown. How easy it all looked in celluloid, viewed from a comfortable seat with appropriate background music. How different in reality.

But now back to Nyamandhlovu; the time had come for me to have a look-see at the district and so it was that I was to meet some of the residents. The Binghams, a charming old world couple – Mrs Bingham gracious and full of wit – Jack, an elegant, immaculate Edwardian figure and grandson of Lord Lucan, a controversial figure in the events leading up to The Charge of the Light Brigade during the Crimea War. Both were extremely kind to me during the time I was stationed at Nyamandhlovu, as was Jack's brother, Lionel, who maintained a separate bachelor establishment on the same farm. I spent many happy weekends at Edwalini.

The farm Spring Grange, where George Mitchell, later to be Prime Minister, was building up a magnificent herd of pedigree Herefords – both he and his wife were delightful hosts. They always had a house full of guests for Christmas, among whom I was fortunate to be one.

Jack Poole late of the 60th led a bachelor existence on Cawston Block. A great character full of wit with a tremendous zest for life. He came out of the 1914-18 War full of decorations of which he rarely spoke. His house when he was there – which wasn't often – was, in the manner of most bachelors, rather untidy. Periodicals and magazines by the dozen strewn all over the floor provided a happy hunting ground for rats which infested the place. They seemed to have a predilection for *Country Life*, which Jack observed, showed how intelligent they were! On a more serious note, rats were a real problem on Cawston Block, for Jack had planted quite an acreage of cotton which was completely ruined by a plague of them in 1925.

Jack left Rhodesia in 1926/27 after what he called a period of mucking about in Matabeleland and in 1929 joined the Sudan Political Service. Being on the Reserve of Officers he was recalled to his regiment in 1939 and had the bad luck, after having been a P.O.W. in the 1914/18 War, to go into the bag again at Calais in 1940. His escape from Germany after tremendous difficulties at the third attempt in 1916 was spectacular enough for King George V to summon him to a private audience. In tribute to him in the *Times* after he died, the Hon. Terence Prittie wrote: 'His active and astute brain was behind some of the most exciting and successful escapes of the war. Those of us who served with him will remember too, his warm heart, ready wit and patient courage. He was an inspiration to all who knew him, not just behind the barbed wire, but throughout a life full of friendship and shared laughter.' What a loss to Rhodesia when he left.

The Prince of Wales toured Rhodesia in 1925 and arrangements had been made for the Royal Train to stop at Morgan's Spur on the way back from the Falls for a duck shoot on the pans there and I accompanied Mr Greer to meet the party. A number of people had come out from Bulawayo for the shoot, including Col. Birney, General Manager of the Railways and Ellman-Brown. On the arrival of the train, we were all introduced to His Royal Highness, after which Col. Birney took H.R.H. off in his Sunbeam car to the pans. All went well until the Sunbeam got stuck in the mud near the pans and in spite of all efforts, proved impossible to extricate. I was travelling with Greer in his Willys Overland immediately behind the Sunbeam and it fell to us to collect H.R.H., who was a little sarcastic about the shortcomings of British cars as against American ones in this particular kind of country.

Admiral Halsey and Captain Dudley North, who were also part of the entourage, shot extremely well, but H.R.H. was not particularly keen. When Ellman-Brown came along saying, 'Come along here, Sir, I think this is the best place,' he was treated to a short but pithy dissertation on the merits of the 'best place' and we all promptly adjourned for a cold beer underneath a shady tree. A pleasant interlude, although I got the impression that the Prince was rather bored and really not interested in the shoot.

Later that year, Greer suggested that I should have a go at taking the Native Language examination in Sindebele and, in order to get some practice, I should try and prosecute in the language – he would put me right where I slipped up. This served me in good stead and enabled me to qualify when the time came. Court in Nyamandhlovu was held in the Native Commissioner's office, a kaytor hut, certainly not very impressive surroundings. The accused squatted on the floor, almost at the feet of the 'beak' who, before the proceedings commenced, would light up the inevitable pipe, blowing out huge clouds of blue smoke, settle himself in his chair and, after a suitable interval to ensure the unfortunate miscreant was duly impressed by the majesty of the law, would remark, 'Well, Seward, let's get started.'

In long cases involving a preliminary examination, Greer would say, 'Lead the evidence if you like but I always find it best to let them tell their own story and if there are any points you want to bring out, you can ask questions afterwards.' And that's how it usually worked out in the end. Greer had a far bigger vocabulary in Sindebele than most Africans who appeared before him and seemed to know instinctively whether or not he was being told the truth. Above all, he had tremendous patience and would spend an enormous amount of time quietly listening and then suddenly spring a question which would completely shatter the composure of the accused or witness. 'Ah,' Greer would murmur, 'now we're getting closer to the truth.' At the same time, I was learning that in dealing with African affairs, patience was the key.

As I mentioned earlier, we had two of Lobengula's sons living in the district and they occasionally came into Nyamandhlovu to pay their respects to the Native Commissioner. Madhloli Khumalo, especially, was a most commanding figure, well over six feet tall, tremendously well built and with quite a presence. The usual crowd of litigants outside the office would greet his arrival with cries of 'Baba, Inkoos Inkulu' and so on. A chair would be produced in the Native Commissioner's office, it was inconceivable that the Khumalo should sit on the floor, and Greer would discuss with him the affairs of the district. Almost without fail, Madhloli would come over to see me in the Police Camp afterwards. Always I would compliment him on the condition of his horse and always, he would talk of everything under the sun except what he had really come for – a tin of saddle soap. I made a point of seeing that he never went away empty-handed.

New settlers began arriving in the district – a Col. and Mrs King together with their son and the Hon. Peter Tufton, who opened up Rochester Farm with the idea of growing tobacco and cotton. They soon became known as the 'tough kings', but somehow or other, never seemed to be able to establish reasonable relations with their African labour or house servants. Mrs King in particular, seemed to have some kind of phobia about Africans and I remember spending a great deal of time investigating her complaint that an attempt had been made to poison them which eventually appeared to be completely without foundation. After this episode the whole family spoke in French whenever Africans were around. Needless to say I came to the conclusion they would not last long in Africa, which indeed proved to be the case, for not long after I left Nyamandhlovu, they all left to return to England.

Two things did stick in my mind about Rochester – the first, a huge wild fig tree on a small rock outcrop in a land that they were preparing for tobacco. Whilst on a visit there, the son, Cecil, asked my advice on how they could get rid of this outcrop and large tree in the middle of the land. I remembered we had a case of gelignite back in camp, left behind by a roads overseer and I suggested that we could use some of this to good effect. Packing forty sticks into jam tins, well tamped down, we blew the whole thing to smithereens, to the consternation and utter amazement of the farm workers. The other was the fact that the Kings had installed water-borne sanitation in the house – this in a land of long-drop, piccanin kias was quite an innovation and the envy of everyone in the district.

Then there were the Barrys, Gerald Barry and his wife Lady Margaret, arrived by train one afternoon to stay with the Binghams. To their consternation, the only transport the Binghams had provided to take them to the farm some ten miles away was a small ox wagon. Gerald Barry explained that his wife had not been too well and the thought of a three-hour journey in a springless ox wagon was rather daunting. I explained that the ox wagon was the only transport the Binghams had but I would be quite happy to run them out in my old Dodge, an offer that was gratefully accepted. Gerald Barry, who served with the Coldstream Guards in France during World War I, joined the Rhodesian Forces at the outbreak of war in 1939 and later commanded a battalion of the Black Watch in Somaliland and Crete, where he earned a reputation as a fearless leader. Unfortunately for Rhodesia, the Barrys decided to return to England in the 1950s.

It was about this time that Police Headquarters decided to have what was called a Police Conference each year. Each district would elect one N.C.O. and one Trooper to attend the conference in Salisbury, to discuss domestic problems affecting what might be called the Corp's internal economy. I was elected to represent Bulawayo District and I well remember Col. Capell, the then Commissioner, holding up his hands in horror at one of the resolutions passed – this to the effect that hot water should be provided in bathroom blocks in Depot and the various district Headquarters. 'I bath and shave in cold water every day,' said Capell, 'and so can you.' There were, of course, the inevitable sceptic mutterings in the background to the effect that they doubted whether the old so-and-so ever had a bath!

There was at this time, a whisky war going on in Salisbury and Bill Over confided in me that he could let me have a case of Johnny Walker Black Label or Dimple Haig for ten bob (shillings) a bottle. No sooner said than done and if any good came out of this particular conference, it was the two cases I took back to Nyamandhlovu with me – if hot baths were out of the question, we could certainly warm the inner man!

Inyati

During the early part of 1926, I received instructions to proceed to Inyati to take over from Sgt. Major Salt who was off on leave. I enjoyed Inyati. The old London Missionary Station is the oldest in the country and there I learned much about the early history of Rhodesia and improved my knowledge of Sindebele. Salt had left behind his Australian cockatoo, a damnable bird that insisted on flying into the 'skoff kia' at meal times and leaving what one wit described as its 'visiting cards' all over the place. I didn't mind this so much but when it started on my car, the 'cards' were having a curious effect on the paintwork and I decided it was time to put Master Cockatoo under lock and key for public indecency.

One day I found Leslie Seymour-Smith, who had been with me at Nyamandhlovu, sheltering under a mopani tree, complete with donkey, tent and prospecting pan. He had the mining bug and was intent on discovering a fortune hidden somewhere away in that arid bush country. Inyati was a district full of prospectors and miners full of enthusiasm, always looking for that elusive 'tail' in the pan. Miners, in contrast to the farmers of Nyamandhlovu who were always pessimistic, were invariably optimistic, another few shots or another few yards of digging and there was a fortune awaiting them. As for mining generally, I came to the conclusion that it was far easier to put money into the ground than to try and take it out. But Leslie did quite well eventually out of what I believe, was the Patsy Mine near

Essexvale. At any rate, he now owns the Leopard Rock Hotel on the Vumba and a very genial host he is to boot.

'Cerebos' Salt having returned from leave, I now found myself under orders for transfer to Depot in Salisbury. In Bulawayo, 'Snitch' Hutchings and Rodney Stone decided we must have a farewell party on the night before I was to leave for Salisbury.

What a night! We went over to the Drill Hall in my car – I certainly remember going there, but nothing at all of the return journey. What I do know is that on waking up next morning, I found the car half way up the barrack room steps with two flat front tyres. Along came 'Snitch'. 'Blimey' he said, 'That's the last ruddy time I'm ever going to go in a car with you, it was worse than any flipping rodeo ride.' Rodney Stone joined us inspecting the damage, casually observing in passing, that the sooner I left tor Salisbury, the better it would be for all concerned. But, it was a good send-off!

Salisbury Depot

Depot, when I eventually arrived, had undergone many changes since my first arrival there, gone were the old wood and iron barrack rooms and troops were now accommodated in comparatively modern blocks with two men to a room and where, wonder of wonders, hot water had at last made its appearance in the bathrooms. Reporting to Capt. Rochester, the then Commandant, I was told I was to take over instruction in Law and Police Duties for both European and African recruits. Ideas were changing however and instead of 'instruction' being confined to reading out passages of the *Police Code Book*, compiled by Capt. Phillips way back in 1913 it was proposed that a complete new syllabus be drawn up. Would I kindly get on with it right away?

Salisbury in 1927 was still very much a 'one-horse' town with a European population of about 8,000 and with sprawling suburbs and very dusty roads. Tarmac had not yet made its appearance. The speed limit was 15 miles per hour, which resulted in my first appearance in Court as an accused when I was fined £2 for speeding along Second Street at 20 m.p.h. Most people cycled to their offices in the morning, whilst rickshaws remained the troops' favourite method of getting into town at night.

About this time there was some excitement in Camp when a recruit was found dead in his bed one morning. Apparently he had been involved in some kind of fracas in one of the bars in town the previous evening and had been hit over the head but it was never discovered who was responsible. A month or two later, a young recruit was murdered by his room mate who stabbed him through the body with a bayonet – a grisly business which I had to investigate at two o'clock in the morning. The recruit responsible was found to be mentally deranged and later removed to a mental institution in England. The only comment from R.S.M. 'Jock' Douglas was, 'It's terrible, getting more like the Foreign Legion every day.'

Early in 1927, having been promoted to Commissioned Rank at the magnificent salary of £30 a month, one of my first duties was to accompany the then Governor, Sir John Chancellor, on a tour of the Umvukwes as a kind of extra A.D.C. I reported to Government House where I received instructions to do a preliminary reconnaissance of the route and the places where H.E. was to stop overnight. This was just at the time of the first tobacco boom, when farmers in the Umvukwes were getting three shillings and six pence a pound for their crop and everyone was on top of the world. 'Beauty' Andrews was the 'tobacco king' and the leading light in the tobacco world. Everyone was looking forward to H.E.'s visit and full of bright prospects for the future. Alas, with the world recession in a few short years, many of the farms were left derelict, their owners working on strip roads and the Lobangwe diversion on the Victoria Falls railway line. What is now known as the Centenary area was completely unoccupied, the last farm in the Umvukwes area being Donji, occupied by Quinton. Beyond that and considered completely in 'the blue', was Tremlett, whose farm could only be reached by careful negotiation of somewhat hazardous corduroy bridges which swayed uneasily under the weight of a car. Now of course, Tremlett's farm is in the middle of a prosperous tobacco area.

In 1927, 'Show Week' in Salisbury was the affair of the year. Dances and dinner parties were the order of the day, culminating in the 'Show Ball' at the Prince's hall, where the music was provided by Dave Sheppard's band. The earliest I got to bed that week was two-thirty in the morning, after Umvukwes had played Marandellas at rugger in the Meikle's lounge, the 'ball' being an oval tray. The game was abandoned when the 'ball' disappeared through a window and 'Robbie' Robinson, the manager, politely suggested that enough was enough!

Carefree, halcyon days – the show itself intimate where everyone knew everyone else. The ground itself was quite small and cars drew up all the way around the ring often with room to spare.

Earlier in the year, it had been decided to send a Police column through the Goromonzi, Marandellas, Mrewa and Mtoko Districts. This was intended as a kind of training exercise in addition to 'showing the flag' in the rural areas.

On this occasion, the column was commanded by Capt. Rochester, with Lieut. Parr as second in command, Lieut. Stanley-Adams in command of No. 1 Troop and myself in command of No. 2 Troop supported by a machine gun Troop and the Askari platoon. Transport, consisting of mule wagons, was the responsibility of an old sweat, 'Conductor' Schlacter, who was assisted by none other than Sgt. Hughes-Halls. My Troop was made up of newly joined recruits who had only been out from the U.K. for a matter of a few weeks and their efforts at cooking in the bush had to be seen to be believed. One of our biggest problems was getting the supply wagons through the rough tracks and quite frequently, we had to make our own tracks through the bush.

At Mtoko, the column split up and I had to take my Troop through the Mtoko Reserve to the Mazoe River, after establishing a base camp not far from an abandoned small working curiously named 'New Fullback', near the foot of a hill called Bombodza. Thereafter we were referred to as the Bombodza Bombardiers! A night spent on the banks of the Mazoe River was memorable by the fact that lions grunting and occasionally roaring upset our horses, so much so that most of the night was spent trying to pacify them. Nevertheless, a couple got away and got badly injured on the rocks in the riverbank and bed.

The following morning an African messenger arrived with a message from the O.C. to the effect that my Troop and I were to return to Mtoko with all possible speed. No reason was given, but I got the Troop saddled up and made our way back to the base camp at Bombodza, arriving there about midday, only to find the place deserted and a facetious note pinned to a tree which read, 'Gone without paying the rent', signed 'Bombodza Bombardiers'. Shortly afterwards, Stanley-Adams arrived with his Troop, but we were completely out of rations, either for horses or ourselves. We decided that, as no reason had been given for the recall, we would spend the night at Bombodza, giving the horses a well-earned rest, and push on to Mtoko before sun-up next morning.

The next day's trek was dull and weary, broken only by our midday halt when Stanley-Adams and myself sat by the side of a small spruit indulging in flights of fancy as to what would constitute a good meal when we got back to civilisation. His tastes centred around all kinds of exotic dishes, mine were more mundane, a good tender rump steak would suffice. Arriving eventually at Mtoko in the late evening, we were greeted by the news of a strike at the Shamva Mine. Some half a dozen three ton lorries were parked at the Police Camp ready to take the troops through to the mine, while I was to be left with a dozen men to take the horses to Shamva.

It was all damned silly really. If the information regarding the strike had been sent to us while we were camped on the Mazoe River, we could have trekked upriver and been at Shamva in the time it had taken us to get to Mtoko.

The strike at the Shamva Mine fizzled out within a matter of days without serious incident, but it rather shook the Government of that time and we were ordered to remain camped by the Mazoe River in case any further trouble occurred. After a couple of weeks spent camped in the shade of M'sasa and M'tuti trees in the Mazoe valley and enjoying the hospitality of one Dr Plowright, whose skills at mixing 'zonke bottle cocktails' still remains in my memory, we returned to Depot.

The following January (1928), I proceeded on leave to the U.K. And it was when travelling on the *Dunlace Castle* I met my future wife, Joan Fall, daughter of Col. C.S. Fall, who later became Deputy Commissioner of the South African Police. Joan was, and for that matter still is, one of the world's worst sailors and did not put in an appearance on deck until the Cape rollers had been left well behind, but our 'Union Castle romance' has survived forty-six years of varied adventure and vicissitudes and is still going strong.

I had traded in my old bull-nosed Morris car with Messrs Over & Co. before leaving Salisbury and had arranged to take delivery of what was called a Morris All-Steel-Dominion-Model on arrival in London, constructed, it was claimed, especially for tropical conditions. While it went well in the U.K., its performance under Rhodesian conditions, as you will hear later, fell far short of meeting 'dominion conditions'.

One of my first trips in the new Morris was to visit Joan, who was staying with her aunt in East Coker, Somerset. Purely by chance, I discovered that Harry Morton, who had been with me in the Police at Figtree, was living at Blackford outside Sherborne, not too far away from East Coker and little time was lost in getting in touch with him. An enthusiastic horseman, Harry was a subaltern in the North Somerset Yeomanry (which he later commanded in the last war) and I spent many happy days with him visiting various point-to-point meetings in the Blackmore and Taunton Vale country when he usually had a good horse or two racing.

In April 1928, I received advice from the High Commissioner's office in London, that arrangements had been made for my attachment to the 1st Battalion, the Argyll and Sutherland Highlanders (presently stationed at Shorncliffe), to receive instruction on machine guns. I duly reported to the Adjutant there, only to learn that the Machine Gun Company was at that time doing firing practice at Lydd, which was not any great distance from my home in Tenerton. Apart from the time spent on the range at Lydd, I found peacetime soldiering a little dull. Back in barracks at Shorncliffe, one had to be in uniform until lunch, after which members of the mess went their various ways. It was an expensive experience, every officer had to provide livery for his servant and contribute towards full dress uniform for both pipe and regimental bands. I recall with some amusement being introduced to the Brigadier who, on hearing the words 'British South Africa Police' said, 'Quite remarkable, I thought you were all Dutchmen'. The Brigade Major, who lived in the Argyll's mess, was Archibald Nye, who became Vice-Chief of the I.G.S. during World War II and afterwards held high office in both India and Canada. He was very interested in Africa and we often talked about the future of Africa in general and Southern Africa in particular. Alas, how many of our pigeons have come home to roost.

Returning to Rhodesia. I found the Mess in Depot undergoing a facelift, with everyone living in tents in the grounds. Not before time and now, for the first time in history, the Mess was being provided with bathrooms and, believe it or not, hot and cold running water. Gone, or in the process of going, were the old hip baths in one's rooms that had more than served their purpose up to now.

Posted back to Salisbury as Assistant District Superintendent Police (A.D.S.P.), under Capt. 'Auntie' Phillips, my first inspection tour gave me the opportunity of testing out my new Morris All-Steel-Dominion model in

Rhodesian conditions. It certainly didn't take long, for on the road to Goromonzi I went over a couple of bumps and the brakes went on and stopped the car. The rear springs had flexible shackles fore and aft and when hitting a bump the whole spring 'flattened' and automatically put the brakes on. There was nothing for it but to cut a couple of small logs and jam them between the spring and the chassis. So much for the Dominion model made specially for colonial conditions. Needless to say, the rest of the journey between Goromonzi, Marandellas, Wedza, Mrewa and Mtoko was boneshakingly uncomfortable. Corporal 'Fatty' Harmer and Howman, the Native Commissioner at Goromonzi, were a good team, while at Marandellas, Posselt, a first class linguist was the Native Commissioner and Sgt. Major Breeden the N.C.O. i/c Police. Marandellas at this time boasted a Village Management Board of which Breeden was the part-time secretary at £7.10/- a month. The Marandellas Hotel, run by Plint, was pretty primitive, even by the standards of those days. It always amused me to find that most of the cutlery and crockery had belonged either to the Rhodesia Railways, the South African Railways, Meikle's Hotel, the Union Castle Line and even the Savoy Hotel in Beira. Spending the night at the old Macheke Hotel, then run by Messrs Webster and Kilpin, I met up with Major Lewis Hastings, who had tobacco interests in the district. A very voluble character, with decided views on almost every subject under the sun and a gifted pen. He is probably best remembered for his colourful contributions to debate in the Rhodesia Legislative Assembly and his book of poems, *The Painted Snipe*. During World War II, he made something of a reputation as a military commentator for the B.B.C., when his pithy analysis made interesting listening. But at Macheke that night, the talk was more mundane – mostly on the shortcomings of African labour.

At Mrewa, 'Werei' Edwards was the Native Commissioner and monarch of all he surveyed and from what I remember, he had spent practically all his service in that district. Thus, he knew everything that went on there and the history of most of the inhabitants. This, in striking contrast to the present state of affairs when young District Commissioners and District Officers are constantly being transferred before they really have time to get to know their districts, quite apart from the inordinate amount of paper work which keeps them 'chairbound'. Many a young policeman learned a lot about the Shona language and customs from 'Werei'.

At Mtoko, Latham the Native Commissioner was away and Corporal Howard was i/c Police and had with him Trooper Pendered, a young recruit who was making great progress in Shona and African customs generally. I remember Pendered only too well for, when I was lecturing in Depot, he asked more questions than any other recruit I recall. He advanced rapidly on joining the Native Department after leaving the Police. Later in the year, I was transferred to Bulawayo to relieve the A.D.S.P. 'Bute' Edwards. Major Pitt-Schenkel was the D.S.P., and was the one Police Officer I know who sported a monocle. Not one of the world's workers, he had a habit of passing any paper from Headquarters which required any thought on to his Assistant, for, as he put it, 'your views'. These being duly forthcoming, he would send it back to Headquarters as representing his own views in the matter, without adding or changing a word. There was an amusing story about 'Pitt' and his monocle. When he was O.C. Hartley District, he had one Trooper Dauncy brought before him for being absent without leave. Screwing his monocle into his eye, he gazed sternly at Dauncy saying, 'You know Dauncy, if this was on active service, I could have you shot.' Dauncy, who was a bit of a wit, murmured, 'I hope you won't be as hard as all that on me Sir!'

Pitt loved parades and one Saturday morning whilst I was with him, he mustered all dozen men in Camp in Bulawayo and proceeded to put them through what he called 'their paces', finally calling on them to 'double' and then turning to me saying, 'Fine body of men, Seward.' Snitch Hutchings the farrier, now getting on in years, thought the proceedings had gone too far and dropped his ride. In a stage whisper, which Pitt must have heard but made no comment, Snitch remarked, 'Now the old bugger will want to charge me for casting away me arms.' It was all rather ridiculous and I couldn't help thinking the sooner the old so-and-so was pensioned off the better.

Returning to Salisbury, I found myself taking over Salisbury town, with the intriguing prospect of earning some £8 a month extra duty pay. There were at this time, special allowances for Town Branch and a further allowance for supervising Railway Police who at that time, formed part of the Force. In addition I became censor of films with a free seat at all cinemas I cared to attend. This job was a complete sinecure, as all one had to do was go through the list of films sent to us by the South African Police, who acted as censors in the Union. At that time, there was no Board of Censors, either here or in South Africa.

Soon after taking over, the first and only strike of European railway men occurred and the Rhodesia Railways came to a complete standstill. To deal with the situation, a large number of European Special Constables were enrolled and Col. Frank Johnson of Pioneer Column fame was appointed as O.C. Special Constabulary. I well remember sitting with him in my office at night, whilst he recounted some of the adventures of the Pioneer Column. A first class raconteur, his stories lost nothing in the telling.

It was about this time that a most amusing incident occurred. Frank Johnson had a certain gentleman staying with him, rejoicing in the name of Col. Bertie Drew-Fisher. The Johnsons had met him whilst staying at the Victoria Falls and invited him to join them at bridge on a couple of occasions, during which time they extended an invitation for him to stay with them at Orange Grove (part of Highlands) when they returned to Salisbury. One day, Drew-Fisher explained to Johnson that he was temporarily hard-up, owing to the non arrival of funds from Kenya, whereupon Col. Johnson took him along to the bank and stood as guarantor for an overdraft of some £100. A couple of days later, Johnson took Fisher to the Salisbury Club for lunch and introduced him to Col. Hugo Watson. Here, disaster was about to overtake the plausible Drew-Fisher, for Col. Watson was a well-known officer of the 60th Rifles who had just arrived from England on secondment to take over the training of the newly formed Rhodesian Territorial Force. On being introduced, Watson immediately said to him, 'You're not the Bertie Drew-Fisher of the 60th Rifles. I know him well.' Nonplussed, the so-called Bertie replied, 'No. I'm his elder brother.' The gaffe was soon blown however, as suspicions led to an exchange of cables between Watson and the real Drew-Fisher in England who revealed he had no brother. On being confronted and realising the game was up, the 'pseudo' Colonel promptly decamped in a car which he had obtained on credit from a firm who had parted with it on the assumption that anyone staying with Col. Frank Johnson was credit worthy and had handed over the car without even a down payment.

Enquiries showed that the so-called Bertie Drew-Fisher had indulged in several other shady transactions and the Police all over the country were alerted and he was eventually arrested outside Bulawayo. I've forgotten what actual charges were brought against him, but his defence in Court was that he had been badly wounded in World War I and had a silver plate in his head, often resulting in amnesia and he was, therefore, promptly X-rayed, when no silver plate was discovered. Sentenced to a term of imprisonment in the old Salisbury gaol, he found himself in the company of another of the same ilk, who was serving a sentence for forgery. It subsequently transpired that the two, with the connivance and co-operation of an African warder, had been obtaining liquor, cigarettes and other luxuries on forged orders from local stores. It was also said, though never proved, that the two had occasionally been let out on some evenings to enjoy the favours of certain 'ladies of the night', in Pioneer Street – presumably using their gifts of the gab to obtain their favours on credit. Those were the days!

A little later in the year I accompanied the Governor, Sir Cecil Hunter Rodwell, as an extra A.D.C. on a trip he made around the Eastern Districts. The party consisted of the Governor, his wife and daughter, together with his uncle Sir Evelyn Ruggles-Brice and Major Blackburn, the A.D.C. We travelled down to Umtali by rail in the Governor's private coach; this was my first visit to the Eastern Districts and I remember being very impressed with Umtali nestling in the tree-clad hills.

Umtali itself seemed to consist of one long untarred street, seemingly with bars and hotels at every corner. Staying overnight at the old Cecil Hotel, we set off next morning for Chipinga, on what was then known as the Sabi Road. The road, or rather a dusty corrugated track, was appalling and it took us most of the day to get there via the somewhat fearsome Three Span Berg, so called because in those days it took three spans of oxen to get the wagons up the steep gradient. In open cars tempers began to get a little frayed until we came on a sign which read, 'Cheer up, only another five miles to the Chipinga Pub'.

A tented camp had been prepared for us a couple of miles outside the village and after dinner that night, the Governor's uncle asked his manservant to bring on the Napoleon brandy. Nothing happened. After some delay I went to find out what was holding up the proceedings and in some trepidation, I went back to the mess tent to report the failure of my mission. The mystery of the missing brandy, especially brought out from England, was never satisfactorily solved, but strong suspicion centred around the Coloured drivers who had probably helped themselves to what they must have thought was first class 'dop'. They probably had a better night's sleep than the rest of us!

John Nielson, a splendid linguist, was the Native commissioner at Chipinga and, following the 'indaba' with the local chiefs the next morning, he had organised a group of Shangaan dancers to put on a wonderful display of their talents. During our stay at Chipinga, visits were paid to the Middle Sabi Estates, at that time presided over by Tawse-Jollie, husband of Mrs Tawse-Jollie, the only woman member of the Legislative Council. The Estate then was mostly planted with sisal, not a very profitable crop at that time and was later stumped out in favour of cotton.

The Tanganda Tea Estate at New Year's Gift had just been started and we had lunch there with Grafton Phillips and his wife. Grafton explained to us that here, at New Year's Gift, tea was being grown for the first time in the world under irrigation. Before they came to Rhodesia from India, the rainfall figures for this area had been carefully studied, but the figures probably pertained to the whole district and the rainfall at Tanganda itself was nothing like sufficient to grow tea, hence the need to resort to irrigation from the Tanganda River. Since that time, experience has shown that tea can be grown very successfully under irrigation and the industry has really expanded in the Chipinga area.

Before we set off for Melsetter, we had been advised that a mounted 'posse' of local farmers would meet us some five miles from the village with spare horses for the Governor and party. Would we be suitably dressed? The Governor donned a new pair of white breeches for the occasion and, having arrived at the Nyahodi River where the mounted posse was assembled, mounted his rather shaggy looking horse and off we went. All went well until we reached the old Melsetter Hotel, where the Magistrate and local dignitaries (all three of them) were waiting to greet us. As the Governor dismounted, there was a rather ominous sound of tearing material and the next thing we saw was his Excellency grasping a large tear in his new breeches and the gubernatorial posterior exposed to public view!

Protocol makes little provision for such contingencies, but on this occasion it was met by a hasty retreat into one of the hotel bedrooms, where running repairs were carried out by means of safety pins – 'safety' being the operative word! The public reception was adjourned and we retired to the camp prepared for us. Not unnaturally, conversation was a little strained at lunch, as it took some time to restore H.E.'s dignity. Melsetter – who can forget the first view of the Chimanimani Mountains, bathed in the light and shade of the late afternoon and setting sun. My first and immediate thought was that when I ever decide to settle in Rhodesia permanently, it will be here. The village, a very, very sleepy hollow, for some reason best known to the powers that be, boasted a Civil Commissioner and magistrate, together with a Native Commissioner. How they ever kept themselves occupied was quite beyond me. Visiting Melsetter on an inspection trip, a Police officer once wrote in his inspection report that he had looked at the Police cells which had not been occupied for months. Nevertheless, with a touch of wit, added that he had instructed the Member i/c to keep the building aired and dusted in case they should ever have occasion to use it.

Among others we entertained was John Martin, the member of the Legislative Council for the district. As a member of the Moodie Trek in the 1890s, he was one of the oldest residents. On his farm Rocklands, now Martin Forest Reserve, he grew an amazing variety of crops: tea, coffee, sugar, maize and many varieties of fruit. Indeed, most people living in the area had, perforce, to be as self supporting as possible, for the nearest shopping centre, Umtali, was a good day's journey away, weather permitting. Only recently, Zeederbergs's mule drawn coach had been replaced by the Railway's Road Motor Service, before which the coach took two days to reach Melsetter from Umtali with a night stop being made at Cashel, then known as Melsetter North.

After three nights at Melsetter, we started off on the long, winding road between Melsetter Village and Melsetter North, a distance of some forty miles with more than five hundred bends over some spectacular mountain scenery. When one considers this road was constructed by hand, where picks, shovels and wheelbarrows were the only items of equipment to move vast quantities of rock and soil, one realises just what an achievement it represents. It took, from what I can remember, almost four hours to reach Tabanchu Farm in Melsetter North. This farm was owned by Major Rowan Cashel, a retired Police officer and some years later, was purchased by Hallam Elton, on which he built the Black Mountain Inn. A camp had been prepared for us and in the afternoon, along came the usual deputation of local residents to pay their respects to His Excellency. While the residents were still paying their respects, a Police motorcyclist arrived with an urgent telegram for the Governor. It was in Government Code and I was instructed to get out the Government Code Book and decipher the message. It turned out to be world shattering news from Whitehall, to the effect that Sidney Webb, His Majesty's Minister of State at the Colonial Office, was in future to be known as Lord Passfield, but his wife would continue to be known as Mrs Sidney Webb!

Major Blackburn, the A.D.C. came along and told me that a couple of local residents had been invited to dinner and bridge with His Excellency. They duly arrived at the appointed hour – in a Rolls Royce car. 'Well, well,' I thought, 'This is quite something,' the first Rolls Royce I'd seen in the country, albeit a rather ancient model, but nevertheless a Rolls. Talk turned to bridge in London Clubs and the Governor came out with quite an amusing story. This concerned a certain woman playing at Almacs, who somehow got involved in a heated argument over a particular hand and ended up with one of the other women calling her a whore. Off went the woman in high dudgeon to complain to the Secretary of the Club about how she'd been insulted. The Secretary, evidently a man of many parts, contained the situation by telling her, 'Well you know Mrs So-and so, I left the Army twenty years ago, but I'm still called Colonel.' As an interesting aftermath, I heard some time later that the owner of the Rolls Royce had left the country in rather a hurry. Apparently everything he bought was on credit which eventually caught up with him and the Rolls was seized by a departmental store in Umtali against a hefty unpaid account.

I mentioned earlier that the area around Tabanchu was at that time known as Melsetter North and some years later when I was sitting at Police Headquarters in Salisbury, the question arose as to what we were to call the new Police Camp, which was being built there. The Post Office didn't like Melsetter North, as they thought most of the mail would end up in Melsetter. Tabanchu was turned down on the grounds that letters would find their way to a place of the same name in Lesotho; if named Umvum-vumvu after the name of the river running through the area, post would undoubtedly end up in Umvuma. Thinking about a suitable name, I thought of old Rowan Cashel and suggested to the then Commissioner, Col. G. Stops, that we should call the place Cashel, after him. He thought it was a good idea. 'Write to Mrs Cashel at once and ask her if she has any objection' he said. Mrs Cashel not only had no objection, but was delighted with the idea and so Cashel came into being. Continuing on our way the following morning, our next stop was back in Umtali, where H.E. was to open the Umtali Agricultural Show. The Show ground in those days was on the site now occupied by the Umtali Sports Club.

It was there for the first time that I met two members of the Pioneer Column, Johnnie Crawford and Jim Palmer, two wonderful characters who I got to know well much later, both with a wealth of anecdotes of the early days. There was the Show Ball in the evening, followed the next day with a visit to St Augustine's Mission and Rezende Mine, where we had lunch with the Manager, Rome.

And so back to Salisbury.

A further Note on Lieut. Col. H.G. Seward

Unfortunately 'H.G.' did not complete his memoirs. He is mentioned at length, however, in the History of the British South Africa Police, and I am indebted to Hugh Phillips for his kind permission to reprint extracts from this definitive History.

Post-war Recruiting Drive

The man chosen to garner recruits for the Police from among the various British Armed Forces at the end of the war was Lieutenant Colonel Henry George Seward, known popularly as 'H.G.' Seward had joined the Police in 1920, having served in the Royal Flying Corps and later transferred to the Army with the Fifth Cavalry Division in Palestine and Syria. In the 1930s he was Staff Officer to the Commissioner, before joining the C.I.D. where he rose to Officer Commanding and Chief Immigration Officer in 1938.

Seward's letter of accreditation, dated 16th July 1945, from Commissioner Ross, and which was to lead him to the Middle East and finally to London, was slightly perplexing (the italics are authors): 'Bearer, Lt. Col. H.G. Seward, B.S.A. Police, accompanied by Lieut. F.R. West, B.S.A. Police, have been authorised *by the Prime Minister of the Union of South Africa* to proceed to the Middle East for the purpose of obtaining recruits for the British South Africa Police, Southern Rhodesia. Any assistance which can be afforded by all concerned will be a matter of high appreciation by the Southern Rhodesia Government.'

The Middle East proved fairly non-profitable if not downright unhelpful. The Commander in Chief, Middle East Forces, was prepared to bring all his authority to bear in order to retain the B.S.A.P. members presently under his command. To him, they were indispensable, no matter what view the Southern Rhodesia Government took. His attitude, though of no help to Ross, is understandable in the light of the troubled situation at that time in Palestine and the need to have experienced men, not only in the Palestine Police, but also in the various occupied territories and sundry Colonial Forces. Thwarted, Seward moved on to London where he found himself involved with the War Office, the Admiralty, the Air Ministry, the Ministry of Labour and all the red-tape that accompanied the release of servicemen at that time. By early 1946, Ross was becoming impatient and demanding that Seward send out at least 75 bodies as soon as possible, though he had little knowledge of, or at that stage preferred to ignore, the difficulties his

Recruiting Officer was facing. Seward was battling with officialdom, selection procedures, vetting, medical examinations and the prioritising of berths on ships; to say nothing of the absence of any clerical assistance to help him. Despite these problems he did not waste his slack – 'spare' would be an incongruous word – time. Seward was determined to expand his knowledge and usefulness to the B.S.A. Police. He wrote to Sir Percy Sillitoe, then Chief Constable of the Kent County Constabulary, and arranged for an educational visit to the headquarters at Maidstone: a similar request went to the Essex County Constabulary, while a liaison trip to MI5 at the War Office served to renew contacts made some years before.

In the light of present day costs, it is diverting to read a part of Seward's plea, made just before Christmas 1945, for an increase in his subsistence allowance ... 'I am finding 29 shillings a day rather hopeless here. The cost of living is probably higher than in Salisbury and entertainment terrifically so – one round of drinks costs anything from 18 to 24 shillings and ordinary everyday living expenses nearly 30 shillings without any extras.'

Back in Salisbury, Ross had finally begun to realise the problems facing his recruiting officer and offered some assistance, at the same time revealing some befuddlement of his own: 'This member (Sergeant Grundy) was originally posted to the Gold Coast Police and then, through some obscure means, was discharged from that Force and found his way over to Civil Affairs in Europe ... He is quite an intelligent man and, I think, should do you quite well.'

At the end of this letter, Ross mentions that a Commission of Enquiry has been appointed into Police Pay, Allowances and Conditions of Service ('too long a story to put in writing') and urges 'H.G.' to set down his views on these matters. Although this Commission will be dealt with in some detail later, the views of Ross (conveyed to Seward by letter in mid-January) cast an interesting light on the Commissioner's feelings at that stage '... I can tell you that the proceedings of the Commission have really developed into an all out attack on the officer class with a general expression of opinion that discipline should be done away with. My attitude is to put up as many suggestions as possible and leave it at that.'

But the priority was finding men and getting them out to Rhodesia and Seward had done his job well: beavering away at officialdom, coaxing and cajoling as necessary. In early March of 1946 he was able to despatch the first group of 13 recruits on the *Franconia* and a few weeks later a massive contingent of 94 left Southampton on the *Alcantara* – having to endure troopship accommodation and other fairly primitive conditions. Further parties were sent in May. The holes in the establishment were at last being plugged.

Bulawayo Municipal Workers Strike
In 1948 a nationwide strike occurred which had its roots with municipal workers in Bulawayo. The Officer Commanding Bulawayo District was none other than Lieutenant Colonel H.G. Seward. His understanding of the problems leading up to the unrest was clear and not unsympathetic. His detailed report had every appearance of being a spirited and well-reasoned reply to uninformed criticism:

On every hand new industries and factories are being set up – building permits were granted for these but accommodation for the increasing labour supply fell far behind the very minimum requirements. In fact it seemed as though no balance was being maintained as between the two – certainly this was the case in Bulawayo where overcrowding in African areas has led to pitiful conditions of overcrowding. The press continued to publish reports of the rising cost of living and every time an African went to a store it was borne on him more and more that the purchasing power of his money continued to decline, and then – in a year of drought – the cost of his basic food, mealie meal, soared away to a figure which shook his economy to the very roots. And all this time he read of cost of living allowances to Europeans and waited patiently for the legislation which was promised after the Railway Strike in 1945 to adjust his own wage difficulties.

This legislation failed to make its appearance until the latter half of 1947, nearly two years after it was promised, and the leaders of the Africans, at least in Bulawayo, carefully noted that it did not make its appearance until the threat of another native strike in the Railways hung over the government's head.

All this, combined with the fact that there appeared to be no one who could keep them in the picture, or who had their welfare really at heart brought about a state of affairs where what might be called the depressed classes in the Colony rose as a whole to express their – up to now – inarticulated feelings of what seemed neglect and indifference to their lot.'

Seward went on to review the logistical arrangements made to deal with the disturbances. These included a rapid call up procedure for the 85 police reservists who were available at the time, and also for up to 200 Special Constables – regarded, because of their lack of training, as a 'last ditch' alternative; plus as many Territorials as could be mustered. A small number of men were also withdrawn from outstations. However, the problems facing a handful of police confronted by a potentially hostile population approaching 100,000, and the latter congregated within a stone's throw of the central business area, requires neither elaboration nor imagination.

Seward's report concluded: 'During the 34 hours the strike lasted, not a single pane of glass was broken, and not a half ounce of mealie meal was reported stolen – and order was restored by 10 on the morning the strike commenced, by unarmed Police – I emphasise this – for not a single B.S.A. Policeman was armed. Our reward – critics on every hand, believing what they read in the Press and from Club Gossips arriving at the conclusion that the Police failed to control the situation. Every member of the Force in Bulawayo is looking to the Government to give the lie to the Press and armchair critics. Police could, by precipitate action, have put the clock back 50 years. However, by their patience, forbearance and restraint, order was rapidly restored and the means used were such that the African still regards the policeman as his friend.'

'H.G.' sent his report to the Commissioner on 30th April, 1948. The Commissioner, in forwarding it on to the Minister, made no additional comment beyond expressing his complete agreement and making it clear that he was well aware of the situation and had acquiesced with all the arrangements made.

Subsequent events are not recorded but Lieutenant Colonel Seward eventually sought permission to retire and is recorded as leaving the Force on Boxing Day of that same year, 1948.

JOHNSTON'S TALE

Contents

Biographical Note	153
Off to Rhodesia	154
Early Days at Concession	163
The Chiweshe Reserve	176
My Own Station: Sipolilo	188
Salisbury: School, Scouts and Home Leave:	223
Return to Rhodesia:	229

List of Photographs and Maps:

Concession Group:	170
Victoria Falls/Mtoko Group:	174
Chiweshe Reserve Group:	184
Sipolilo Groups:	194, 196
Zambesi Valley Group:	206
African Police Training School:	222
Training Recruits:	230
Southern Rhodesia Soccer Team:	232
African Police Children:	235

Map of voyages:

	156
Southern Africa, 1946:	162
Southern Africa, 1980:	221
Cycle Tour of Britain:	227

Biographical Note on Dennis Sabin 'Johnny' Johnston, MBE.

This is the only Tale in this book of which the author is still alive and very much active.

'Johnny' Johnston led an adventurous life which took him into the Royal Navy during World War Two, then joining the B.S.A.P. in the first group to be attested into the Force after the War, the famous 'Alcantara Draft' (his Recruiting Officer in London was Lt. Col. Seward, author of the previous Tale). He not alone had an interesting career as a policeman but also found time to be captain of the Southern Rhodesia soccer team. He became a fluent linguist in African languages and after service in the Police he went to Nyasaland and was very much involved in African education. He established and built two boarding schools on the self-help system, with the pupils making and burning the bricks, terracing the site with hand tools, dredging sand and gravel from the Shire River, making the furniture and clothing, and growing much of the food required.

In 1958 he received the M.B.E. for services to Community Development in Nyasaland. He rose to be a Permanent Secretary in the Ministry of Community and Social Development in the Malawi Government.

After Malawi he became a teacher and leader of many Mountain Walking expeditions to all parts of the world. These included the Atlas Mountains, Karakorams, Himalayas, Khyber Pass, Rockies, China's Holy Mountain, Alps, and in many other countries. After returning to Britain and even though now (2008) 83 years of age, he still leads walking tours in places like Dartmoor. He also teaches part-time at his local colleges, who send groups of students to Malawi each year.

We are indebted to him for permission to publish here the B.S.A.P. section of his Memoirs.

JOHNSTON'S TALE

Dennis Sabin 'Johnny' Johnston
Trooper (3967)
British South Africa Police

Off to Rhodesia.
On a dull, misty morning our Troopship, the 'Alcantara', slipped quietly out of Southampton docks. It was the 28th March 1946 and we were the first post war batch of British recruits, and the largest contingent in the history of the Rhodesian Police.

The 'Alcantara' group was a mixed bag of young ex-servicemen, of various ranks and considerable war experience. Matelots who had served on the icy seas of Russian convoys and Naval battles of the Far East, and riflemen and tank crews who had fought in the dusty deserts of north Africa, and the steamy jungles of Burma. Some had been paratroopers during the 'D-Day' landings, and a few were highly decorated airmen who had flown throughout the world. Several had been prisoners-of-war of the Japanese and Germans, and one of these, Basil Taylor, became my best mate. Bas, a fellow Dartfordian, was one of the older recruits at 26, and I met him a few days before sailing, through the Church and his brother Alan. Captured in 1940, whilst serving with our local regiment, the Royal West Kents, Basil had spent the rest of the war, hewing coal and salt, in the mines of Germany and Poland. He lived life to the full and died of cancer, in Rhodesia, at the age of 33; probably due to the harsh years spent in prison camps.

Camping in northern France had been the extent of my travels, and now this great adventure was to take me over 9,000 miles, to an exciting country in the vast continent of Africa. With just a few pounds in my pocket and a suitcase, filled with clothing unsuitable for the tropics, I was ready for anything. Taking almost a month, the voyage was full of excitement and new experiences and, after years of austerity in war-time Britain, the 'Alcantara' was comfortable, despite sleeping in a crowded hold, queuing for food and washing our own cutlery.

Turning east at the majestic Rock of Gibraltar, and entering the calm, blue waters of the Mediterranean, carefree days were spent playing games and swimming, under a hot sun and cloudless skies. Still not half way, we reached Port Said in the ancient land of Egypt; the northern entrance to the Suez Canal, and the gateway to the exotic, mystical East. It was at Port Said that lithe, young Arab boys dived skilfully for pennies, thrown from the ship, and where persistent Arab salesmen tried to scale the ship's side from their bum-boats, and were roughly hosed into the sea by the vigilant crew. Over a thousand African troops came aboard here, en route to Mombasa, and they slept on deck and were raucously happy to be returning home. I was fascinated by their colour and features, and they all looked the same.

A tremendous feat of engineering, the Suez Canal was masterminded by a French engineer, Ferdinand de Lesseps. Opened in 1869, it had taken ten frustrating years to cut the hundred miles channel, through the inhospitable desert and shifting sands of the Suez Isthmus. It meant that the Mediterranean was at last connected with the Red Sea, and saved about 5,000 miles over the Cape of Good Hope route to India. With the temperature hovering at 100 degrees Fahrenheit, the 'Alcantara' manoeuvred into the narrow, high-banked waterway for the twelve hours' cruise, via the Bitter Lakes, to Port Suez at the southern end of the canal. Then came the dreariest section of the voyage; over a thousand miles through the stifling Red Sea, with the desolate Islamic states of Saudi Arabia, Egypt and Sudan, to the east and west. It was amongst these barren deserts of Arabia that Islam, one of the great religions of the world, emerged in the 7th century A.D., and spread rapidly during the next three centuries. Mecca, the holiest city of Islam and the birthplace of its founder Mohammed, was many miles from the eastern shoreline, but there was excitement amongst the African troops as we passed, and the Muslims amongst them carried out their prayers with increased enthusiasm and agility.

Leaving the scruffy port of Aden, at the southern extremity of the Red Sea, we rounded the 'Horn of Africa', entered the Indian Ocean, and hugged the Somali coast for some 1,600 miles to Mombasa, the main port of Kenya. Here our friendly African troops disembarked, after a sleepless night of monotonous drumming, deep-throated chanting and energetic tribal dancing. North of Mombasa, we had crossed the equator and volunteer victims were lathered, shaved and tipped backwards into the pool, as part of the traditional 'Crossing the Line' ceremony. Another 1,800 miles

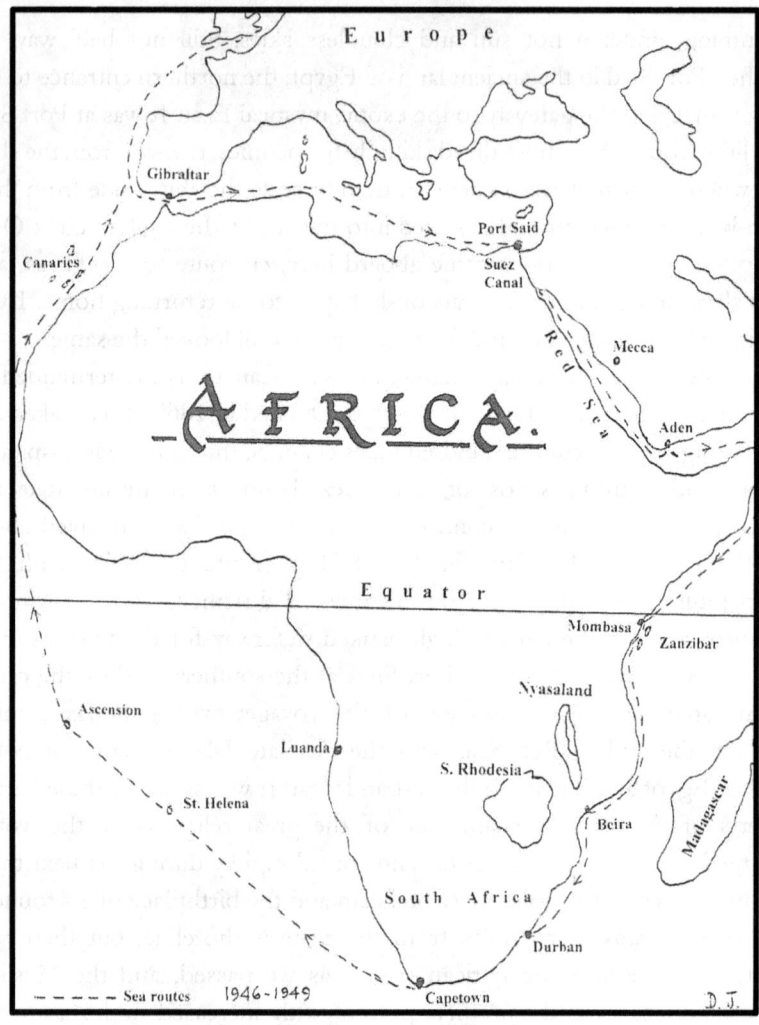

and, on St George's Day, the 23rd April, we reached our destination, Durban, in South Africa's province of Natal, and home of the Zulu people.

With the African sun shining brightly, the good ship 'Alcantara' steamed slowly into Durban docks, to the singing of a large European lady, attired in a voluminous white dress. It was a wonderful and unexpected reception and, during the war years, this lady had become a legend, as she welcomed many allied troopships to her friendly and pro-British city. Before being whisked away to the basic facilities of Clairwood Army Camp, we gratefully munched gifts of oranges and grapes; rarely seen in Britain during the war.

The 1,000 miles rail journey northwards to Southern Rhodesia, passed through the scenic Drakensburg mountains of Natal, the suburban sprawl of Johannesburg, and the parched areas of the Transvaal and Bechuanaland. After crossing the boundary, over the River Limpopo, we arrived at Bulawayo, the main city in Matabeleland. Here a few went boating and one of the lads, David Logan, was tragically drowned when his boat capsized. Another few hundred miles, through flat, dry and sparsely populated veldt, brought us to Salisbury, the capital of Rhodesia and now known as Harare, capital city of Zimbabwe. We had been travelling just over a month, and a unique form of transport was waiting for us at the railway station; open-sided carts, each pulled by four mules, and reminiscent of the Boer War! Trotting through the wide, modern streets of Salisbury, with a whip-cracking African driver, was an embarrassment to some of our sophisticated ex-commissioned colleagues!

The headquarters of the British South Africa Police, alias the Rhodesian Police, was sited on the prosperous side of the city and reached by Montague Avenue, with its shady lines of red-flowering flamboyant trees. Usually known as 'depot', it was the training school for new recruits, and our home for the next few weeks. The misleading title, 'British South Africa Police', needs clarification. Cecil John Rhodes, a genius at gold and diamond extraction, and a fanatical Empire builder, founded the 'British South Africa Company' to exploit the sparsely populated lands between the Limpopo and Zambesi Rivers. In 1890, a motley group of adventurers and prospectors formed a 'pioneer column' and, accompanied by several hundred men of the newly formed British South Africa Company Police, they occupied the dusty scrublands and raised the Union Jack, near present day Harare. Later, the territory became a self-governing colony and was named Southern Rhodesia, in honour of Cecil Rhodes, and the police force dropped the word 'Company' from its title.

Our few possessions were unloaded from the quaint mule carts, and an unsmiling, red-faced Sergeant, in riding breeches, brusquely allocated rooms. Returning to the small parade ground, one case was still on the ground. 'Why hasn't this case been taken to a room?' yelled the officious Sergeant. John Alyward, an ex-Naval officer, claimed the bag and added in a refined English accent, 'Er ... Sergeant, I haven't managed to find a boy yet.' After nearly exploding, the Sergeant told him, in ripe barrack room language, to get it moved!

Kit issue was the first priority. Khaki shorts and tunics, riding breeches, puttees, leather gaiters, spurs, peaked cap, felt bush hat, pith helmet and various badges were some of the equipment we carried off, in large brown kit-bags, to our small rooms. Then there were the various items of saddlery: reins and bit, surcingle, saddle wallets, gun bucket and the all important saddle. Another piece of equipment was a bandoleer; a series of small leather pouches, worn across the chest, for storing clips of rifle bullets. Another relic of the Boer War!

After years of war-time storage, the saddlery and leather equipment was stiff and covered with mildew, and hours of massage, with saddle soap, was needed to bring it up to military standard. Fortunately, help was at hand as the bush telegraph had been working overtime, and a hotchpotch group of under-nourished African men had gathered in hope of employment. Many had worked for Troopers pre-war, and were experienced at dhobeying and polishing. All were shabbily dressed, barefooted and anxious for employment but, as our pay was about £18 a month, it was obvious that our servants or 'boys' would receive a pittance. I succumbed to the pleading eyes and pleasant smile of a small, emaciated man, wearing clean but well-patched shorts and a threadbare shirt, who looked as if he deserved a job. Chari Mupranga hailed from an isolated village, in the district of Mtoko, where his two wives and five children lived and grew their own food. He had worked for Troopers pre-war, and produced a few scruffy, dog-eared references from a dirty stained envelope. Of indeterminate years, good and faithful Chari was a slow, hard-working batman, with minimal cooking skills, but we made a compatible team for the whole of my Rhodesian service. His lack of English was an incentive for me to learn Chishona, and his one excusable fault was that he usually got drunk on pay day!

Pre-war batches of recruits were different to our contingent, in that they had come directly from civilian life. We were all ex-servicemen, reasonably disciplined and proficient at 'square bashing', with and without rifles – the age-old method of transforming raw recruits. Our instructors had a fairly easy task, and the aim was to get us out to the under-manned towns and districts as soon as possible. Obvious and obscure nicknames for recruits soon emerged; 'Bomber', 'Spike', 'Spud', 'Tubby', 'Shiner', and the more racist, 'Taffy', 'Jock' and 'Paddy'. 'Clubs' had been my Naval nickname, and now I was 'Johnny' for my Rhodesian years.

Depot was always a hive of military activity and, from early morning 'Reveille' to late evening 'Last Post' our lives were dictated by bugle calls. It was a place of good order and discipline, where the grass was always cut short, weeds dare not grow, hedges neatly trimmed and boundary stones freshly whitewashed. Recruits, smartly attired in starched uniforms, polished leather and gleaming badges, marched to lectures, drilled on the dusty parade ground, or trotted and cantered in their military formations on their well-groomed horses. Every day the sun shone relentlessly, and we were permanently thirsty and our backs damp. From the outset, I felt that I belonged to an elite band of men and, although the Regiment had been in existence for just over 50 years, less than 4,000 had enlisted before me.

At daybreak, an African bugler sounded 'Reveille' and we would creep from under our mosquito nets, dress and hurry with our saddlery for first parade at 6 a.m. It was the best time of the day; cool air, clear blue skies and before the tropical sun became uncomfortably hot. Early days at the riding school were a mixture of pain, comedy and sheer fright, as many of the recruits had never ridden and the reluctant horses, after a few restful years, realised that they would now have to work for their fodder. On the first morning an officious Sergeant shouted, `Those who have ridden before, one step forward, MARCH.' A few, hoping to impress, admitted their skill and were promptly allocated the frisky horses. Then, to gain confidence, we were encouraged to speak to our suspicious steeds, stroke their necks, examine their teeth and crawl under their bellies. This resulted in a few crafty nips and kicks, as the wily horses sensed the fear and inexperience of their timid masters.

Resembling a large, open-air circus ring, the novices' riding school had a high, reed fence and a deep, sawdust floor to cushion unauthorised dismounts. Initially, saddles were banned and, to teach us to grip with our knees, we sat on blankets strapped to the backs of our animals. The more artful horses would puff out their stomachs, to prevent the surcingle from being tightened, which meant that the blanket swung round and the rider slipped off. `Taffy' Morgan was one of the less agile riders, and his undignified falls always prompted the unsmiling instructor to yell, 'and who told you to get off, lad?' After a few days of bouncing round the ring with only a blanket, we progressed to the more comfortable and safer saddles. Again the more wilful horses would puff out their stomachs, so that the saddles swung round when the rider's weight was placed in the stirrups. The trick was to give the horse a sharp dig in the ribs, and quickly tighten the girth strap!

Our first ride out of Depot was an important occasion, as we were now likely to be viewed by the public. Saddlery inspection completed, we responded to a series of yelled commands; 'Stand to your horses', 'Prepare to mount' and 'Mount'. Sitting proudly on our steeds, the gate was opened and we walked out in immaculate columns of four. 'Prepare to trot', shouted the instructor, and our horses responded to the well-practised pressure from our heels. All was proceeding with precision, when one of the alert horses noticed that the gate had swung open. Its ears pricked up, round it turned and away it galloped back to the stables, with the unfortunate rider clinging desperately to its neck. Other horses thought this a wonderful idea and, despite our efforts to control them, we were back to the shade of the stables in record time, to endure an unprintable tirade from 'sir'. Occasionally, a frisky horse would decide that the pace was too slow, and would gallop off with its rider. This usually prompted the instructor to shout, 'send us a card when you get there, lad.' During 'animal management' sessions, we inspected shoes, examined teeth, checked for cuts and abrasions and took body temperature, by inserting a large thermometer in the animal's rectum. Often a horse would object to such humiliating behaviour from a mere 'rookie', and would relieve itself at the crucial moment. Carefree riding in the open veldt, away from internal combustion engines and other 'civilised' noises, was always a thrill and I loved the combined aromas of hay, sweat and manure. But, I also have memories of hot legs and protruding veins, caused by tight woollen puttees, thick cord breeches and the tropical heat!

Sport played an important role in Rhodesian and Police life and, within a couple of days of arriving, football trials were held in the cool of the evening. The dry, well-maintained grounds meant that fast, ground-passing soccer was played, instead of the tough, physical style often necessary on uneven, muddy grounds. With two other recruits, I was selected to play for the Police 1st XI, during our first weekend in the country, when we trounced a strong R.A.F. team, and delighted our sports-mad senior officers. It meant that I was destined to be stationed near Salisbury for the whole of my service. For the next five years I played regularly for the Police, and progressed to representative matches for Mashonaland and Rhodesia, which often meant interesting visits to other African countries.

Arriving in sparsely-populated Mashonaland in 1890, the early white pioneers raised the Union Jack at a spot they called 'FORT SALISBURY', after Lord Salisbury, the amenable British Prime Minister of the time. Then they quickly scattered and staked out their extensive farms and numerous gold claims. Much of the surrounding country was flat, uninhabited wilderness, which was a great advantage when Salisbury was mooted. They had a free hand to plan as they wished, and to use the expertise of South African engineers and architects, with experience of African conditions. Towns were built on the grid system, American-style, and the roads sufficiently wide to allow cumbersome, canvas-covered carts, pulled by teams of slow-moving oxen, to manoeuvre easily. These wide, straight roads proved to be invaluable when ox-power was replaced by the internal combustion engine. To my surprise, Salisbury was a pleasant, modern city, built from scratch in just over fifty years. Privileged white people lived in large detached villas, set in spacious, well-tended gardens, and any Africans seen in the affluent residential areas were certain to be the house servants, nannies or gardeners of their white masters. Litter-free and tarmacked, the streets and avenues were lined with shady, scarlet-flowered flamboyant trees or lavender-blue jacarandas, and bore names of places and people that reminded them of home. There was even a 'Rotten Row'.

At the end of a long, depressing war, thousands of British people sought new lives and opportunities in other countries and Rhodesia, a vibrant, care-free land, still in its infancy, was an attractive proposition. With a scarcity of cheap sea passages and air travel non-existent, the more determined folk, tired of rationing and the British climate, had only one option; the adventurous, and often horrendous, overland journey through the uncertain wilds of northern and central Africa. In the cool of evening, some of us would stroll down to Cecil (Rhodes) Square to welcome and chat with these tough, colourful characters. Most had spent months on the journey, and their battered, gaudily painted vehicles had carried them across the wastes of the Sahara desert, and through several thousand miles of unknown and often hostile country. These lean, enthusiastic travellers, and their young families, were all in the pioneer mould and well-suited to this new, exciting country. The fact that they had white skins was a definite advantage!

A welcome piece of news emerged during our training; our salaries were raised to £260 per annum or £21 – 13 – 4d a month! With no taxes, insurance or licences to pay, plus free uniform and transport, I was never consciously short of cash and, after paying my Mess bill and Chari, I managed to save a few pounds each month towards my sea passage back to Britain for leave. Boozers, smokers, snappy dressers and those with girl friends found the pay scandalously inadequate! Once out in the bush, expenses were minimal as much time was spent on patrol, living off the land or hospitable tobacco farmers. Materialism had not arrived in the outback of Rhodesia, and money was of minor importance.

True to her word, Lady Roborough did write to His Excellency the Governor and, towards the end of training, and fearful of telling even my best friends, I had tea with the King's representative and his wife. A few months later he died and, dressed in full ceremonial uniform, I was one of the Police squad on duty at his graveside.

(Note: The author was billeted at Lady Roborough's mansion in England during part of his war service and she was a friend of the Governor of Southern Rhodesia).

Early Days at Concession.
Now a 'trained' Trooper, and empowered by Parliament to uphold the law, I took up my first posting, early June 1946, at Concession, a small settlement some 35 miles north of Salisbury, and close enough to play soccer for the Police team. Also known as Amandas, it was reached by a 'strip' road through a mixture of virgin bush, tobacco farms and the very big Mazoe citrus estates. 'strip' roads were a unique Rhodesian invention of the '30's, which halved the cost of construction. The two parallel strips of tarmac, each about 18" wide and the width of a car apart, were a great improvement on rough, dusty tracks, but concentration was needed and there were clouds of dust when vehicles moved over to pass.

Concession was a typical 'pioneer' village; dusty, earth roads, a small hotel and bar, a Meikle's store for basic supplies and an unfenced single railway track, which Africans used as a convenient short-cut through the bush. It was the centre of a scattered tobacco farming area and a few lucrative chrome mines. Just before my arrival there was a major scandal, which set the tongues wagging at 'sundowner' parties throughout Mashonaland. The important white Native Commissioner-cum-Magistrate, and the District Medical Officer, had swapped wives and children, resulting in the rapid transfer of the former. Then a Greek storekeeper, named Capaluto, was found decapitated, and a few well-fed Native detectives, conspicuous in their suits and shoes, mingled with the locals in search of clues. The crime was never solved.

Apart from a few modest, single-storey Government offices and bungalows for senior officials, the Police Camp was the largest complex with its Charge offices, married quarters, and the mosquito-proofed Troopers' block. Stables, an earth tennis court and a small, circular corrugated iron swimming tank, completed the amenities. Station transport comprised a couple of heavy B.S.A. motorcycles and an ancient Chevrolet truck, as well as horses for the Troopers. My mount was a dapple-grey, named 'Alack', while his brother, 'Alas', patrolled the arid wilds of Matabeleland in the south of the country. Each horse had its regimental number burnt on its hoofs and, if an animal died on patrol, a hoof had to be hacked off, as proof of death, before burial. In the distant past, unscrupulous Troopers had been known to sell a few 'dead' horses!

My preferred mode of transport was a slow-moving horse but, as I had been ordered to Salisbury each weekend to play football, the art of Jupiter ing had to be quickly mastered. I had never ridden a motorcycle or driven a car before arriving in Rhodesia, but a few spins round the camp and I was proclaimed competent to tackle the 35 miles of 'strip' road. Crash helmets were unknown, but we did wear leather gaiters, which prevented an exhaust burn if we fell off. They were also effective protection against snake bites.

Wise and experienced, Inspector 'Merv' Harries was Member-in-charge, ably assisted by married Sergeants Peter Hawke and 'Death' Murray. Having done their share of patrolling and field work in their younger days, they now enjoyed family life and carried out administration and court prosecuting duties.

Troopers rarely stayed at a station for more than a year, and I served with seven during my first year at Concession. All were British except Vaughan, a self-important, born-and bred Rhodesian, who had never seen the sea! His servant was treated like a slave; taking off his master's clothing and boots, and even being called to stoke the fire during winter nights, to save Vaughan rising from the comfort of his chair. African staff dreaded a motorcycle patrol with him, as he rode at break-neck speeds and often skidded in the thick, powdery dust.

Charlie Anderson, a tall, southern Irishman, was a fiery character. His spare time was spent propping up the hotel bar, and he never accepted social invitations or played sport. He lived on a short fuse and anyone who really upset him would be called 'a bloody Orangeman'; such was his hatred of Northern Irish Protestants. Unable to pronounce the African name of his servant, he re-named him 'Shamrock! Brian, Chris, Butch, Doug and Bomber were other Troopers who came and went. Fortunately, they preferred working in the 'European' areas and returning to the comfort of the Police Camp each evening. This suited me as I found working amongst the indigenous people, camping in the bush and travelling by horse, push bike or foot, far more rewarding.

The Police force was a prestigious job for African men, and our Constables were a reasonably educated and disciplined group. Most spoke heavily-accented English and were our guides, advisers and interpreters. These tactful, loyal and hard-working men patiently endured our inexperience, and perhaps our arrogance and, at times, must have felt that we needed a good kick! It was impossible to operate without them, and they did most of the work and solved most of the cases. In 1946, they were still wearing sandals, instead of boots and puttees, and progress had not been made to the term 'African'. So we had about a dozen 'Native' constables, who came under the watchful eye of 'Native' Sergeant Mubayiwa. Despite his long service and experience, he was junior to the most recently joined 'white'!

Tucked away at the back of the camp, amongst a few grey-barked eucalyptus trees, were the modest quarters of the African staff; two small rooms each, into which they managed to squeeze a wife, children and a few possessions. Second wives of some of the older constables stayed in the home villages, as a 'one-wife-at-a-time' rule applied in camp. Beyond their single-storey quarters, the virgin bush had been slashed back to make space for growing maize and vegetables, and where their agile, bright-eyed offspring played happily in the dust.

Concession was a busy station and urgent calls were answered by dusty jaunts, along narrow tracks by motorcycle, with a 'Native' constable perched precariously on the pillion. Police work in the outback was a way of life and, unlike our taller colleagues in the Town Police, there were no set hours, shifts or overtime. We were on call 24 hours each day, and often worked long hours. On the plus side, we had a fascinating job and didn't have to cook, wash dishes, sweep floors, wash and iron clothes, or tend the garden!

With servants to perform all the menial tasks, the small white community had time to socialise, and they were particularly kind to young, single Troopers. We were often invited to 'scoff', as they knew that our personal servants were employed for their dhobeying and polishing skills, rather than their cooking. Tennis was the main game and there were informal tennis gatherings at weekends. Our ball boys were unique, and unpaid, and wore broad arrows on their white canvas shirts. All were volunteer African prisoners from our small gaol, who enjoyed a few tit-bits of food and preferred the fresh air, to being locked in their hot, stuffy cells.

We were a welcome addition to the small community and, as patrolling Troopers, were potential purveyors of District scandal. During school holidays, the small white population doubled with children arriving home from boarding schools, and there would be invitations to extra tennis parties and barbecues, as company for the youngsters. They were well mannered and unsophisticated children, who tended to live sheltered lives and, apart from their family servants, had no contact with Africans. Occasionally, I took a few of the boys rock scrambling on a snake-infested kopje, which was reputed to be the abode of evil spirits and taboo to local Africans. Except for a few snakes, the only animals we ever saw were suspicious, hyper-active troops of baboons; known to the youngsters as 'bobby-johns'. Taking it upon themselves to educate their ignorant young English friend, I learnt about slow-moving, swivel-eyed chameleons, insect-eating 'praying' mantises, harmless and poisonous snakes, and a variety of ants. Large, black scorpions were always avoided, and I was informed that the females were sadistic cannibals who, after mating, stung their partners to death and ate them!

Shortly after my arrival, we thought we had a second European murder on our hands. A distraught African servant, having braved the dark bush and marauding animals, arrived at camp after midnight and reported that his white employer's wife had been shot. Fully armed, we bumped along miles of dusty track, in our battered truck, to the Blackburn's tobacco farm. Quietly surrounding the dimly-lit bungalow, we crept on the wide verandah and, by the light of a fading pressure lamp, could see a European slumped on a large settee, with a hunting rifle across his thighs. He woke from a drunken sleep as we barged in, and then his dishevelled, but unscathed wife, appeared in a well-worn dressing robe. With typical Rhodesian hospitality, she offered us drinks and explained that, during a petty argument, he had become violent and had fired a few shots into the ceiling. She apologised for the trouble they had caused and we returned, through the dark African bush, to camp and a few hours sleep before pre-breakfast duties.

Next day, during a scorching but enjoyable horse patrol, I realised it was my 21st birthday! This was confirmed a couple of weeks later, when a batch of cards arrived from home, via a slow-boat to Cape Town. At about this time, I helped our African driver, Chigoya, decipher the instructions for his newly-acquired paraffin stove, and I was rewarded with a few driving lessons. Shortly after, 'Merv' Harries asked me to drive him to Meikle's store at Amandas. On returning, he announced that I had passed my driving test! Few things were complicated in post-war Rhodesia. During the war years, with a depleted Police force, isolated farms and mines were rarely visited but, with an influx of eager recruits, regular patrolling commenced by horse and motorcycle. To show the flag, I visited the rich tobacco farms of the

Umvukwes, the citrus and monkey nut farms of Glendale, and the bleak chrome mines to the north. Most of the farmers and miners were of British descent, but there were other nationalities; Dutch Boers from South Africa and a few Portuguese and Greeks. All were proud to be known as Rhodesians, but with names like Bezeuidenhout and Papathanasoplous, spelling and pronunciation was sometimes a problem! Always welcoming and generous with food and drink, these folk had spent the war in comfort, and it soon became obvious that white Rhodesians lived privileged lives, with servants to attend their every wish. What a contrast to frugal, war-weary Britain that we had left just a few months before.

An erratic, primitive telephone system served the farms, but generally communications were poor or non-existent. Once we left camp, we were on our own and did what we thought best. There was a variety of situations and cases; illegal hunting, stock theft, cannibalism, witchcraft and suicides, to name a few. Organised criminal gangs and sophisticated offences, common in capitalist countries, were unknown. Some complaints were trivial and I remember a blonde Rhodesian lady reporting that she had found black, curly hairs on her hair brush! Rapes, serious assaults and murders sometimes occurred at weekends, when the locals drank vast quantities of traditional beer, made from maize or millet, and often spiked with lethal chemicals. Permission to brew large quantities of beer had to be obtained from the Native Department, but illegal brewing in the bush was common. If discovered, our constables had the unenviable task of tipping over large drums of precious, but illicit beer.

Rhodesia's remarkable and rapid development was made possible by a cheap African labour force, and a discriminatory piece of legislation, the "Masters and Servants' Act. Servants worked on short contracts and they soon got to know the good and bad employers. Desertion was common and workers from distant Nyasaland and Mozambique were popular with employers, as they were less likely to desert or leave at short notice. Just after the war, African Workers' Unions began to emerge and strikes became more common. At Marandellas, the African hotel staff went on strike, and were duly charged under a section of the 'M & S' Act. They received short prison sentences and were hired back to the hotel, where they worked in prison garb and without pay!

The antics of house servants were a source of amusement. One cook allegedly had pieces of toast between his toes as he warmed his feet, and another strained the soup through an old sock. Borrowing the 'master's' clothes, to cut a dash at a village dance, was common, and a spate of cat thefts was connected with a wedding feast. Coming from a culture with few breakable possessions, the sense of touch of servants was not highly developed, and fragile crockery and ornaments often came to grief.

Servants' pay was comparatively poor and was supplemented by a ration of maize meal, and a low grade 'bony' meat, known as 'boys' meat. Many were illiterate and sought help from their more educated brothers when writing to friends or making requests to their employers. One such request read:

Dear Madam and Sir,
I humbly ask your time and generous, as I am desperate to beg a temporary loan/gift of 7 shillings.

This consideration of expedient loan/gift will be reflected in extra special faithful service to you and your beloved family.

Asking in the name of Jesus Christ, of whom you are good resemblance.
Your hardworking Cook,
Zobushe

Most African servants were loyal and indispensable employees, who ran efficient households, and many Rhodesian families were happy to entrust their young children to the care of 'native' nannies. Life without African help would have been very difficult.

Rhodesia was full of unusual characters and the Concession area had its share of eccentrics. Most immigrants were of good yeoman or artisan stock, but occasionally wayward members of the British aristocracy were banished to the Colonies and paid a remittance to stay there. One expensively educated freak, named Ferguson, could always get extra cash by telling his noble relations that he had booked his passage home. 'Fergie', an unkempt bachelor, liked to maintain standards befitting his class. He wore a jacket and black tie to dinner, but usually with scruffy grey flannels and plimsolls. His pet baboon carried his shooting stick and umbrella.

Others included a talkative Welshman named Version, who was known as 'DA1 VERSION' and a corpulent drunk, Bill Fuller, who was referred to as 'FULLER and FULLER'. One tobacco farmer, a retired Colonel, devised a novel system of remote-control supervision. He would set his African labourers to work in the fields and, before retiring to the cool of his bungalow, he would take out his glass eye and balance it on a special stick – to 'keep an eye' on them! The bachelor Tulley brothers were successful maize farmers in the Glendale area. One went on holiday to South Africa, and returned with an attractive, young Afrikaans wife. Within a few months the other brother absconded with his sister-in-law and fled the country. A plausible Rhodesian rogue, named Bolton, was the only European I remember being held on remand in our small, basic lock-up at Concession, and he was convicted for stealing cars and non-payment of hotel bills. Several years later this inveterate crook was still up to his tricks, and I recognised him at Zomba Prison in Nyasaland. He had changed his name, but my knowledge of his previous conviction helped to land him a hefty sentence in Salisbury European prison.

In the early days of Rhodesia, there was a shortage of white women and, despite the stigma, some whites took 'native' wives. With just a mule and a few possessions, Jacob Van Der Merwe arrived from South Africa in the 1920s. With hard work, he developed a successful maize and monkey nut trading business, and also built-up a harem of African wives.

Ostracised by the local white community, it was rumoured that he had sired over thirty children. He generously supported a Salvation Army village primary school I used to visit, and where twelve of his well-cared for mulatto children attended. They were the only pupils who wore shoes!

Another eccentric was Alistair Hudson, an ex-British Naval Commander. Without mining experience or geological knowledge, he had staked out a small gold claim, and employed a few Africans to dig, crush and sift. He liked his drink and was amazed that a non-smoking, teetotaller Trooper was loose in the country. Confident that he would eventually strike it rich, he lived in a pole and mud hut, enjoyed the near perfect Rhodesian climate, and managed adequately on his small Naval pension.

Thousands of miles from the Mother country, the English-speaking community quickly assimilated local words, and Rhodesians were influenced by nearby South Africa for both vocabulary and accent. I soon learned that, as an Englishman, I was a 'rooinek' or 'red neck', and within a few months other words became second nature. A valley was a 'vlei', a rocky hill a 'kopje', a stream a 'spruit' and a verandah a 'stoep'; all words borrowed from the Afrikaans language of the Dutch Boers. Local slang words developed; food was 'scoff', the cinema was the 'bioscope', and tennis shoes were 'tackies'. Few whites bothered to learn an African language, and used an ungrammatical 'lingua franca', called 'kitchen kaffir', to communicate with their workers. 'Munt', or the more derogatory 'Kaffir', was the general term for an African, and was used throughout southern Africa. 'Kaffir' is an Arabic word meaning 'unbeliever', and probably filtered down from the Muslim Arabs of East Africa. It is still used in Islamic countries to describe persons who are not Muslims, Christians or Jews.

Two main African languages are spoken in the country. In the arid south, the Matabele, an off-shoot of the war-like Zulu nation, speak Sindebele, with its peculiar 'clicking' and 'sucking' sounds. Chishona, the other main language, is spoken by the Mashona and related tribes, who make up about 75% of the population. This was the language I was determined to learn. I quickly learned two slang words used by our Constables; 'mtututu' meaning a motorcycle, because of its 'tututu' engine sound, and 'macatchem', a vaguely recognisable English word, they used for handcuffs. Another 'African' word came to light when I asked the word for cheese. 'Bootsu', came the reply, 'no word for cheese, but smell like boots'! Our Constables were always pleased to unravel my linguistic queries, and within a few months, I could hold a simple conversation and begin to delve into African customs. My abnormal interest in the language earned me the African nickname 'Muzezuru'; 'one of the Zezuru tribe'.

During my first few months at Concession the weather was perfect:

Staff at Concession

R.H. Alack

pleasantly hot days, with cool mornings and evenings, clear blue skies and no rain. One major problem at this time was that the bush was tinder dry and devastating veldt fires were common. Travelling at high speeds, the fires were extremely dangerous, and the roar and crackle of the blaze was terrifying. There was a rapid exodus of wild life; the speedy buck and smaller mammals were the first to flee, followed by hundreds of rats, which were killed by the locals and highly esteemed as food. Then flocks of small birds preyed on the thousands of grasshoppers and other insects, set in motion by the fierce heat and, in turn, they were watched greedily by the larger birds of prey. Many of the fires were started deliberately by local Africans, whilst smoking out wild bees or flushing out wild life to provide food, but prosecutions were rare. Becoming progressively hotter as the rainy season approached, the hottest month was October; known as the 'suicide' month. When the first torrential rains came, I stood fully clothed in front of the Troopers' block and enjoyed the deliciously, cooling water; the first rain I had seen since leaving Britain, and the heaviest I had ever experienced.

Within a few days of the onset of the rains, farmers, villagers and our Constables'

With Native Constable Zivanayi

Butch, Johnny, Norman and Chris prepare for Royal Visit 1947

families were busy preparing their fields for crops of maize, beans and monkey nuts. Even young children, armed with child-sized hoes, worked happily alongside their parents to ensure their food supply. Then, as if by magic, grass sprouted, unfamiliar veldt flowers and trees bloomed, and the dusty countryside was rapidly transformed from lifeless dry browns to a variety of fresh greens. Dry river beds became rivers for a few months, and were often difficult and dangerous to cross by horse, and muddy District roads made motorcycling a slow and slippery operation.

Just before Christmas 1946, I witnessed my first child birth. A buxom and grotesquely tattooed woman, of the Senna tribe of Mozambique, was in camp on a charge of witchcraft. Late one night, I was duty Trooper when Sergeant Mubayiwa knocked on my door and excitedly announced that the 'witch' was in labour. Normally, one of the Constables' wives would have acted as midwife, but they were scared of this fearsome-looking lady, who spoke a strange language. Our temperamental truck failed to start, and Mubayiwa hurried away to get help. Then, to the light of a small hurricane lamp, she lay on the ground and, with a series of excruciating grunts and groans, she gave birth to a son; an indelicate experience for a virgin Trooper! Helped by my First Aid manual, I nervously tied and cut the umbilical cord, and steeled myself to clean her as much as possible. My towel was a write-off! In the meantime, a few bleary eyed Constables, roused from sleep, managed to push-start the truck, and I was able to transport mother and child to the small dispensary at Amandas. Next morning, before breakfast, I trotted down on 'Alack' to see my handiwork by the light of day. Sleeping blissfully in a metal cot, the browny-red mite had been named 'Joni' by the African nurses. A short news item, 'Trooper midwife in action' appeared later in the local paper, and attracted wry comments.

A 'Hogmanay' party on New Year's Eve, with good company, excellent food and energetic Scottish dancing, brought 1946 to a happy conclusion. It had been an eventful year; from the Royal Navy and war-weary Britain, to the vast continent of Africa, and an exciting job with a famous Police force.

1947 was also full of interest: adventurous patrols in the Chiweshe Reserve, a Royal Tour, temporary transfers to Victoria Falls and Mtoko, and my eventual elevation to Trooper-in-Charge of my own remote station, Sipolilo. I also became the first post-war recruit to pass the Government oral and written Chishona language examinations. It was a momentous year for our African policemen. They were now 'African' instead of 'Native' Constables, and their sandals were replaced with prestigious boots and puttees.

During April, 1947, King George VI, Queen Elizabeth and Princesses Elizabeth and Margaret, toured Rhodesia. With other Troopers and African Constables from Concession, I spent several days on duty in Salisbury and Bulawayo, the two main cities. In Salisbury, I was on stable duty when the young princesses rode two well-behaved Police horses, and most of us were not impressed with their superior demeanour and affected accents. Also, being near the King on several occasions, I was surprised that he wore make-up!

The impressive city of Bulawayo, the 'place of killing' of Lobengula, the Chief of the Matabele, was of greater interest to me. Formerly an African settlement in the midst of almost treeless veldt, it was rapidly transformed, by the 'white' City Fathers, into a modern city with tree-lined streets, wide enough for an ox-wagon and a full span of twelve oxen to turn in. A few miles south of Bulawayo are the Matopos Hills, where Cecil Rhodes, and a few other Rhodesian heroes, are buried at a spot known as 'World's View'. It was amongst this rocky wilderness that Mr Rhodes held his famous Indaba, with leaders of the Matabele people, which ended the abortive Matabele Rebellion of 1896. Baden-Powell was Chief Staff Officer of the forces suppressing the rebellion, and it was in the Matopos that there developed some of the inspiration that led to the formation of the Boy Scout Movement. Later that year Princess Elizabeth married Philip, son of Prince Andrew of Greece.

Following the Royal Visit, I was one of the Police escorts at the repatriation of 800 German internees, from their camp at Norton, and then a few days relief duty at the Victoria Falls Police Post. Now considered one of the great wonders of the world, the breath-taking falls on the Zambesi River, with their rainbows and towering columns of spray, are known locally as 'mosi ao Tunya', the 'smoke that thunders'. David Livingstone, the famous explorer and missionary, was the first white person to view the falls in 1856 and, following the custom of the time, named them after Queen Victoria. Just over a mile wide, the swift waters of the Zambesi plunge over 350 feet to the frothy chasm below, and meander through deep gorges on their long, winding journey to the Indian Ocean. There was little work for the Police, except to keep the tourists happy, pose for photographs and rescue them if they fell over the unfenced edge. One American tourist was obviously impressed with the Falls, and sent a telegram back to the United States. It read, 'sell Niagara'!

Living in a small insular community, I knew very little about world events, and generally Rhodesians were too busy with their own affairs to bother about other countries. I never listened to news on the wireless and rarely saw a newspaper. Mum and Dad occasionally mentioned home news when they wrote, and they reported the 'Big Freeze' in Britain, during the early part of 1947, when I was experiencing my first 'hot and wet' season. During August 1947, I made a note in my diary about events in India. The *Rhodesia Herald*, Salisbury's daily newspaper, reported that India had been partitioned, and that East and West Pakistan had been created, specifically for the Muslim communities. There were horrific photographs recording the massacres that took place between Hindus and Muslims, when they met travelling to their new countries. Such momentous events meant little to me and, at that time, I knew little about these two great religions. Much of 1947 was spent on extensive patrolling of Chiweshe Reserve and trips to Sipolilo, and these two places have their own chapters in this narrative. Just before my transfer to Sipolilo, I spent two and a half weeks as Acting Member-in-Charge at Mtoko, a border station north-east of Salisbury, on the road to Mozambique and Nyasaland, as two of the staff were in hospital with malaria. This temporary transfer delighted my 'boy', Chari, as it was his home district, and some of his relations visited us bearing edible gifts.

Statue of David Livingstone and self Victoria Falls 1947

Baobab Tree on which Livingstone carved his initials 'D.L. 1856'

Trooper 3967 at Mtoko

Chari and his wife and mother-in-law

There was very little crime, and most of the African constables' time was spent checking passes and searching 'foreign' African travellers, on their way to work on Rhodesian farms and mines. It was a quiet station but my diary reveals that in two and a half weeks, as well as keeping the paper work under control, I shot a leopard in a trap, took part in a hyena shoot, and played in a tennis match with the troopers at Mrewa, a station near Mtoko. Also, whilst riding in the bush, I heard a baby cry and discovered that an African woman, with a baby tied to her back, had sadly committed suicide by hanging herself from a tree. Chari added to the excitement when he was attacked by a drunken axe-man, at a beer drink, and sustained a deep wound to his thigh. There was always lots of action, even at a 'quiet' Rhodesian station!

Before the advent of Europeans, Southern Africa lay unexplored and unknown to the outside world, and the indigenous peoples, blessed with a near perfect climate, enjoyed lives of ease. Their needs were few and, being conservative in custom and habit, there was little incentive to improve their means of shelter or subsistence. Also, reading and writing was unknown to them, and the history of the world has shown that without these skills men and nations make no cultural progress.

The Chiweshe Reserve

In the 1890s, when white settlers arrived in the lands between the Limpopo and Zambesi rivers, later known as Rhodesia, they grabbed much of the best land for their farms, and their claims were backed by Cecil Rhodes' powerful mining company, plus a tough mounted police force with modern rifles. Within a few years, white Rhodesians, who made up about 5% of the population, became owners of about 40% of the fertile farmland! However, the indigenous people had to live somewhere, and so the early white rulers set aside large areas of land, called 'Native Reserves', for the exclusive use of the African population.

One such area, the extensive Chiweshe Reserve, came within the Concession police boundary and, early in my service, I carried out several extended patrols of the Reserve – the first since before the war. Only a handful of officials and missionaries had access to the Reserve, and so it was a unique experience, and a culture shock, to witness how Africans lived in their traditional villages, under their tribal chiefs and headmen. Incredibly, most white Rhodesians had little idea how their black brothers lived in the Reserves. My patrols, during 1946-47, each lasting from a week to ten days, are among my happiest Rhodesian memories. Travelling and camping amongst the Mashona villagers, I discovered a primitive world where the indigenous people lived in the fashion of their ancestors, without clock or calendar, the need to know birthdays or exact ages, or to record births and deaths. Living close to nature, their simple lives were ruled by the sun and the seasons, and they existed without electricity, piped water or a means of communication, except by word-of-mouth or the tom-tom.

There was one major difference in the Mashona way of life since the European occupation. They were no longer in danger of periodic, blood-thirsty attacks from the dreaded warlike Matabele tribe from the south, who in the past had stolen their food and cattle, and taken young girls as wives, and young men as recruits for their war impis. Thus, although heavily laced with discrimination, the European administration brought law and order, and frugal-living missionaries introduced Christianity, together with the skills of reading, writing and a number system; all previously unknown. In the past, the tribe owned and controlled the land, and the concept of individual ownership was unknown. Boundaries meant very little to them and, if harassed by stronger tribes or their land became exhausted, they could easily move to fresh pastures. With the European occupation and consequent control, their days of wandering and settling in new lands were over forever.

Predominantly subsistence farmers, the villagers spent much of their time laboriously digging their land with small, back-breaking hoes, and growing crops of maize, millet, beans, and a variety of vegetables. Each extended family possessed a cluster of small, thatched huts, built of poles and mud, which seemed to sprout from Mother Earth. Boys, girls and adults had their own sleeping huts, in which they slept on woven bamboo or reed mats, on hard earth floors. In a separate hut, without a chimney, women cooked over an open wood fire. Men and women always ate separately and, using their fingers and communal bowls, they lived on a monotonous diet of stodgy maize meal and a relish of beans or vegetables. Meat was a luxury and any available fruit was always eaten raw. Most villages had a few large shade trees but, being reliant on wood for cooking, the immediate scrub was often denuded of trees, and women and girls had to walk ever-increasing distances for fuel. Sanitation was often suspect, but some of the more enlightened villages, with a nudge from the Native Department, had sensibly progressed to squat-type, communal pit latrines, with a small can of water for washing.

Women, unsophisticated and without make-up or jewellery, were the back-bone and drudges of village life, and their busy days were spent on strenuous, repetitive survival tasks. With babies tied to their backs, and modestly dressed in lengths of printed cloth wrapped round their bodies, they carried water from stream or hand-dug well, and skilfully balanced the heavy, home-made clay pots on their heads. They also collected firewood, pounded maize for flour, cooked meals, worked in the fields, cared for their children, and became worn out before their time. At an early age, girls commenced their apprenticeship for a lifetime of servitude, and it was common to see young children cheerfully working at the pounding mortar, balancing heavy pots of water, and wielding small hoes in the fields. This unequal division of labour was the custom, and women accepted their beast-of-burden role without question. In the past, the main occupation of the men had been to hunt and fight, and protect the women and children, but now they hunted, built huts and cattle kraals, and spent hours discussing village problems under the shade of a tree, usually with the aid of a pot of beer. One Government regulation worked in favour of women; they were exempt from carrying identification passes. For men, over the estimated age of eighteen, it was an offence to be found without the unpopular legal document.

Most of the village men were barefooted and poorly dressed in ill-fitting khaki shorts or trousers. They had few possessions, except for basic tools, primitive weapons and various pots and baskets. Some of the younger men, who worked for Europeans, and had escaped the restrictions of tribal life, were better attired. Despite the heat, they paraded in long trousers and jackets, proudly wore trilby hats at jaunty angles, and often sported fountain pens and sunglasses; sure signs that they had a foothold in the white man's materialistic world!

With wild animals hunted almost to extinction, cattle and goats were valuable possessions, and often more important than a young child. Children were easy to replace, but the death of a cow was a major disaster. Young boys, crack shots with stones and catapults, tended the under-nourished, and often tick-infested, animals as they scavenged amongst the dry, dusty scrub for sustenance. At dusk, the animals were herded into thorn-fenced enclosures as protection against predatory leopards and hyenas. In contrast to the well-fed, pampered 'ridge-backed' dogs kept by white Rhodesians, the cringing village dogs were mangy and skeletal, and best avoided for fear of rabies.

Realising the advantages of education, many parents sent their children to the small, pole and mud Primary Schools dotted around the Reserve, and it was always a great joy, and a humbling experience, to visit them. Sitting on rough wooden benches and using slates balanced on their laps, large classes of enthusiastic, well-scrubbed children learned literacy skills, which had been denied their parents. Accompanied by home-made drums and rattles, the children would sing lustily, and in perfect harmony, songs of 'Welcome' in the Chishona language, and often I would be the first white person they had seen. One catchy song, I thought to be in Chishona, turned out to be a rendering in heavily-accented English; 'If I can't get a pretty girl to be my wife, then I shan't get married at all'! In the cool of evening, if my camp was near a school, I played football with the agile, bare-footed youngsters and their teachers, using my inflatable ball instead of their usual tennis ball; a rare treat! Education was not compulsory, but literacy was seen as a means of material advancement, and disciplinary problems were rare.

Accompanied by an African constable on a cycle, my first 'tenderfoot' patrol was by horse, and I soon discovered that an extended horse patrol had its disadvantages. With no stabling in the villages, there was the nightly fear of predatory leopards and hyenas, as well as poor grazing. Cycling was more practical and, without map and compass, I would disappear into the sparsely populated bush for exciting adventures amongst the local people, and miles from any white person. Compared with a tent, I found that an African hut was cooler and much safer from marauding animals, despite the occasional rodent, and an amazing variety of insects, that expected to share it with you. Once in the hut and tucked under a mosquito net, the small tropical nuisances were soon forgotten. After a day in the scorching African sun, along rough dusty paths, and little shade, washing was a problem. Stagnant pools were avoided because of the water-borne disease, bilharzia, but a wash in a flowing stream was a bonus, and a small bowl of warm water in the privacy of my hut was a luxury.

At the end of each day, the Rhodesian sunsets were invariably magnificent and, after a short period of twilight, the evenings became cool and peaceful. Nobody wandered after dark, and a campfire was an effective way of warding off wild animals and mosquitoes. It was magical to sit by a wood fire, under clear, starlit skies, and blissfully watch the 'Southern Cross' glittering at one end of the 'Milky Way'. With little else to do, pleasant hours were spent chatting and improving my language skills and, at times, enjoying the rhythmic dancing and harmonious singing of the happy, unsophisticated children. The vast open spaces, the attraction of the unfamiliar and the slow pace of life, suited my temperament, and I was often filled with a child-like happiness. Despite their comparative poverty, the villagers were happy, contented folk, who laughed easily and were not disgruntled, covetous or prone to begging. Their needs were few and their simple lives were ordered by age-old laws and customs. They were undoubtedly better off than many peasants living in the harsh climates of some European countries.

Apart from a supply of tea, sugar and powdered milk, I lived on local food; eggs, maize flour and cobs, and seasonal fruit, such as papaya, guavas and mangoes. Occasionally, I was able to buy a tin of condensed milk from a village store. This was a great treat and, once opened, I would stir it generously into my maize meal porridge and tea, and eat the remains with a spoon, before armies of ants picked up the scent and advanced! Bartering was still common and, as the villagers had very little money, their modest stores sold a few basics, often on credit; printed cotton material, paraffin, slabs of soap, coarse salt and cheap cigarettes, sold singly. Despite their impoverished lives, villagers often gave presents of eggs, fruit and, occasionally, an anorexic chicken. Following tribal etiquette, a shy, pre-pubescent girl, still growing her teeth, would gracefully kneel and offer the gift with two hands. It was good manners to receive the food with two hands, thank her with a 'ndatenda kwazo', and offer a small gift, such as coarse salt.

A network of narrow paths and tracks, pounded by thousands of bare feet and eroded by the seasonal rains, connected the many small villages, and were best suited to travel by horse, cycle or foot. It was these that I used to visit Chiefs and headmen to 'show the flag', listen to problems, and offer help. Most were courteous, dignified men who were witnessing the inevitable breakdown of the tribal system, as their young men travelled to the towns and found the ways of the Europeans more attractive. There was also the emergence of a small but influential African middle-class, who had benefited from a mission education, and were destined to usurp the power of the hereditary leaders. Expecting the chiefs to be attired in colourful tribal regalia and monkey skins, it was always a disappointment to find them dressed in drab European clothing and barefoot. In the absence of motorised transport, cycles were treasured possessions and used almost exclusively by the men. Women with large bundles on their heads, and babies on their backs, usually walked! A few richer peasant farmers had progressed to ox-drawn ploughs and wheeled carts, but heavy wooden sledges, made from the fork of a tree, were still commonly used to transport crops, and were dragged laboriously along the dusty tracks by oxen.

Howard Mission, the main educational centre of the area, was administered by down-to-earth Salvation Army officers, and reached by a good earth road, on the southern boundary of Chiweshe Reserve. Here African officers trained for missionary work, and selected students from primary schools attended one of the top secondary schools for Africans in Mashonaland. As there was great sports rivalry between the few secondary schools, I often acted as an impartial referee at inter-schools soccer matches and athletics meetings. Howard was an oasis of learning where teenage boys and girls proved that, given the opportunity, they had the ability to attain high academic standards. Within a few years, they had to make the transition from primitive village life to the discipline of an academic establishment, as well as mastering English, and adjusting to the baffling mysteries of a foreign culture. Girl students at Howard, in smart uniforms, hair braided in intricate patterns and wearing shoes, were a pleasing reminder that the higher education of young African women was not being neglected.

With their newly found freedom from tribal and family restraints, they radiated happiness and confidence compared with their less fortunate village sisters. Many were also well-proportioned, from devouring regular school meals, and escaping the strenuous daily round of village life and early marriages.

My first visit to the Mission was through an unusual case of infanticide. A young, buxom African servant had managed to conceal her pregnancy and, whilst squatting at a pit latrine, gave birth to a child, which dropped in the sewerage and drowned. Suspicions were aroused when a trail of blood was spotted leading to her hut. Later, the unfortunate mite was retrieved by a small African boy, who volunteered to be lowered into the depths of the latrine. The distraught girl was given the benefit of the doubt, and no action was taken. It proved to be a busy day, as I was asked to shoot a rabid dog, before visiting a set of abandoned twins, who were being cared for at the Mission hospital.

Despite sleeping under a mosquito net, and only occasionally forgetting to take my anti-malaria pill, I succumbed to my first and most frightening attack of malaria towards the end of a long patrol of central Chiweshe. With my companion, Constable Gavaza, we had been visiting chiefs and headmen during the day, and I had gradually developed a splitting headache. Assuming it was due to the scorching tropical sun and lack of fluid, I drank several cups of milky tea in the shade of my hut at base camp, and was soon asleep under a mosquito net on the cool, earth floor. During the early hours of the morning, I woke in the dark hut with teeth-chattering rigors and nausea. Failing to light the small hurricane lamp, and certain that my end was nigh, I called for Gavaza who, realising that I was quite ill, cycled off for help. Fortunately, there was a small rural dispensary a few miles away, and he returned just after dawn with a young African nurse, who found my temperature to be 104° F. and diagnosed malaria. My 'Angel of Mercy', Emily Mkwananzi, was a tall, competent Matabele lady in her early twenties, who spoke perfect English, and was conducting ante-natal clinics in the area. She cycled off and somehow got a message through to the Mission, and later I was carried along paths, on an improvised stretcher, to a point where a truck was able to transport me to hospital. I wrote and thanked Emily for her help and, weeks later, I received a reply from Bulawayo, in Matabeland. Homesickness had caused her to return home and work amongst her own people. She enclosed a photograph of herself, taken with a few of her patients, as a reminder of my first attack of malaria.

My saddest moments in the Reserve, were visits made to the graves of two young Police Troopers who had died on patrol, in the thirties. Both were buried at remote places in the Reserve, and far from human habitation. The grave of Trooper Edmonds was a rough heap of stones, under the shade of an acacia tree, and a small metal plaque nailed to the trunk merely gave his name and date of death. At a lonely, rocky area to the north, was the simple grave of No. 3005, Trooper D.S. Bain, who had tragically drowned whilst crossing a flooded river on his horse. His former Scout troop, the 219th Liverpool Scottish, had donated a simple memorial stone, engraved with his name, date of death, and the Scout 'I have gone home' sign. Local Africans avoided the area and, as I tidied the lonely grave and knelt to pay my respects, I felt very close to Trooper Bain. Far from his family and friends in a distant land, it was an isolated but beautiful resting place for a servant of the Empire.

My farewell expedition, to a remote area of the Reserve, proved to be an unusual experience; a poisoned well and the exhumation of the dead! An alert Constable had gleaned from campfire chatter, that eight villagers had died, under suspicious circumstances, after drinking from a well at Nyamawuchu Kraal, in Chief Makope's country. Knowing the area from a previous patrol, I was detailed to supervise the exhumation of the bodies, in readiness for examination by the station medic, Dr Rittey. Zivanai, a likeable and experienced Constable, was my companion and, after being dropped off by truck a few miles from the village, we completed the journey, by cycles, along narrow footpaths. None of the deaths had been reported officially, and the unexpected arrival of a European 'majoni' caused surprise and horror when our intentions were revealed. To disturb the spirits of the dead was sacrilegious, and certain to bring misfortune on the village. Just before sunset, a procession of apprehensive villagers accompanied us to the foot of a boulder-strewn granite kopje, known as 'Nyamashumba' or 'Lion's meat', where seven piles of stones marked the graves. A smaller heap of stones, by a dried-up river, marked another grave. It was the resting place of a small child who, by custom, had to be buried near a river, lest its mother became barren. Reluctantly, the headman agreed that the exhumations could start the next day.

Later that evening, a few young men warmed their tom-toms by an open fire before beating a slow, monotonous rhythm. It was the signal for villagers to assemble round the blazing fire, and commence mournful wailing. Suddenly, the drumming stopped, and the local witch-doctor, adorned in animal skins and monkey tails, made a dramatic entrance before the docile villagers. To slow hand clapping and drumming, he leapt and shrieked before his gullible audience, as he worked himself into a frenzy, and sprinkled 'protective' powder into the flames. Obviously, we were unwelcome visitors and, as I slept in my small mud hut, many miles from the nearest European farm, my loaded revolver was close at hand and a comfort. During the night, a rat devoured much of my candle! Next morning, before the fierce Rhodesian sun became too hot, we quietly made our way to the rocky graveyard, with a few young volunteers. Before digging commenced, the witch-doctor gave another theatrical display of dancing and shrieking, as he stressed to the spirits that the white men were to blame. Producing a greyish powder from a small duiker horn, he chanted as he rubbed it on the bare torsos of the youngsters. Now fully protected from evil spirits, they set to work with great speed and energy, removing the small rocks from two graves, and quickly revealing much larger boulders, which had been levered into the graves from the kopje above. It was a more difficult task than we had anticipated and, at the end of the first day, only two bodies, crudely wrapped in sleeping mats, had been uncovered.

Obviously, it would take several days to exhume all the bodies, and 'Merv' Harries and Dr Rittey were due in 36 hours!

That evening, whilst I sat fascinated by another display of monotonous chanting and energetic dancing, Zivanai was busy with his own investigations. He discovered that a swaggering scoundrel, Joel, had been engaged in an acrimonious power struggle with the elderly headman. Some villagers suspected that Joel had poisoned the well, and this theory was strengthened when Zivanai found an empty bottle of lethal cattle dip concealed in the thatch of his hut. Beneath the stars and to the light of a large fire, Joel was roughly paraded before the assembled villagers and, with bowed head, he meekly admitted that he had poisoned the well! It was an incredible and unexpected admission, and he was immediately arrested by a jubilant Zivanai, who dramatically fixed steel 'macatchem' to his wrists.

The nearest telephone was about ten miles away and, early next morning, Zivanai volunteered to cycle to the tobacco farm, to get a message through to Camp. To the delight of the village elders, I agreed that the bodies could be reburied. Later that afternoon, Zivanai returned and reported that the white farmer had contacted Camp, and we would be collected the following day. Grinning broadly, Zivanai presented me with a box of supplies from Mrs MacDonald, the farmer's wife; a currant loaf, biscuits, a tin of corned beef, potatoes, cigarettes and a bottle of lime juice. He had obviously explained to the good lady that a young English 'tenderfoot' Trooper was living like a pauper at an African village! Anxious for my well-being and safety, Mrs. MacDonald had penned a few instructions. I must boil all water, sleep under a net, and not eat any 'native' food or use their utensils. Her concern and kindness was appreciated!

'Tenderfoot' Quarters
Native Constable Gavaza

Thanks to Mrs Mac., I ate well that evening, and her expensive cigarettes pleased the hardworking young grave diggers. A happier atmosphere now prevailed throughout the village, and the celebration dance was a joyous occasion with loud drumming, singing and dancing. Certain that his medicine had been successful, the witch doctor was the star performer. I watched from a rickety seat of honour, the beer flowed freely, and a few got drunk.

Next morning, with hapless prisoner Joel in tow, we cycled to our rendezvous, and were trucked back to camp. I was transferred to Sipolilo shortly after the Nyamawuchu saga, and I cannot recall the outcome of the case. In down-to-earth Rhodesia, not yet plagued by expensive lawyers and western morality, Joel was probably hanged!

Customs and Beliefs.

Living amongst the indigenous people during my 'Chiweshe' days, I became absorbed with the African way of life and, as my language skills improved, I was able to tactfully enquire and make a simplistic record of a few interesting customs and beliefs.

Birth. Bearing children was the pinnacle of a woman's existence. To be barren was a terrible humiliation, which allowed the husband to claim a younger sister. If a husband were thought to be impotent, another man in the family would be secretly invited to make the wife pregnant. Untrained

Malaria Hut 1947

Nurse Emily

School children

but experienced village midwives assisted at births, and were paid in kind by the husbands, who never attended births. Children with a deformity were allowed to die, and those born with teeth, known as 'crocodile' children, were stifled at birth. Twins were regarded with horror and the weakest abandoned, as artificial feeds were not available. No record was kept of births and deaths.

Childhood. Babies suckled until their teeth had formed, or until the next baby arrived, and were always strapped to their mothers' backs, whilst daily tasks were performed. Within the extended family, children had many important adults in their lives and, from an early age, they were taught that mutual help was paramount. They had to behave in ways conducive to the well-being of the group, and too much individuality and attention seeking was considered a serious flaw.

In a country that expected drought and famine every few years, adults who tilled the land and cared for the animals were more important than non-productive children. Thus, children were the first to suffer; a concept not easily understood by western cultures, whose morality is tempered by affluence. Children were easily replaced and were not considered a full person until all the first teeth had grown.

The 'survival of the fittest' was the guiding rule. Very young children who became blind or deformed were often abandoned, as they would be a drain on slender family and tribal resources. During my years in Africa, I never saw a Down's Syndrome person amongst the indigenous population.

Marriage. Everybody married at the right time, and not to marry was considered a blasphemy and against all laws of Nature and the Spirits. It was not possible to live alone or in sin as in western cultures, and homosexuality and lesbianism had no place in their lives. A marriage dowry or 'lobola' was paid to the bride's parents, in cattle or other animals, as an insurance of good intent and behaviour by both parties. Marriages were not required to be registered but, encouraged by missionaries, Christian marriages were registered with the church, but had no legal binding.

Witchcraft. The Bantu were animists who held that important spirits lived in the forests, kopjes and wild animals. They brought rain, gave fertility to women and the land, and ensured victory for the tribe in time of conflict. When things went wrong, the witch doctor was the tribe's representative to negotiate with the spirits on their behalf. He dressed to impress the people, and his paraphernalia included horns, bones, fly swish and various secret powders and potions. Superstition played a major part in village life.

Religion. With the coming of the missionaries, many people found Christianity attractive with its sermons, hymns, rituals and festivals. Often there was conflict with the old traditions of animism and the supernatural.

Eating. Meals were usually taken in the open, crouching or sitting on a reed mat or small stools. Before eating the right hand was washed and meals were eaten with the fingers. At the end of the meal, a bowl was passed round and the right hand washed. Their food was what they grew or hunted in the bush, and consisted of two meals a day of solid carbohydrate and protein. Obesity was a sign of beauty and status, and dieting was unknown!

Traditional Beer. Brewed from maize or millet and resembling a thin gruel, was the main drink. Consumed in moderate quantities it was a valuable antiscorbutic for people who lacked sufficient quantities of fruit and vegetables in their diet. At communal harvesting and threshing activities, helpers were rewarded with beer from the owner of the crop.

Medical. Most people knew the medicinal properties of plants, and often the 'witch doctor' was a knowledgeable herbalist. However, most treatments were very basic and many died of what would now be considered simple ailments. Many were connected with poor water supplies, lack of toilets and basic hygiene. Stress-related illnesses were virtually unknown but parasitic diseases, such as hook worm, tape worm, round worm and bilharzia, were endemic. Bloodshot eyes were common and caused by poor hygiene, smoky fires and the fierce sun. Spectacles were unknown before the arrival of missionaries. Villages were generally kept tidy and swept with brushwood brooms, and most rubbish was bio-degradable. Huts were used mainly for sleeping and sheltering from bad weather, and villagers spent most of their time in the open air. Sickness was often attributed to the misdemeanour of a family member, and wrong-doers were invited to confess their sins at family assemblies. At times criminal cases came to light as a consequence of these confessions. At Chinehasha village, a young girl student confessed that she had been seduced by her teacher. The outraged father was suspected of burning down the pole and mud school, and the teacher fled the district.

Law and Order. The Chief, headmen and elders were responsible for law and order and much time was taken discussing the merits of each case. Unwritten laws were passed down from generation to generation by word-of-mouth, and punishments were often harsh. Common sense and innate decency were important criteria, and the well-being of tribe was the main consideration. Only serious cases were reported to the Police, and the villagers usually sorted out their own difficulties. At times traditional bush justice prevailed and, at one village, a young boy lost his temper and set fire to the family granary. Villagers were assembled to witness a severe thrashing administered by the father, using a hippo hide whip.

Currency. Prior to the European occupation, money was unknown. Bartering was common practice and beads or cowrie shells were sometimes used as a form or currency. For many years, 'copper' coins, issued by the Rhodesian Government, had holes in their centres, so that they could be strung together like a necklace. This was useful for people without pockets in their simple skin coverings or clothing.

Initiation Ceremonies. With puberty, young people lived in the bush with their tutors and were taught tribal laws, behaviour and responsibilities. It prepared them for life within the tribe and was the only form of education available. There were separate ceremonies for boys and girls, and often involved circumcision.

Sipolilo

Winding northwards through the arid, rock-strewn Umvukwe hills, the earth road from Msoneddi gradually worsened, and ended abruptly at Sipolilo, a small backwater outpost and the most northerly Police station in Rhodesia. It was wild undeveloped country where material comforts were few, and where remote primitive areas could only be reached by foot or cycle.

The Police district encompassed a vast section of the sparsely populated and oppressively hot Zambesi valley, with the legendary Zambesi River forming Rhodesia's northern boundary with Northern Rhodesia. A few miles north of Sipolilo, a rugged path zig-zagged some 2,000 feet down a steep escarpment to the low-lying and unhealthy Zambesi valley. On the healthier plateau was the Native Reserve of the Makorekore tribe and, further south, a group of farms pioneered by young, hardworking ex-servicemen, who had painstakingly cleared the virgin bush to grow lucrative tobacco and maize crops.

Without electricity and prone to water shortages, Sipolilo comprised a couple of government bungalows, the Native Commissioner's offices, and the Police camp. Without a hotel or rest house there were few visitors: a doctor once a month, a missionary visiting primary schools and, very occasionally, a Police farrier to check the station horse. The dreaded Annual Inspection brought another visitor; a high-ranking officer from distant Salisbury, to make spot checks and keep us on our toes. There was not even a store, and basic supplies came from Salisbury by a dilapidated bus owned by the enterprising Chidavaenzi brothers. Joshua and Solomon were part-time Salvation Army officers, with little formal education, and some of their profits were used to pay for their younger brother's education, at the exclusive Fort Hare Native College in South Africa. Calling at the family's humble village one afternoon, I met the scholarly brother who was on vacation. Lounging on the verandah of their mud brick hut, he was dressed in a well-pressed suit, and reading Shakespeare's *Macbeth*, as part of his English literature course!

My first visit to Sipolilo was in October 46, when I drove the 80 dusty miles from Concession, with rations for the small gaol and a drum of petrol for their motorcycle. I was immediately attracted to its raw beauty, isolation and slow pace of life. The Member-in-Charge, bachelor Sergeant 'Sox' Vincent hated the place. A few months before, he had been a war-time Captain in the Rhodesian African Rifles, and this was a far cry from the status and camaraderie of the Officers' Mess. I found him a morose character, who was prone to heavy drinking during bouts of depression and, after a nervous breakdown, he was transferred to a more civilised environment. I took charge of the station for a few weeks, before the arrival of Sergeant Jock Lesley.

Other Europeans at Sipolilo at that time were South Africans Tony Buckley and Piet Jordaan, who were married and lived with their young families. Tony held the exalted position of Native Commissioner, Magistrate, and Chief Tax Collector, and Piet was his deputy. Neither had experienced war service, as Tony had a withered leg and Piet had been too young, but both were attuned to the bush, and well-suited to the lonely but peaceful life.

Hoping to view the Zambesi valley during my temporary posting, I woke early one morning, saddled-up Jupiter, the station's good-natured chestnut gelding, and cantered towards the Zambesi escarpment. The air was sweet, the sun pleasantly warm and I had the world to myself, but it proved to be too far and, frustrated and sweating profusely, I returned to camp. Tony heard of my disappointment and, at dawn next day, we set off in his car and bumped along the deeply rutted track to the edge of the escarpment. As the sun revealed its first shafts of light, we sat in silence and I had my first sighting of the mysterious valley, hundreds of feet below, with the Zambesi River hiding itself some 70 miles to the north amongst thick, forbidding bush. It had its own strange primeval beauty, and a journey to the famous river became an ambition.

This short posting gave me my first experience of prosecuting. A cowardly African youth had viciously assaulted a young village maiden, and was sentenced to six strokes with the cane which, the Magistrate specified, should be administered by the temporary Trooper-in-charge. Corporal punishment was normally administered by the senior African gaol guard, with the unlikely name of Dopi Goodfly, and he explained the procedure. A rattan cane was soaked overnight to increase flexibility, and a wet cloth was placed over the frightened young man's bottom, before striking the buttocks and avoiding the spine. It was an unpleasant duty and Dopi implied that I had been far too lenient!

Sergeant Jock Lesley duly arrived, laden with booze, a few possessions and his personal servant, Whisky. Sadly, I returned to Concession with its busy routine and low-powered electric lights, instead of a hissing paraffin lamp and candles. Jock, a proud Highlander, had served as a piper with the Highland Light Infantry and had the reputation as a hard drinker. He quickly fell out with the Chidavaenzi brothers who, as Salvationists, politely refused to transport his beer and whisky supplies. On moonlit nights, Jock loved to dress in his kilt and regalia, and play reels and dirges on his bagpipes as he paraded round the camp. On one occasion he unlocked the astonished prisoners to teach them the intricacies of Scottish dancing! Other eccentricities were attributed to Jock; shooting the button off the flag pole with his .303 rifle when trying to dispatch an imaginary vulture; a drunken spear fight with a visiting Scottish doctor; mini-golf by paraffin lamp, with Whisky playing caddy; and yelling to the longsuffering Whisky for help when awaking, with what Jock believed to be paralysis, after going to bed with both legs down one pyjama leg. Whisky was never shocked by his employer's antics, and even allowed Jock to name his new baby boy, 'Soda'. Jock did not get on with puritanical Tony Buckley and, after a few months, he was suddenly transferred and I took over the station in September 1947.

Sipolilo was a 'sergeant' station and I never knew why I was singled out to be Trooper-in-charge, or why I didn't ask for extra pay! I was delighted to have the opportunity to work at such a unique outpost and, undoubtedly, Tony Buckley had something to do with my appointment. In contrast to my predecessors, I was young, amenable and a teetotaller! In 1900, a few years after the founding of Southern Rhodesia, there was tribal conflict in this remote area over the appointment of the next Chief Chipuriro. Colonel Jack Flint of the Mashonaland Mounted Police, set out from Marandellas to resolve the problem, and one African policeman was killed. A temporary mud-brick Police camp was established about a mile from the present camp, and during my time, the remains of this old camp and two neglected graves were still visible. Thomas Wilson of Durham, who died of blackwater fever in March 1905, and Corporal J. Marais, a South African, who was killed a couple of years later, when his horse rolled on him. Both were members of the British South Africa Company Police, the forerunner of the modern Rhodesian force. A healthier site was chosen in 1915, when a modest brick and corrugated iron building was erected and a permanent Police Post established. It was named Sipolilo, a corruption of the local Chief's name, Chipuriro. When I took over, the buildings still had a 'pioneer' appearance and bits had been added with scant regard for aesthetics or expert planning. As well as the Charge Office, there were two small bedrooms, a lounge/dining room, a kitchen with a wood burning stove, a minute bathroom and an outside 'bucket' toilet. Because of the basic accommodation only bachelors served at Sipolilo. Our water was drawn from a nearby well, and transported in two drums, fixed on an ancient cart and pulled by two oxen. It was then poured into a storage tank, and gravity fed to the kitchen and bathroom. Another 44-gallon drum, with a fire underneath, was the hot water supply. Just before I left, a bore-hole was sunk and the slow plod of oxen gave way to a noisy, throbbing engine, which pumped the water to the tank.

Our nearest post office was at Msonneddi, 45 miles to the south, and mail was taken and collected twice a week; once by a messenger on a cycle and also by courtesy of the Chidavaenzis' bus. Another means of communication was by the erratic station telephone; a solid antique, probably dating from the early days of telephony. Wiring was concealed in a strong mahogany box, fixed to the wall, with a heavy brass receiver suspended on its side. We shared the line with a few other European subscribers over a wide area, and contact was made by a code of long and short rings, made with a small handle on the box. Any calls outside our area had to be made through an operator at Msonneddi. Our signal was three short rings and it was possible, but taboo, to eavesdrop on other conversations. Sometimes the line was out of action, as the locals found that telephone wire was useful for making bangles and necklaces.

Norman Dyer was the other trooper when I arrived and, having survived long spells with Sergeants Vincent and Lesley, was soon transferred to a more civilised station. 'Norm' was replaced by Bill Lowe, and later Brian Weeks, the well-educated son of an Admiral, came for a few months. All were post-war English recruits and excellent colleagues, who were content to undertake the office work at camp, and patrol the white farming areas by motorbike, when they needed a change of scenery. Neither was interested in a slow-moving horse, which gave me exclusive use of Jupiter, for the more intriguing African areas. Eight African constables and two gaol guards, under reliable African Corporal Jackson, were other members of staff. Cpl. Jackson was the station time-keeper, and his many duties included raising the 'Union Jack', winding the station clock and, as there was no bugler, striking a piece of metal hanging from a tree, to regulate our lives. Times were always approximate at Sipolilo.

A couple of hundred yards from our quarters, about a dozen short-term prisoners were incarcerated in a small rudimentary gaol. There was little stigma attached to a spell in 'Kingi Georgi Hoteli', and most inmates were impecunious villagers who opted for a few days' gentle labour and free food, in lieu of a fine. They cheerfully removed sanitary buckets, performed gardening duties around the Government buildings, and grew maize and vegetables, which we all shared. On one occasion, a crafty prisoner from Mozambique managed to elude the guard, and it was obvious that he would quickly descend to the valley and disappear into Portuguese territory. To avoid bureaucratic forms and procedures, his name was ticked off daily in the register and he was duly 'discharged'. It was a dangerous practice, but the secret was kept by the staff and appreciated by the careless guard. Our meat supply was what we managed to shoot locally. Swift, delicate duiker buck and larger bushbuck were common in the surrounding bush and, like most Afrikaaners, Piet Jordaan was an expert stalker and hunter and organised our shooting forays. When the maize crop was ripening, wild pigs were particularly destructive, as they rooted around with their tough, sharp tusks and could destroy a field overnight. A different technique, using torches, was employed during night shoots and roast pig was delicious. Most Africans hate snakes and often we were expected to shoot them. During the 'suicide' month, a huge python took up residence in an acacia tree near the staff huts, and I was persuaded to shoot it. It was over ten feet in length, and provided Chari with an unexpected source of protein. Villagers often had food for sale and, just after my arrival, two young daughters of the local headman offered milk in a dirty whisky bottle, sealed with the remains of a maize cob. Although ridiculously cheap, the milk was rather watery and, after a tuberculosis scare, we reverted to the more hygienic powdered milk. We continued to purchase eggs from the girls, and each egg was carefully immersed in a can of water which they carried with them. If the egg sank to the bottom it was deemed fresh and edible, but if it floated it was bad. Unscrupulous egg sellers had been known to hard boil their bad eggs to cause them to sink!

Life at Sipolilo, away from the complications and materialism of the large towns, was a pleasant, peaceful existence, but for many it would have been considered a punishment station. The lonely life was certainly not suited to those who hankered after clubs, bars and bright lights. Pre-breakfast duties commenced at 6 a.m., checking the horse, issuing prisoners' rations and attending to routine paper work, before the sun became too hot. During the day, a mixture of supervisory duties, court work and patrols kept us occupied and, in the cool of the evening, I exercised Jupiter in the surrounding bush, or played football with some of the staff.

There was little social life, but usually once a week we had a good meal with the Buckleys or the Jordaans, and 9 p.m. was a late night! As Magistrate, Tony was empowered to inspect the gaol and relevant records, and at times liked to assert his authority. Every few weeks he would inform me, by official note, that an inspection was imminent and, after taking a cursory glance at the various books, he would produce a towel and ask if I would give him a haircut!

There was little for our African staff to do after hours, and they responded enthusiastically to forming a football team with the Native Department staff. Using volunteers and a few prisoners, we quickly made a reasonable ground near the camp, and played regular matches with barefooted village teams. Our ground, considered the best in the area, and the only one correctly marked, became the focal point for local sporting activities, and hundreds of appreciative villagers, starved of entertainment, walked miles to watch the events. Inter-schools activities were also staged and required very little organisation; a water supply, a couple of trench latrines with grass fences, and help with judging the choir singing, dancing and sports activities. They were joyous occasions for the easily satisfied youngsters and, as the festivities lasted all day, they brought their own pots, firewood and food for the midday meal. A competition for the best constructed shelter, using poles, grass and bark string, was a devious way of providing several shady, open-sided shelters for the spectators!

Far left: Charge Office and Quarters

Left: Rear View

RH 461 Jupiter

Some of Staff

Out riding one Sunday morning, I passed near the pole and mud Salvation Army 'citadel', at Chimanikire village, where the locals were assembling for morning service. The unexpected arrival of a European law enforcer caused a stir, and much amusement, when Jupiter started to feed on the recently thatched roof. Although welcoming, the officials were a little uneasy at my presence, as they invited me to sit with them on a raised platform and look down on a sea of quizzical brown faces. The ice was broken when I joined in some of the Chishona hymns and choruses, which I had learned at Howard Mission. The services were an enjoyable social occasion for the villagers who, dressed in their best clothes, packed the church and sang enthusiastically to home-made drums and rattles. It was always a delight to listen to the harmonious singing, and watch the uninhibited congregation as they swayed and clapped rhythmically to the music, often with babies breast feeding or on the backs of their mothers. I attended the church whenever possible and was sometimes invited to read the lesson in Chishona. In lieu of a monetary collection, corn cobs and fruit were donated and sold for Church funds, or given to the elderly. Without a radio or gramophone, African singing at Church or primary schools was the only music I heard at Sipolilo!

Police work in the outback was like an open-air university, with an abundance of learning experiences and unusual cases; the death of a young student who tried to abort using chloraquin, a case of bestiality involving a goat and an isolated garden growing a large amount of Indian hemp or cannabis, are examples. One morning, a very young baby, wrapped in dirty rags, was found abandoned on the Charge Office steps. Without fuss or written record, the fortunate mite was adopted by a local Christian couple, who named her 'Rufaro' – 'Joy'.

Generally, the African people were hardy and uncomplaining. Whilst out riding one day, I passed close to a group of chattering women who had stopped work in a maize field. Thinking that one of them had fainted, I asked if they needed help and was informed that she was in the throes of childbirth! Fearful of being attacked by a predatory leopard or hyena, few people ventured out after dark and we rarely had night calls. One very dark night, an African arrived with a spear still lodged through his calf. He had limped from a village brawl so that we could see the evidence. The medical orderly could not be found so, helped by Corporal Jackson, I gently extracted the spear and doused the fleshy wound with a warm iodine solution, before binding with a cloth. Remarkably, the wound healed quickly and the assailant was duly gaoled. Far from the influences of Islam, Christianity was the only effective religion in Rhodesia, and the Salvation Army and the Methodists held sway in the Sipolilo area. During the dry season, a strange all-African religious sect arrived and organised a weekend rally a few miles from camp. A cluster of temporary grass huts mushroomed and curious villagers, always receptive to events that added colour to their mundane lives, flocked to witness the proceedings. Bearded leaders, wearing long white cloaks with crude red crosses, preached their version of the Gospels, and led hymns and choruses appropriated from the more orthodox denominations. Soon there were rumours that these strangers were advocates of free-love, and were in reality a bunch of lecherous tricksters. It was alleged that, as part of the conversion process, couples prayed together in separate huts, and vulnerable young women were then seduced.

With experienced Corporal Jackson following on his bike, I rode over on Jupiter to the rally and chatted amicably with the apprehensive leaders. Finding no evidence of improper behaviour, we concluded that the more orthodox churches had probably prompted the rumours, and were envious of the charismatic appeal of the 'bearded baptists'. It was at this rally that I saw my first albino; a person having a congenital absence of colouring pigment in the skin and hair. With distinct Bantu features, the unfortunate teenage girl had tight, sandy coloured hair, a white and brown blotchy skin and pink eyes; a sad sight, but she seemed happy and was accepted by the community.

Ngwerume thatching

Staff Huts

Corporal Jackson and Family

Ceremonial Uniform

When the torrential rains commenced, the perilous state of the mud brick walls and thatching of a few staff huts was revealed and, with ample free labour, we decided to rebuild them. At the end of the rains, large "Kimberley' mud bricks were moulded and the huts quickly erected. Unfortunately, none of our prisoners were skilled at the superior 'Barotse' style of thatching, which I was anxious to adopt. Then, out of the blue, a skilled 'Barotse' thatcher was remanded for alleged cattle theft, and he was soon put to work. Ngwerume was a likeable rogue and undoubtedly guilty, but there was little evidence against him, and we were obliged to release him before the thatching was completed. Amazed that he had escaped punishment, he agreed to stay and finish the task. For re-building the huts at no cost to the Force I was later commended by the Officer Commanding, Salisbury District. I kept quiet about the thatching being done by a remand prisoner, particularly as remands were not supposed to work!

The dry half of the year was also the Rhodesian soccer season, and my weekly sporting trips to Salisbury probably saved me from becoming a bush-loving recluse. Leaving at dawn on the day of the match, it was a long, juddering motorbike journey and I aimed to reach the capital city before the sun became too hot. After the luxury of a cold milkshake, I would sit for a while in the cool, tranquil atmosphere of Salisbury Cathedral, before heading for the Police headquarters, and the raucous chatter of the Troopers' mess. After the match, and with my fluid level back to normal, I would roar off into the dark African night for the 115 miles trip back to

Sipolilo, with a couple of fresh crusty loaves safely in the panniers; a welcome change from Chari's stodgy home-made bread. Although I enjoyed the thrill of playing for a successful team at well-supported matches, I was always pleased to return to the peaceful life in the outback. During the 1948 season, the Salisbury Police team, strengthened by postwar recruits, won three of the four main Rhodesian trophies, and narrowly lost the fourth trophy, the Austen Cup, Rhodesia's equivalent to the F.A. Cup.

From its remote source in north-west Zambia, the mighty Zambesi flows eastwards for almost 1,800 miles, before discharging its waters in the Indian Ocean. On its long, meandering journey through the Tropic of Capricorn, the river plunges over the Victoria Falls and, for about 400 miles, forms the boundary between present day Zambia and Zimbabwe.

In 1497, whilst searching for a sea route to India, the Portuguese mariner, Vasco da Gama, found the mouth of the Zambesi, and reported seeing Arab dhows laden with cargoes of gold, ivory and slaves. Anticipating riches in the hinterland, Portugal proclaimed the Zambesi area a 'sphere of influence' and, in 1505, a small settlement, Tete, was established on the river, some 300 miles westwards from its mouth. With Tete as their base, prospectors gradually explored the eastern Zambesi, but failed to find the legendary gold. Jesuit missionaries followed the gold seekers and, by 1650, a Catholic mission was founded at Zumbo, at the confluence of the Luangwa and Zambesi Rivers. Their sacrifices were in vain and, due to tropical diseases and unfriendly tribes, the mission was abandoned by the end of the 17th century. Losing interest in the remote interior, the Portuguese concentrated on lucrative slave trading from their coastal settlements, and thousands of African slaves from Angola and Mozambique, were shipped to Portuguese Brazil, to work on the plantations.

It was left to David Livingstone, the Scottish missionary, to explore the central Zambesi area, during his epic walk across southern Africa, between 1854-56. Starting from Loanda, in Portuguese Angola, Livingstone and his army of bearers followed the Zambesi eastwards, and he became the first European to view the magnificent 'mosi ao tunya' falls, which he named 'Victoria' after the reigning monarch. Entering Portuguese territory at Zumbo, he visited the ruins of the abandoned Jesuit mission station, before continuing along the Zambesi to Quilimane, on the east coast of Africa.

With the discovery of diamonds in South Africa in the 1870s, the 'scramble for Africa' began in earnest. European powers met in Berlin, to discuss boundaries and 'spheres of influence', and the Zambesi River became a convenient boundary, between the newly invented countries of Northern and Southern Rhodesia. In the subsequent carve-up of Africa, Portugal claimed a vast irregular-shaped piece of south-east Africa, which they called Mozambique. To the British, it was known as Portuguese East Africa.

Some 50 miles of the Zambesi River, and a vast area of the Zambesi valley, came within the Sipolilo Police District, and my journeys during 1947/48 provided a unique insight into this uncharted and undeveloped area. Low-lying, stiflingly hot, and rife with malaria and sleeping sickness, this remote part of Rhodesia was deemed unsuitable for European settlement, and there were no mineral bearing rocks to entice prospectors. Lacking economic potential, the valley remained a sadly neglected area, with no roads, schools or hospitals, and the primitive valley tribes were left undisturbed by the march of progress.

During the 19th century docile, peace-loving tribes sought sanctuary in this unhealthy and hostile environment, to escape the oppression and slaving tendencies of ruthless warrior tribes. They settled in small, isolated communities, under their traditional chiefs, and their simple lives were regulated by strict, unwritten tribal laws. Living in pole and mud huts, often built on stilts and with a protective stockade, they grew enough food to sustain a monotonous but adequate diet, and hunted without restriction a variety of wild animals in the virgin bush. Due to the deadly tsetse fly, they had no domestic animals, except a few scraggy chickens, and, during the long dry season, water was often scarce and water holes had to be dug in the dried-up river beds.

Away from the evils of materialism, and knowing no other way of life, the isolated valley folk lived close to nature. A few of the more adventurous men made the long journey to Salisbury to work as night soil labourers, before the city had piped sewerage. Considered inferior and shunned by the sophisticated plateau tribes, these rustic 'Zambesi boys', were the only Africans prepared to undertake such nauseating work. At the end of their contracts, they would return to their primitive villages laden with cloth, tools and utensils, and regale their families with unbelievable stories of the strange customs of the pale-faced occupants of the vast European 'kraal'.

Only the fittest children survived in such a hostile environment and no records were kept of births and deaths. Infant mortality was high, and babies with disabilities were abandoned and devoured by scavengers. With no schools, children quickly absorbed the customs and skills of village life. Girls helped with survival chores; fetching water, collecting firewood, cooking and tending younger children. Boys became experts with bows, arrows and spears, and could manage sharp knives and axes at an early age. Older boys joined exciting hunting groups and learned to stalk, drive animals into ambushes, and recognise the spoor and droppings of the many wild animals. It became second nature to the youngsters, to recognise edible and medicinal leaves, bark and roots, and which timbers were best for bows and arrows, implement handles and firewood.

A few weeks after my arrival at Sipolilo, a serious stabbing, at a valley village was reported and I decided to embark on my first visit to the mysterious valley. My companion was Tambo, a quiet, middle-aged constable of the old school, who spoke little English. Since arriving at Sipolilo in 1937, Tambo had never known a white policeman travel to the valley.

Because of tsetse fly, horses were not allowed in the valley, and cycling was our only option. Tambo carried a few possessions in a small haversack, whilst his inexperienced, young white companion carried a mosquito net, a cotton sheet bag, a supply of tea and sugar, and a revolver. Reaching the escarpment as the yellows and reds of sunrise flooded the cloudless sky, the timeless valley below was shrouded in a swirling mist. My excitement was not shared by unemotional Tambo, who knew what lay ahead. Descending over 2,000 feet to the valley was painfully slow, as we slithered down the steep, eroded path with our cumbersome cycles. There was little shade from the relentless sun and, as we approached the flatter valley floor, the heat became more intense. Tambo, dressed in a thick uniform jersey, had still not raised a sweat, whereas I was sweating profusely, burning under the scorching sun, and wondering whether I would survive. With our water supply exhausted, we made reasonable progress, along a narrow, serpentine path, through dense bush and long elephant grass and, by mid-afternoon, we reached a dried-up river bed. Quickly finding a small pool, Tambo drank thirstily from the brownish water, before relaxing under the shade of an acacia tree. Noticing the recent spoor of wild animals, I was more cautious and carefully strained the suspect liquid through a handkerchief, before drinking and filling my bottle.

Our arrival had been watched by local hunters and, as we rested, they appeared silently from different directions and surrounded us. Small in stature and scantily dressed in loin cloths, they submissively laid their bows, arrows and spears in front of us, before squatting and clapping their hands in a humble salutation. They were the first humans we had seen since leaving Sipolilo, and they had been watching the water hole, and hoping to replenish their meat supply. Guiding us to their poverty-stricken village, a few poorly dressed women, and numerous pot-bellied children, emerged cautiously from their huts, to gaze incredulously at the perspiring, young white man. Showing a modicum of modesty, the unwashed young girls wore small frontal aprons of skin, while the boys were completely naked.

Now too late to continue our journey, I was offered a small windowless hut, with a flimsy grass door, and hot water to make tea. Exhausted and badly sunburnt, I was soon tucked under my net and lulled to sleep by the gentle sounds of the African night.

It was still hot and humid the next morning, but refreshed by sleep and tea, we made an early start for Kalamba village, near the Dande River. Again, progress was tediously slow as we battled through the tinder dry undergrowth, and carefully avoided vicious thorn bushes that encroached over the path. Our silent approach startled various animals; chattering monkeys, browsing kudu, and bushbuck, and troops of hyperactive baboons, engaged in noisy arguments. At one point, two women emerged from the bush, with breasts uncovered and balancing huge bundles of firewood on their heads. Staring with disbelief at a white man on a cycle, they dropped their loads, screamed with fright, and fled into the undergrowth.

At Kalamba village, the elderly headman was lying in the shade on a reed mat, and looking extremely weak. Dressed in a dirty loin cloth, he had been speared through both arms, and blood and pus oozed from his wounds. Apart from bathing with suspect water, he had received no treatment since the assault, and his only chance of survival was to seek help at Sipolilo dispensary; a journey of about two days. Making him comfortable on a make-shift stretcher, a group of volunteers set off on their errand of mercy.

Facts of the case came to light. The assailant, a Mozambique African, had been offered customary shelter but, during the night, had attempted to rape the headman's young daughter. Caught in the act, he speared her father, and managed to evade pursuing villagers, before fleeing to the safety of Portuguese territory. Fearing the old man would die, the village elders sent a messenger to inform us at Sipolilo.

Returning to the 'hunters' village by late afternoon, we again accepted their hospitality. A large kudu had been killed, and young and old had assembled to eat charred meat, and sip local beer. It was a magical African scenario: a starry night, the flickering flames of a huge fire, and the smell of wood smoke and roasting meat. A few youths warmed their tomtoms by the fire and, gradually overcoming their shyness, the younger children were persuaded to entertain us with dusty, shuffling dances and singing games. Before our arrival, none of the youngsters had seen a white person, or a cycle.

At dawn, two muscular youths showed us a shorter route to camp, and helped push our heavy cycles up the steepest part of the escarpment, to the cooler plateau. In the comfort of camp, I reflected that I had seen more wild life in three days, than my previous eighteen months in Rhodesia. Several important lessons were learnt. Severe sunburn and prickly heat could have been avoided by wearing a shady pith helmet and a long sleeved shirt. It had also been unwise to visit the valley, in temperatures of over 100 degrees Fahrenheit. Despite the difficulties, I was determined to reach the mighty Zambesi during the cooler months, hopefully with my experienced friend Tambo.

A few days later, we learned that the old man had died on his way to Sipolilo, and the stretcher party had returned home for the burial rituals. Life for these uncomplaining valley tribes was extremely difficult, and now we had a murder charge on our files.

The Zambesi at last!
Towards the end of May 1948, Tony Buckley offered a chance of reaching the Zambesi. He had received a vague message that white hunters had crossed the Zambesi, from Northern Rhodesia, and had been illegally

hunting elephant and rhino, with automatic weapons. It was a legitimate excuse to visit the Zambesi river, even if the poachers had long since departed. As the vulture flies, the distance from Sipolilo to the Zambesi River was about 80 miles but, as native paths are very meandering, 90 miles was a more realistic estimate. One minor problem was that the Mashonaland soccer season had resumed, but I was confident that I could make the return journey to the river, without missing a match. Sadly, Tambo was recovering from malaria, and a younger man, Constable Uto, was nominated as his replacement. Although lacking experience of the primitive valley, Uto was one of the new breed of African policemen; mission educated, intelligent and ambitious. His selection, by hard-bitten Corporal Jackson, was probably a ploy to toughen him up!

We planned to travel by 'native' paths through virtually unknown country, without a map or means of communication, and the only certainty was that, if we headed northwards, we would eventually reach the Zambesi. Lacking a compass, the ever-present sun would be a reliable direction indicator. Protected against the tropical sun, by a pith helmet and long-sleeved shirt, and armed with both revolver and a heavy .303 Lee Enfield rifle, we left camp to a dazzling sunrise on the last day of May 1948.

Written, in abbreviated form, shortly after our return, the following account was based on the hastily scribbled notes of a young, inexperienced observer.

Day One.
Excitement as we reached escarpment to a beautiful sunrise. Heat gradually increased on the slow, slithering descent of over 2,000 feet, to the valley and Chief Chitsungu's country. Now lost contact with 'civilised' world and will rely on primitive villages for food and drink. Late afternoon, tired and thirsty, we arrived at the temporary camp of African workers preparing for a tsetse fly survey. Given the use of two grass huts, and a meal of 'monkey' stew and stodgy maize 'sadza'. Ate wild honey, mixed with wax and dead insects, from a sticky enamel mug. Many insects, so jammed cotton wool in my ears and slept.

Day Two.
Except for the chatter of startled monkeys, there was an eerie silence as we cycled mile after mile along narrow, twisting paths through long stretches of

dry elephant grass and virgin bush. Towards midday the heat worsened, and the numerous mopani trees provided little shade, as their leaves close together, like butterfly wings, to avoid the direct sunlight. Hunters guided us to a cluster of thatched mud huts, called Kalumbe. Welcomed by the elderly headman, deeply wrinkled and wearing a dirty sarong. Surprised to see a white policeman; the first he has ever seen. Inquisitive villagers, with frightened children hiding behind their mothers, gathered to stare at the strange, over-dressed white man. Rested in shade on roughly carved stools. A shy young girl, naked except for a small, frontal piece of animal skin, knelt gracefully and offered an earthenware pot of refreshing millet beer, and two unused drinking calabashes. Fascinating village activities; preparing arrow heads for evening hunt, weaving baskets, making pots, and twisting bark into string for bows. Older women have deeply slashed tattoos on their faces and arms, made by knife cuts filled with ash and plant juices. Sun still high, as we made for Kachari village. Two strong youths pushed our cycles through a sandy area, and carried us over the thigh-deep Hunyani River, near Mushumbi pools; a popular wildlife watering hole.

Slow, tiring ride through thorn bushes, creeping vines and elephant grass; all designed to hinder progress. Late afternoon reached Kachari's, a large, orderly village with extensive maize and millet gardens. Naked boys excitedly pushed our cycles to the village meeting place, where curious villagers quickly assembled. Kachari, a dignified man with a mop of grey curly hair, and dressed in an ankle-length sarong, greeted us and the customary pot of beer was offered. Kachari was surprised that we had travelled from Sipolilo in two days. Given use of a small hut, with a bed made of hide thongs, stretched over a rough pole frame. Headman's daughter brought a large bowl of warm water, for a refreshing 'stripped' wash, the first since leaving Sipolilo. Sat with headman and elders after a meal of maize porridge and boiled egg.

Village often troubled by elephants, wild pig and baboons at harvest time. Deserted village, seen earlier, was abandoned three rainy seasons ago, after a mother and her two children had been killed by lions. Now near the Mozambique border, and advised to take a short-cut through Portuguese territory, to reach the river in two or three days.

Slept well, despite mosquitoes.

Day Three.
Early start and guided to 'Portuguese' path by young boys, who were thrilled to be allowed to handle and aim the unloaded rifle. Headed north-west, in fierce, dry heat, through tropical wilderness, and vicious thorny undergrowth. Followed a narrow path to the Angwa River, and paddled across the cool waters. Squalid collection of huts nearby and frightened villagers ran and hid in their poorly-built shacks. Contrary to custom, nobody greeted us. Found to be a settlement for mentally defectives, herded together by the Portuguese authorities. Grey with dust, and cringing with apprehension, a few apathetic adults emerged from their huts to stare in disbelief. Several had large, untreated tropical ulcers on their legs. Known as Gwebe, it was a wretched, depressing settlement. Set off in afternoon heat, and hoped to reach 'civilised' Rhodesian territory before dusk. Numerous agile monkeys, baboons and well-camouflaged antelope in the open bush. Several vultures were riding the thermals and searching for carrion. Uto indicated recent lion spoor, so loaded the rifle as a precaution. Found a faint path which passed a small boundary stone. We were back in Rhodesia! Met men, walking single-file, with baggage on their heads. Lowering their loads, they squatted and slowly clapped their hands, as they chanted, 'Changamire, Changamire'; a greeting usually reserved for chiefs. All returning to work on a tobacco farm in the Umvukwes; a five or six days' walk.

Very sandy path, so walked with cycles towards Chanamu village. Spotted by excited young boys, who pushed cycles through the stockade. Our unexpected arrival surprised the villagers. Men gathered to clap hands and chant a greeting, and women, singing happily at their pounding mortars, stopped work to stare in amazement. Very little clothing worn by adults and younger children naked. I was wearing shirt, trousers, leather gaiters, pith helmet, and a heavy rifle slung across my back! Welcomed by Chanamu, a middle-aged chief, with a wispy beard and a cast in one eye. Women quickly placed reed mats in the shade, and offered a pot of beer and a clay bowl of 'masawi' berries, which resemble cherries. Allocated a small hut, with a candle and a bowl of warm water. A typical hut has an earth floor, and no windows or furniture; a quick sweep and the housework is done! After dark, squatted round fire with men, while wives served 'sadza', beans and vegetables. Uto ate from the communal bowl, using his fingers. I was given my own bowl of food and wooden spoon. Village elders thought I was the first European to visit the village, but an ancient, grey-haired matriarch disagreed. She remembered two 'mabuno' (Afrikaaners) visiting when she was young. They hunted elephant and rhino, and one was a magician who could take out his teeth and put them back again! When resting, men use small wooden neck-rests, resembling miniature stools. Invited to a noisy but enjoyable 'Vasikana' (girls) dance round fire. Youths beat drums and shook rattles in a monotonous rhythm, as the gyrating girls sang, clapped hands and made expressive arm movements. Except for short frontal aprons, the exuberant young dancers were naked, and their lissom bodies glistened with perspiration. Slept well despite a sunburnt face and prickly heat rash.

Day Four.
Much activity at sunrise; pounding flour, collecting water and firewood and hoeing the gardens. Shown crops damaged recently by elephants. Their clumsy movements cause more damage than actual feeding. Villagers use fire brands and drums to scare the elephants, as spears are ineffective and nobody owns a gun. Uto's back tyre punctured as we headed for Chief Chapoto's village. Attracted by the moisture on our backs, several large flies inflicted painful bites. Browsing kudu and eland scattered as we approached, and snakes on the path slithered rapidly into the bush. Evidence of elephant activity; trees uprooted, foliage stripped, mounds of manure and wide trampled trails. Native paths are never straight, and wide detours are made round fallen trees, gullies and impenetrable bush. My urine is dark and concentrated, and must drink more often. Arrived late afternoon at well-maintained village, and received by Chief Chapoto, an elderly, dignified man, sitting on a roughly carved 'throne', with a faded cloth wrapped round his emaciated body. He had not heard of white hunters, but complained about the large number of tsetse flies. Presented with millet beer and a small bowl of masawi berries. Meat is an important part of their diet and, after a successful hunt, strips of meat were drying on a wooden rack, with swarms of flies helping the drying process. Women, with cheap printed cloth covering their bodies, sat in the shade, busily weaving palm sleeping mats and moulding clay pots. Trousers and shorts are never worn by women and, despite the scorching sun, nobody wears a hat. Sat by a smoky fire with the Chief and elders, as he related the tribe's recent history and customs. Before the British arrived in Rhodesia, they lived in the Tete area of Mozambique,

but left because of the cruelty and forced labour schemes of the Portuguese. Moving westwards along the Zambesi, they settled amongst the primitive Kanyemba people, on the south side of the river. Having learned many skills from the Portuguese, they were considered a superior tribe, and their leader became Chief Chapoto. He was always carried on a stretcher, like an important Portuguese official. Polygamy is practised and a dowry or 'lobola' paid. By custom, girls are betrothed as children and marry at puberty, within the tribe. As they have no watches or calendars, the sun and moon are their indicators of time.

Horses not allowed – Tsetse Valley Fly Area

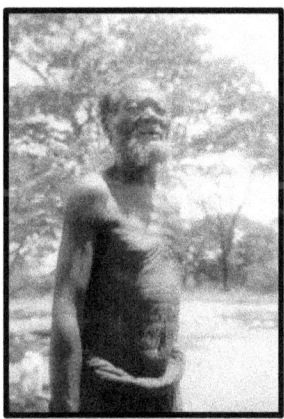

Tribal Chief

Water Carriers

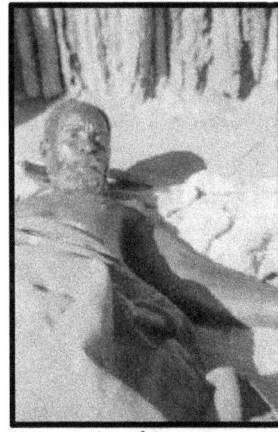

Victim of Spearing at Beer Drink – later died

Away from the influence of Christianity and Islam, the people are animists, and the witch doctor is influential. All are illiterate and exact ages are unknown. Despite their lack of possessions, they are a very practical people, with a good community spirit. Women spend their whole lives in the home village, but some men travel to Salisbury to work as 'Zambesi boys'.

Simple acts amused the curious children; writing my diary, sketching one of the boys, and revolving the cycle wheel and applying the brake. None had ever seen a pencil! Village men were intrigued by my rifle and revolver, and have previously only seen muzzle-loading guns. Evening meal was of maize 'sadza' with a tasty, 'monkey' soup. Fire is made by friction, and food is cooked over open fires. Watched young children play a guessing game; imitating the actions and sounds of wild animals. Others played a form of draughts, using large seeds and holes in the ground. Many have 'sticky', blood-shot eyes, but are sturdy and happy. Shoes are rare, and the soles of their feet are hard and cracked. Early bed to conserve candle.

Day Five.
Left at dawn, but uncomfortably hot. Slow progress because of sand paths. Flat tyre at Malamba village, but have lost our pump and there are no cycles or pumps at the village. Only a few hours to Zambesi, so left our cycles with the headman and walked. Two strong lads, Vasiko and Mala volunteered to carry our baggage and act as guides. Without our heavy cycles, good progress was made despite the sweltering heat. Gradually, the bush became less dense, and the distant hills of Northern Rhodesia closer. Nearer the river, villages and gardens are larger, huts more substantial, women fatter, and naked children fewer. White people are rarely seen, and I attract curious, but friendly stares, as we trudge through the well-kept villages. Suddenly, the great African waterway looms ahead, glinting in the sun, and winding slowly between sandy islands.

Reached a small village at the water's edge, known as Kanyemba, and welcomed by a tall, uniformed African, Wilson Mulanga, who speaks Chishona. Given a pole and mud hut, with an earth floor, and an unimpeded view of the Zambesi. Tea on verandah, as the golden sun sank slowly behind the distant hills. Enthralled by the natural African scenario, thatched huts, graceful palms, bulbous baobab trees and narrow dug-outs gliding along the river.

Everything very 'African'; no roads, brick buildings, shops or even cycles. Zambesi narrows to about 200 yards here, and the silt-laden waters must have plunged over the Victoria Falls yesterday! An ambition fulfilled, and well worth enduring the physical effort, the scorching heat, and primitive living conditions.

Wilson, from Mrewa, recruits local Africans for the copper mines of Northern Rhodesia. We are the first policemen he has ever seen at Kanyemba, and is surprised we have cycled and walked from Sipolilo, without bearers or tents. He had not heard of white hunters in the area. As the only wage earner at Kanyemba, he is held in high esteem, but his office is a humble mud hut. During the war, he served in Burma with the Rhodesian African Rifles, and is envious of my .303 rifle. At the evening meal Uto and Wilson shared bowls of 'sadza' and fish, and ate the heads and tails! Locals live mainly on fish; a real luxury for Uto. Escorted to my hut and given a small hurricane lamp, instead of the usual candle. Advised to keep a close watch on my valuable firearms, as I would be on my own. Mosquitoes buzzing during the night, and the occasional blood-curdling yelps of hyenas.

With Wilson at Zumbo Mozambique

Above left: Preparing our canoes
Above: Zambesi children

My hut on river at Kanyemba

Day Six.
Woke at dawn and sat on the verandah. A wrinkled, middle-aged man, wearing a ragged army greatcoat, brought a can of boiling water for tea. He had slept on the verandah, guarding me! Watched groups of hippos, swimming in the misty river below the hut. Mist gradually dispersed to reveal thousands of birds on the river flat; pink-legged flamingoes, herons, egrets, and other species unknown to me. Watched white-headed fish eagles, gliding gracefully and suddenly swooping to catch fish.

Crossed by dug-out to a village on north bank with Wilson. Now in Northern Rhodesia, but no formalities. Uto stayed at Kanyemba as nervous. A canoe was overturned by hippos yesterday, and he cannot swim. Villages here are more affluent than inland valley villages. People are subsistence farmers growing maize, cassava and sweet potatoes. Their huts, built on stilts, are clean and well-maintained. Strong fish odours, as fishing is the main occupation of men. Fish drying in the sun and over smoky fires, as rarely eaten fresh. Friendly people pounding flour, thatching and weaving fish traps. All wear simple clothing. Well-washed women have bangles, earrings and necklaces, and plait hair in various styles. Curious about me as white policemen are never seen. Shown large hippo spoor outside a stockade. Vegetarian hippos visit at night in search of food, and often raid crops. At harvest time, men and boys sit on raised platforms, and rattle tins and beat drums to scare them. Elephants, wild pig and baboons also seek easy meals in the gardens. Hippos are occasionally killed for meat, and hippo foot is a great delicacy. Whips are made from hippo hide, and the large incisors used for ivory carving. Crocodiles, well camouflaged and floating like logs, are a constant danger to inattentive young girls drawing water at the river. No chance of escape from the jaws of crocodiles, who kill their victims by drowning. Some villages prefer to dig safer water holes.

Very hot, but late morning joined Wilson on a trip to Feira, a Northern Rhodesian settlement a few miles upstream. Large dug-out canoe with four young paddlers, who smeared an oily substance over the bows; a secret medicine to ward off hippos and crocodiles. Powerfully built and happy-go-lucky, the paddlers took up the rhythm. Deep-throated chanting as the almond-shaped paddles were dug deeply into the water, and two resonant taps with the paddle against the side of the canoe, as they returned for another stroke. Away from the villages, numerous crocodiles were basking on the mud flats. Also groups of hippos, suspicious and motionless in the river; the first I have seen at close quarters. Several miles of strenuous paddling, against the flow of the river, and Feira came into sight.

A sleepy town, with a pot-holed, earth road from the crude jetty, and a mixture of mud huts and corrugated iron shacks. Friendly group of Africans greeted us with gentle hand clapping. As we drank tea in a scruffy shack, a small truck, driven by a European, arrived in a cloud of dust. A tall, rangy man, with a strong South African accent, introduced himself as Dr George Booth, of the N.R. Medical Service. Leaving Wilson to his duties, George drove me to his bungalow, with commanding views of the Zambesi. He had watched our progress through binoculars, and was surprised to see a European passenger. He is employed on sleeping sickness research and, seeing bites on my face and arms, advised a check-up in Salisbury. Whilst washing, I saw myself in a mirror for the first time since Sipolilo; matted hair, blood-shot eyes, and a thin sunburnt face! Delicious cold orange drink, with appetising salad lunch, before visiting his hospital. Basic male and female wards, set in gardens with flowering bushes, but a depressing atmosphere. Scores of dispirited sleeping sickness victims, very thin and resigned to their fate. Most die with dignity in hospital, rather than primitive villages. From the bungalow, witnessed fascinating river scenes through his binoculars. Drank tea from a china cup(!) while George drank brandy. He works six-monthly periods at Feira, and is devoted to his work, but is rather lonely and the only European within several miles. He fell asleep, so I scribbled a note and walked back to the river, to the curious stares of locals. Saw a cycle, the first since leaving camp.

Our return canoe journey, with the flow, was much easier. Paddlers took rests and excitedly pointed out a variety of wildlife amongst the sandy islands. Steered close to a group of wary hippos. One baby hippo was balanced precariously on its submerged mother's back. Hippos with young can be dangerous, and sometimes overturn canoes. Hoped the secret 'canoe' medicine was still effective! Away from human habitation, many large crocodiles wallowed in the slimy mud. Locals drive fish into wicker traps, placed across the shallow channels. Fiercest and largest Zambesi fish is the tiger-fish, and the strange electric cat-fish kills its prey with an electric shock.

Another spectacular African sunset; varying shades of yellow, orange and red. After dark, nobody leaves the safety of the stockades, and an uncanny silence settles over the river. My humble abode smells of damp earth, and I share it with annoying mosquitoes and an assortment of insects. Persuaded Uto and Wilson to canoe downstream to Portuguese Zumbo tomorrow. During the rainy season of 1856, David Livingstone, with over a hundred bearers, had walked this part of the river, and had visited an abandoned church at Zumbo. Livingstone is unknown to most Africans, and has been branded the first white 'tourist' by some educated Africans! Wilson is not allowed to operate in Mozambique, so potential workers come secretly to Kanyemba.

Day Seven.
Guarded by a younger man last night. Tea on verandah and watched a gorgeous sunrise gradually illuminate the timeless Zambesi. Vultures circling high in the sky, searching for scraps left by hyenas and jackals. Early start downstream with Wilson, Uto and the same young paddlers. Leisurely journey, with flow of river, through uninhabited country. River widens past Kanyemba, exposing islands and abundant wildlife. Scores of primeval crocodiles wallowing in the thick mud, and floating amongst the reeds. Uto nervous as we drifted near a group of suspicious hippos, with just their ears and eyes visible. Watched four lumbering elephants wade confidently to mid-stream, before plunging and rolling in the cool waters. Steered closer, but ignored by the enormous animals. Along the high alluvial banks, colourful kingfishers, and scores of red bee eaters, flitted busily in and out of their sandy nests; an ornithologist's paradise.

Built at the confluence of the Luangwa and Zambesi Rivers, Zumbo is a sleepy border town, and Mozambique's most westerly outpost. Under Portuguese influence for 400 years, but little development. The boundaries of N.R., S.R. and Mozambique converge here.

As the dug-out was moored to a rickety pole jetty, a crowd of curious Africans gathered, and gently clapped their hands as a salute. I felt overdressed and very hot, with a heavy rifle on my back and revolver at my side. More brick buildings than Feira, but the atmosphere was not so welcoming. Two barefooted Africans, in khaki uniforms, approached and saluted smartly. Taken to a ramshackle bar, and offered wine and cigars. A small truck arrived and took me along a dusty, tree-lined track to white washed offices, where a faded Portuguese flag hung limply from its pole. An enthusiastic welcome and salute from a smiling, overweight Portuguese official, dressed in immaculate white shorts, shirt and peaked cap. In broken English, he introduced himself as Alberto Coutinho, administrator of Zumbo district. Having worn the same clothes all week, I apologised for my scruffy appearance. Driven to a spacious, Colonial-style bungalow and introduced to his plump, olive-skinned wife, and shy seven-year-old daughter. Offered a bath and given an extra-large pair of white shorts and shirt to wear. Filthy clothing taken by a servant. Emerged shaven and refreshed, and my baggy clothing amused his young daughter. Sat in cool lounge, with ceiling fan and several animal trophies on the walls. Alberto struck a brass gong, suspended from two large elephant tusks, to summon a uniformed servant with drinks. An elderly African butler spoke Chishona, and translated when Alberto's English failed. Alberto amazed that we had travelled from Sipolilo without bearers, and shocked that I had stayed in village huts and eaten local food. Lunch of fish, vegetables and fruit salad, served by attentive servants. Because of the severe heat and basic living conditions, Alberto's tour of duty is only 18 months, before leave in Portugal. Supplies come from Tete, 250 miles downstream, by river and motor transport. Daughter learns by correspondence course, helped by her mother. Alberto offered to show me the ruins of the 17th century Jesuit mission, after the usual siesta.

Blissful rest in a cool guest room, before being driven by Alberto to the Jesuit mission ruins, near the Luangwa River. Africans stopped and bowed as his car passed. Ruins overgrown and some stone has been removed, but thrilled to think that Livingstone had visited 92 years before, and had noted in his journal, '... found ruins of a small church, a cross and a broken bell, as a reminder of human failure'. Alberto had not heard of Livingstone. On our return, a servant presented me with freshly laundered clothes, and polished gaiters and boots!

Given a cycle pump, and a supply of coarse salt and sugar by the generous Portuguese family. Wilson and Uto waiting at the jetty. A wonderful, natural African vista, as the perspiring paddlers battled against the flow to Kanyemba. Saw elephants, hippos and crocodiles, and thousands of birds feeding, as the sun gradually sank behind the Rhodesian hills. Wilson hates the repressive Portuguese regime. Compulsory unpaid labour schemes cause many Mozambique Africans to seek work in the Rhodesias and South Africa. A memorable day!

Day Eight.
Just after dawn, a sad farewell to Kanyemba friends, and the misty Zambesi. Long walk ahead. Mala and Vasiko carried our baggage and guided us to Malamba village. Good progress through dry, open bush dotted with grotesque baobabs, and numerous tall, termite mounds. Many excitable monkeys and grumpy baboons feeding in the acacia woodlands. Reached Malamba late morning, and given an enthusiastic welcome. Gave headman and young guides gifts of salt. Mended puncture in heat of day, and amused an audience of children by using the cycle pump as a water pistol! Shown short-cut and reached Chief Chapoto's village late afternoon. Another friendly welcome. Usual maize porridge and egg, before watching men making fire by friction, and preparing a huge fire for village dance. Noisy but interesting dances by children and adults, accompanied by drums, rattles and a primitive xylophone. Early sleep, after a tiring walk and long cycle ride.

Day Nine.
Decided to avoid Mozambique 'short-cut'. Early start and found a good path through mopani and acacia forests. Rested at a small settlement, near the Angwa River, where several men were building a pole and mud hut. Huts are re-built every few years because of heavy rains and destruction by termites. Two cheerful youths pushed our cycles along a sandy path to the Angwa River, and carried us across. Taken to a large village called Gwanda, and welcomed by the headman, who had never seen a white policeman. Women and children ran away and hid, but gradually emerged to stare. Chat round fire with group of men, all of the Chikunda tribe. Like most Africans, their hardened fingers can hold burning embers without pain. An abundance of game for meat, but leopards are a danger to careless children. Virtually no crime and the Chief and headmen sort out problems, as Sipolilo is too far to report offences. Having faced the scorching sun all day, my eyes are sore, so an early night in a hut with a crude bed, and the usual menagerie of insects.

Day Ten.
Woke early and taken to watch small groups of elegant kudu and impala and bushbuck drinking at the river. Antelope is the favoured meat, but only

killed when needed. Left Gwanda village before the sun became too high. Met two travellers returning from Salisbury, laden with tools and utensils. Told that a 'murungu' (European) had a tented camp, at the foot of the escarpment. Late morning, carried over the Hunyani River by two strong youths, wearing just loin cloths. Good path to the Dande River, and crossed easily between pools. No punctures since leaving the Zambesi.

Reached tsetse fly camp and welcomed by ranger, Jock Fraser; a sprightly man, wearing a large slouch hat. Invited to stay at his camp. Jock, from Glasgow and ex-army, was supervising a tsetse fly survey, and lives in reasonable comfort; a large tent, a portable toilet and a canvas bath! He has several servants and a dozen survey workers. All fond of Jock and, being a crack-shot, he keeps them well-supplied with meat. Enjoyable 'scoff' and singing by the crew, round a blazing campfire. Jock enjoys brandy, and has a fund of amusing 'valley' stories. One time, he shared a delicious meal with a valley Chief, and enquired what meat they had eaten. 'You remember that young upstart who ran away with my junior wife?' replied the Chief, with a smile. 'That was him.' Jock has never been to Feira or Zumbo, and was surprised that we had travelled without food, bearers, or even a first aid kit. A foolhardy young tenderfoot! He is an expert on the tsetse fly. They are found only in Africa, resemble large houseflies, and live on blood sucked from animals and humans, which cause fatal 'nagana' in domestic animals, and sleeping sickness in humans.

Day Eleven.
Comfortable night on a camp bed, instead of the hard ground. A servant busily swatted flies, as I ate the best breakfast of the trip; oat porridge, scrambled eggs and pancakes, with honey. Sun was high when seen off by Jock and his crew. Gruelling ascent of mountainous escarpment, and a tedious ride to camp with the sun in our faces. Arrived at camp late afternoon badly sunburnt, and with an uncomfortable heat rash.

With Uto's help and friendship, I had reached and travelled on the mighty Zambesi! A memorable journey, and a humbling experience, amongst incredibly poor but hospitable people. It was good to be back in camp, with the luxury of chairs, a comfortable bed, 'European' food, and hot water. After a much-needed bath and change of clothes, Trooper Bill Lowe dropped a bombshell. By missing the Force football match, I had incurred the wrath of the Officer Commanding, Salisbury District, Captain 'Plum' Funnell, and was ordered to report to him immediately. It was already dusk and, after a strenuous day, cycling and climbing in the tropical heat, 'immediately' would have to be the following day.

Next morning, fully rested but a little apprehensive, I roared off into the sun and dust, for the 115 miles bone-shaking trip to Salisbury, with my football kit packed safely in the motorcycle panniers. Dreading interrogation by such a senior officer, I deemed it prudent to have a short, 'military' haircut by a Salisbury barber, before making for the Troopers' Mess. Various rumours had been circulating about my vanishing act into the primitive valley, and some colleagues thought I had probably been murdered for my valuable firearms.

Showing signs of severe sunburn, I was paraded before a stern-faced Commanding Officer, and ordered to explain my untimely disappearance. Nervously, I stressed that a combination of circumstances had been against me; unknown and hostile territory, extreme heat, punctures, and no way of communicating my predicament. Amazingly, he was sympathetic and, after a minor rebuke and short lecture on 'esprit de corps', I was ordered to rest, as I was in the Force football team the following afternoon! A Londoner by birth, 'Plum' had advanced rapidly through the ranks to his present exalted position, and his original cockney accent had become more refined with each promotion. His present 'plum in the mouth' English accent, accounted for his Force nickname. He also insisted that 'Funnell' should be pronounced 'Foonell'. Fortunately, we won our match and all seemed to be forgiven. Before returning to Sipolilo, tests for sleeping sickness and bilharzia proved negative.

Quickly settling to camp routine, I was delighted to revert to travel by horse and motorcycle. Poor food, painful sunburn and cycling marathons, in the stifling heat of the valley, soon became a memory. I even thought of a final jaunt to the Zambesi, before my three years contract expired. Physically unable to visit this remote part of his domain, Native Commissioner Tony Buckley, quizzed me about the villages and people I had visited. I suspected that he had concocted the 'illegal hunting' story, to give me an excuse to fulfil an ambition.

At the end of the 1948 football season, a final journey was made to the valley and river. Knowing what to expect, there was not the same sense of excitement as previous trips, and I was better prepared with sunglasses, sun lotion and a small torch. Young and ever-cheerful, Constable Juta was my companion. Although it was his first trip to the valley, he had the uncanny knack of discovering better and more direct paths to the Zambesi. Nearing the end of the dry season, the few rivers had ceased to flow, and the parched vegetation gave little shade. With just one puncture, our frustrations were minimal, and the return trip to the magical river was completed in eight days. It was still oppressively hot, but the priceless experiences in such a remote area, outweighed the hardships. Old friends and villages were revisited, and we were welcomed with genuine friendship, generosity and joyful dancing.

At Kanyemba, Wilson's wife proudly displayed their seventh child, a boy, which they had named Joni. She confided that Wilson was about to marry a second and younger wife, which distressed her. My old 'wattle and daub' hut, with superb views of the Zambesi, was again put at my disposal, and a guard posted at night. Since my last visit, crocodiles had become troublesome, and two young girls had been killed whilst fetching water. Wilson responded enthusiastically when I suggested a crocodile shoot and, despite his lack of practice, he was an excellent shot. He organised a dugout canoe trip to Zumbo, with the same energetic paddlers, and I spent a pleasant day and night with Alberto Coutinho and his family. I was able to return his cycle pump and avail myself of the rapid 'Coutinho' laundry service. Our only failure was to find a 'fossilised' forest, near the Mozambique border, which had been reported by white hunters in the thirties. Without a map, we were not quite sure where to search or what we were looking for, and enquiries about 'miti se dombo' – 'trees like stone', produced blank expressions from villagers. Juta, with his suburban upbringing and outlook, was thrilled to see such an abundance of wildlife, but was shocked by the primitive lives and extreme poverty of the valley tribes.

Guns played an important role in Rhodesian and Police life, but I was never happy 'shooting for the pot', and disliked the compulsory Police musketry practice. On our return journey, and against my better judgement, I was responsible for the destruction of a magnificent elephant; an act I have always regretted. Elephants had again been troublesome at Chanamu village, and the arrival of an armed policeman caused excitement and expectation. Preferring succulent village crops to the dry grasses and leaves of the bush, clumsy elephants had again trampled and destroyed a large area of their precious food supply. After a short rest and a much-needed drink, the headman showed us the heartbreaking damage done to their laboriously produced crops, and pleaded for help from white hunters.

Chatting in the shade, later that afternoon, terrifying feminine screams were heard in the distance. 'Nzou, nzou' ('elephant, elephant'), shouted the villagers, as they sprang into action and rushed for their spears. Quickly grabbing my .303 rifle, I followed them to the stockade entrance. Several hysterical women were hurrying towards us, screaming, 'Nzou, nzou, vana vedu vapera' ('elephants, elephants, our children are dead'). Breathlessly, they explained that, whilst collecting firewood, a group of elephants had appeared, and they had become separated from three young girls. Just then, more loud screams were heard, and the terrified girls emerged from the bush and sprinted across the fields to the safety of the stockade. Within minutes, three lumbering elephants came into view and, despite the loud yells and frantic spear waving of the anxious villagers, plodded unhurriedly towards the crops. Instinctively, I loaded the rifle, and fired two shots over the elephants' heads. Two of them stopped in their tracks, before turning slowly and ambling off into the bush. The third larger animal continued fearlessly towards the luscious food supply, and defiantly commenced its destructive feeding.

Guided by the headman, we approached silently up wind of the huge animal and stood, about twenty yards away, with a perfect sideways view. Although slightly agitated, the giant tusker continued to trample and munch the succulent maize stalks. 'mukati munzeve, mukati munzeve – in the ear, in the ear', whispered Chanamu and, succumbing to the tense situation, I raised the rifle and fired two rapid rounds to the middle of its ear. Obviously in pain and trumpeting loudly, it quickly raised its trunk and its huge ears fanned out, as it slowly turned towards us. Encouraged by Chanamu, I manoeuvred cautiously to a better position and fired two further ear shots. Staggering unsteadily, the elephant's enormous legs suddenly buckled and, to the ecstatic yells of the jubilant villagers, the unfortunate animal collapsed slowly on its side, in a cloud of dust.

Excited villagers quickly encircled the massive mound of flesh and bone and, as Chanamu raised his arms, they sat quietly as he took charge of the proceedings. Sitting near the dead animal on his ceremonial stool, his senior wife placed a leopard skin cap on his balding head, and gently draped a bright red cloth round his shoulders. With quiet authority, he issued orders and, as if by magic, men appeared with an assortment of knives and axes, and women and girls hurried to fetch a variety of buckets and bowls. Blowing a small horn trumpet, and naked except for a skirt of monkey tails, the influential witch doctor made a dramatic entrance. By custom, he had first call on the dead animal and, flourishing a large knife, he deftly cut out the genitals and most of the trunk, in readiness for future medicinal concoctions. Watched by the hushed crowd, two muscular youths, armed with an axe and machete, callously hacked and levered the huge off-white tusks from the jaw, and laid them gently in front of Chanamu.

Butchering of the huge animal then commenced. Dressed only in loin cloths, barefooted men skilfully cut and chopped their way through a sea of blood and soft meat, and heaped it on palm mats ready for distribution. Before dusk, the vast amount of meat had been shared between families, and the blood stained carcass was left for scavenging hyenas, vultures and moisture seeking flies. My immediate concern was whether I had acted illegally and, although saddened by my actions, I consoled myself with the thought that I had prevented the destruction of the only food supply of a large number of people.

Back at Sipolilo, sympathetic Tony Buckley dismissed the unfortunate episode as 'justifiable killing', and I conveniently forgot to record the incident in my patrol diary. Within a few days, Chanamu and a group of villagers arrived at Sipolilo, and ceremoniously presented the huge tusks to the Native Commissioner. My gift from the village was a magnificent, but malodorous, pair of spiralled kudu horns.

Time never dragged at Sipolilo, and I was fairly certain that I would spend the remaining few months of my contract at my beloved bush station. However, shortly after returning from the Zambesi, I sat the University of South Africa's Chishona examinations in Salisbury, and within a few weeks I was on the move.

Sipolilo and Zambesi Update.

Great changes have taken place along the river and valley, since my days at Sipolilo, in the forties.

In an attempt to eradicate the tsetse fly in the Zambesi valley, the Rhodesian

Government resorted to an ill-advised policy of extermination. Between 1953-57, over 150,000 wild animals were slaughtered, but the dreaded fly continued to flourish.

During the 1950s, Kariba Dam was constructed across the Zambesi, as part of a massive hydro-electric scheme to provide electricity for the expanding economy of the Rhodesias. As Lake Kariba formed behind a vast concrete wall, over 16,000 wild animals were rescued and re-located, under 'Operation Noah'. Within a few weeks, Lake Kariba stretched back over 200 miles and, downstream at Tete, the river level dropped about 15 feet, and its width changed from nearly two miles to about 400 yards. The primitive ferry crossing at Tete, which had taken me about thirty minutes in the early fifties, now takes a few minutes.

In an attempt to provide electricity for impoverished and undeveloped Mozambique, the Portuguese authorities also constructed a dam on the Zambesi, at the Cabora Bassa rapids. Lake Cabora Bassa formed, and reached 150 miles upstream to near Zumbo. Portuguese efforts to modernise came too late and, in 1975, after 470 years of decadent and brutal rule, they were ousted by communist-inspired rebels, under Samora Machel. His party, Frelimo, became the only legal political party in Mozambique.

In 1965, when Ian Smith, the Prime Minister of Southern Rhodesia, proclaimed a 'Unilateral Declaration of Independence', many African 'freedom fighters' fled to Zambia and Mozambique, to continue fighting for African control of Southern Rhodesia. Much of the Zambesi valley became a war zone, with Sipolilo becoming an important military outpost. New buildings were erected, modern communications installed, and a good earth road zig-zagged down the escarpment, and continued to Kanyemba on the Zambesi. The journey to Kanyemba, which took me four days in 1948, now takes a few hours. At Mushumbi Pools, some 55 miles north of Sipolilo, a Police post was established, complete with an airstrip. After fourteen years of bitter fighting, the African majority, under Robert Mugabe, gained independence in 1979, and the country became known as Zimbabwe.

Sipolilo has been renamed Guruve, meaning 'wild pig'. Zumbo has kept its name, but Feira is now known as Luangwa. Vast areas of the Zambesi valley have been designated as National Parks, and tourists canoe the river in fibre glass boats, and stay in luxurious safari camps to view the protected

game. Incredibly, some elephants have been tamed, and African 'mahouts' ride and control the noble beasts!

Salisbury – School and Scouts.

The African Police Training School, Salisbury.
There was good and bad news towards the end of 1948. Success in the University of South Africa's Chishona language exams was rewarded by promotion to Staff Sergeant, and an immediate transfer to the capital city. It was shattering news as ultra-modern Salisbury, despite its many facilities, could not be compared with the excitement, freedom and slow pace of life of my own small station in the Rhodesian outback. Apart from a quick visit to play football, and a place to purchase a properly baked loaf of bread, I had always regarded Salisbury as a place to avoid at all costs.

My transfer coincided with the onset of the first heavy rains and, as an instructor/linguist at the African Police Training School, I became a slave to a training timetable, noisy bugle calls, starched uniforms, shining buttons and highly polished boots. There was also the daily presence of a high-ranking Commanding Officer, Captain Herbert Van Niekerk, a Rhodesian by birth and a fluent Chishona linguist. Despite his South African Boer ancestry, 'Van' spoke of Britain as 'home' and had developed an upper-class English accent, compatible with his commissioned rank.

Situated on the outskirts of Rhodesia's capital city, the A.P.T.S. had the appearance and atmosphere of a well-ordered African village. Surrounding a large gravel parade ground were immaculate rows of traditional thatched huts, where staff wives were always busy pounding corn, fetching water, and tending their numerous offspring. At the back of the school, over a hundred enthusiastic African recruits were accommodated in single-storey barrack blocks, where they spent much of their spare time polishing leather equipment, and starching and ironing their khaki uniforms. All were members of the Mashona and Matebele tribes who, only fifty years before, had been deadly enemies.

As well as training African police recruits, the school was base for the renowned Police Regimental Band, and also a group of 'foreign' Africans who made up the anachronistic 'Platoon'. In the early days of Rhodesia, when the loyalties of local tribes were suspect, highly-trained Africans from Nyasaland and Northern Rhodesian tribes, made up the 'Platoon', which could be set against rebellious locals, if the need arose.

Now most of these 'foreigners' were employed as drill instructors, orderlies and buglers, and also mounted guard at Government House, the home of His Excellency the Governor.

Promptly at 4 p.m. each day, and with time for a round of golf, the school's few white employees left for their homes in Salisbury. I remained and became the only European resident, amongst several hundred Africans. Surrounded by a well-manicured lawn and a few mature eucalyptus trees, my small but comfortable, one-bedroom bungalow was tucked away at the edge of the school, and had the luxury of electricity and a shady verandah. 'Chari' was delighted with my transfer, as it meant a wage increase, access to subsidised beer, and a Sergeant to care for instead of a lowly Trooper. He was also relieved of cooking chores, as I ate in the Sergeants' Mess, at the European Depot; a pleasant cycle ride of half a mile, through an avenue of aromatic jacaranda and flamboyant trees.

My Bungalow — African Police Training School, Salisbury, 1956

My duties were far from onerous. Before breakfast, and sporting a swagger-stick, I strolled amongst the squads on the parade ground, as the experienced African drill instructors yelled at their sweating young charges, and vied with each other to produce the smartest squad. It was the best time of the day, when the air was cool and sweet, and before the hot tropical sun rose high in the blue Rhodesian sky. After breakfast and barrack room inspection, I taught basic law and Police procedure, in a mixture of Chishona and English, and the afternoon was taken up with physical education, sport and recruit welfare.

Part of the day was spent at the primary school for staff children, where I helped the younger children with vernacular lessons, and senior pupils with their English studies. Dressed in simple school uniforms, barefooted, and at various stages of tooth loss, they were happy, industrious girls and boys, and a joy to work with. My first contact with African Scouting was with the school's Cubs and Scouts. Lacking a Scoutmaster, I took over the Troop and found the youngsters enthusiastic and quick to learn new skills. Most of them spoke the language of Nyasaland, Chinyanja, and I began to learn a second Bantu language.

Long Leave in Britain.
After four months at the A.P.T.S., my three-years contract expired and, although it had been a rewarding experience, the thought of a career with a semi-military organisation was daunting. Now with a good language qualification, I toyed with the idea of transferring to the prestigious Rhodesian Native Department, but decided to make a final decision during leave in Britain.

Another opportunity emerged a couple of weeks before leaving for Britain. Bob Langley, Commissioner of the Bechuanaland Protectorate Police, visited the school and offered me a commission in the Bechuanaland Protectorate force. On the 2,000 miles train journey to Cape Town, Bob met me at the small station of Palapye and drove me to Serowe, the tribal capital of the predominant Bamangwato people. Set amongst arid, featureless country on the fringes of the Kalahari desert, the quaint Police training school was more primitive than I had anticipated, and I was not tempted. It was intriguing to watch jockey-sized African mounted troopers going through their paces at the riding school, particularly as only Europeans rode horses in Rhodesia. Interestingly, the Police employed primitive bushmen, as guides in the vast Kalahari desert.

In Cape Town, I joined Basil Taylor and other colleagues, who had managed to save £90 for a budget berth on the Union Castle mail ship, the *Stirling Castle*. Having a spare day, Basil and I trudged to the highest point of impressive Table Mountain, for magnificent views of the Cape of Good Hope, where the waters of the Atlantic and Indian Oceans mingle. On the well-trodden path, we passed Jan Smuts, the famous Boer War leader and recently retired Prime Minister of South Africa. Now in his late seventies, he was still sprightly and alert, and enjoying the mountain stroll far more than his perspiring bodyguards. Although only 3,568 feet at its highest point, Table Mountain was the first real mountain I had ever climbed. Taking two weeks, and over 6,000 miles to reach Britain, we cruised generally north-westwards into the Atlantic Ocean, and blissful days were spent overeating, playing deck games and swimming in the tropical sunshine. Compared with the cramped troopship conditions of the *Alcantara* in 1946, our inside four-berth 'budget' cabin was luxurious.

In mid-Atlantic, and about 1700 miles from Cape Town, the remote island of St Helena was our first port of call. Discovered by Portuguese mariners in 1502, it is a natural fortress, with volcanic cliffs rising over 2,000 feet from the sea. There were no inhabitants until 1673, when the island was settled by Britain, and became a staging post on the important Cape sea route to India. Most islanders are descendants of various Asiatic races, brought in as workers by the British East India Company, before the Suez Canal was built. In 1815, after the Battle of Waterloo, St Helena was chosen as a place of exile for the defeated Napoleon Bonaparte and, during the Boer War, it was used as a prisoner-of-war settlement.

With no natural harbour, visiting ships anchor off-shore and essential supplies, mail and visitors are transferred by lighters to Jamestown, the only large settlement. Few ships call at St Helena, and the arrival of a supply ship was a festive occasion for the friendly islanders, and a holiday for the school children. St Helena stamps are collectors' items, and a queue of passengers quickly formed outside the small post office. Most took up the offers of local boys who, for a few pennies, took their place in the queue, while they drank tea at a nearby cafe. 699 steep stone steps, known as 'Jacob's ladder', lead more energetic visitors to open fields above Jamestown. Several of us made the long climb, and were rewarded with superb views and a refreshing sea breeze. Descending the steps to the heat and humidity of Jamestown, we were quickly overtaken by local boys who, with small cushions on their stomachs, slid down the metal handrails at breakneck speeds.

Napoleon's 'prison', a palatial mansion called Longwood, is the island's main attraction. Guarded by a garrison of 3,000 British soldiers, the defeated emperor lived in great luxury and at enormous expense, and died on the island, from stomach cancer, after six years incarceration. Napoleon is reputed to have designed the attractive gardens, which have sunken paths, so that he could not be seen by prying eyes.

With little employment on the island, many of the young people leave to work in South Africa or Britain and, as we returned to the ship by long boat, we were joined by four giggling, mulatto maidens. Attired in old-fashioned hats and dresses, and struggling with heavy leather portmanteaus, it was the first time they had left the island, and were excited at the prospect of working in London as house servants.

Almost two days cruising from St Helena, and another volcanic island loomed in the morning mist. Named 'Ascension' by a Portuguese admiral, who found it on Ascension Day, 1501, it is a forbidding, secretive place, and an important British intelligence gathering centre. Occupied by Britain in 1815, cruise passengers are not allowed ashore, and the only permanent residents are a few dead workers, who succumbed to yellow fever in Victorian times, and are buried amongst the cinders and twisted lava. A mini-golf course, with 'browns' made up of sand and oil, helps the few isolated contract workers while away the lonely hours between spying duties.

Crossing the equator, and passing close to the African mainland near the Cape Verde islands, our final call was Las Palmas, the main town of Spanish Grand Canaria. Now out of the tropics, only 1700 miles remained as we headed for England. Temperatures dropped, coats were needed on deck, and only the hardy were tempted to swim in the cold sea water of the tourist class pool. Early morning, on the fifteenth day, the *Stirling Castle* edged its way through swirling mist into dreary Southampton docks, with its vast corrugated iron sheds, and polluted, oil-stained waters. It was cold and the rain fell steadily, as a few unsmiling dockers, in flat caps and ill-fitting garments, secured the ship's ropes to the quay-side bollards. As we made our way through the cold, soulless Customs sheds, I was absolutely certain that I would return to the sunny climes and exciting life of Rhodesia.

After three years in 'God's own country', it was good to see family and friends, but my over-riding impression was that houses, roads and fields all seemed to have shrunk. Britain was still recovering from the austere war years; National Service was still compulsory for young men, shoes, sweets, meat and clothes were rationed, and unpopular identity cards were carried. Compared with vibrant Rhodesia, with its eternal sunshine, vast open spaces and freedom, everything seemed dreary, archaic and claustrophobic. After a few days, Basil and I cycled through the grimy, sprawling suburbs of London to Rhodesia House, and re-attested in the B.S.A. Police. We also booked our return passages to Beira, in Mozambique, via the Suez canal.

Momentous changes had taken place in Britain during my three years' absence. Prime Minister Clement Atlee, and his Labour government, had embarked on a programme of nationalisation and social reforms, and had launched the flagship of their 'Welfare State', the National Health Service. Britons would now have health care from 'the cradle to the grave', based on medical need and not the ability to pay. Treatment, medicines, dental care and spectacles were all free. Coal mines, electricity, the railways, and the Bank of England had been nationalised, twelve national parks established, and the school leaving age had been raised to 15 years. On the sporting front, the 14th Olympic Games, the 'Austerity Games', had taken place in London in 1948; the first since Hitler's flamboyantly successful 'Nazi Olympiad', held in Berlin in 1936. Still recovering from World War II, sporting giants, Russia, Germany and Japan did not compete, and American athletes dominated most events. Britain managed just three gold medals in rowing and yachting.

Also during my absence, the British Empire, the most powerful in history, had begun to disintegrate with the partitioning of India in 1947, and the creation of East and West Pakistan, as separate homelands for the large Muslim communities. Burma and Ceylon had also gained independence, and many other parts of the Empire were clamouring for self-government. Nearer home, Southern Ireland became a republic and left the Commonwealth.

A cycle tour of Britain was the highlight of home leave. On the ship, several colleagues had shown interest in a proposed cycle tour of Britain but, once home, the number dwindled to three: Basil, Jack and me. We joined the Youth Hostels Association and, with heavy 'commando' rucksacks on our backs, and riding solid, upright cycles, we set off from Dartford, Kent, to investigate various unknown areas of our native land. Fortunately, there was little traffic to hinder our progress, as motorways had yet to be invented, and ordinary people still travelled by rail, buses and cycles. Towns and villages were free from traffic and parked cars, and signposts, dismantled during the war years to confuse the enemy, had reappeared and helped us find our way between towns. Another bonus was that sweets and chocolate rationing had recently ended, and we were able to indulge in quick energy boosters. Jack lasted just two days before heading back to his native Leicester. Armed with a small scale map of Britain, and a list of Hostels, Basil and I continued the marathon in a clockwise direction. With the minimum of planning, and keeping to secondary roads, we followed the south coast from Hastings to Bridport, in Dorset, then northwards through Wales to Snowdonia, and eventually to the Lake District and Scotland.

At Bridport, there was a joyous reunion with a family with whom Basil had been billeted in 1940, prior to leaving for the battlefields of France. At Bluith Wells in central Wales, we spent two days with a prisoner-of-war colleague, who had laboured with Basil in the coal mines of Poland. At the Pen-y-Pass Youth Hostel, at the top of the Llanberis Pass in Snowdonia, the basic dormitories were crowded, as it was the weekend and the weather forecast was good. Scores of walkers, heavy-booted, and with rucksacks full of emergency clothing and supplies, assembled at the Hostel to climb Snowdon,

CYCLE TOUR of BRITAIN 1949

TOTAL MILEAGE 1,084.

the highest mountain in England and Wales at 3,560 feet. As we had recently 'conquered' South Africa's Table Mountain – eight feet higher – we decided to try our luck. Shod in flimsy Rhodesian 'velt-schoen' and carrying heavy rubberised ground-sheets, in case of rain, we set out along the reputedly difficult 'Pyg' track route, without map or compass, but always making sure that we had 'experts' in our sights. It was not a difficult mountain, and later we discovered that our point of departure was 1170 feet above sea level.

Never seeing the sea in land-locked Rhodesia, we decided to spend more time near the coastal areas, and aimed for the seaside town of Rhyl, on the north coast of Wales. Catering for the masses of Mersey-side, it was a dreary resort, but we found a cheap bed and breakfast establishment, where Basil enthralled fellow guests with stories of wild animals, and the trials and tribulations of living in the African outback. On the *Stirling Castle* our particular friends had been a middle-aged Scottish couple, who owned a boarding house in Blackpool and had invited us to stay with them. Heading for Blackpool, their 'boarding house' proved to be a popular fish and chip shop, so we ate well for a couple of days.

Heading northwards in perfect weather, we cycled the lengths of both Lakes Windermere and Ullswater, and were enthralled with the outstanding beauty of the English Lake District. After climbing Helvellyn, we set off for Carlisle and Gretna Green, hoping to reach the Scottish Highlands, and perhaps climb Ben Nevis. For nearly four weeks we had enjoyed sunny 'Rhodesian' weather but, once in Scotland the monsoon erupted and, near Glasgow, we reluctantly decided to head back to Kent.

Before heading south, we spent a couple of enjoyable hours at the impressive David Livingstone Museum, at Blantyre, the birthplace of the great explorer. Here I learned that my hero had suffered twenty-two bouts of malaria during his 33 years in Africa, and he was never aware that the anopheles mosquito caused the debilitating disease. Ironically, the only time Livingstone travelled through the Suez canal was in his coffin, en route to burial in Westminster Abbey. His heart remained in Africa, having been removed by his faithful bearers and buried under a tree at Chitambo village, in present day Zambia.

Being much flatter, our progress down the eastern side of England was much quicker, and I was anxious to get home to prepare for a Scout Camp in the French Alps. Our total mileage for the five weeks tour was over a thousand miles.

Camping with brothers Ernie and Roy, and the 5th Dartford Scouts in the Chamonix-Mont Blanc area of France, was another wonderful experience. Dominated by Mont Blanc, at over 15,000 feet, the jagged, snow covered pinnacles of the Chamonix Aiguilles mountains were the backdrop for our activities. Such awe-inspiring peaks and alpine grandeur probably triggered my life-long love affair with walking and climbing in remote mountain areas.

Sailing from London, the *Umtali*, a one-class ship of the Natal Line, followed the route taken by the *Alacantara* in 1946. Through the Mediterranean and the Suez canal, and fascinating calls at Islamic Aden, bustling Mombasa and Dar-es-Salaam, and the exotic spice island of Zanzibar, before disembarking at Beira, in Mozambique. During the voyage, the British pound devalued by 30% and, more dramatically, Chinese communists, under Mao Zedong, assumed control of China. Laden with China's entire gold reserves, Chiang Kai-shek and the defeated Nationalist army fled to the island of Formosa, which they renamed Taiwan.

Several expatriate civil servants, from the Nyasaland Protectorate, were travelling on the ship, and it came to light that the Colonial Office paid their travelling expenses, whereas we had paid our own! They enthused about the country, with its vast inland lake and mountains reaching up to 10,000 feet, and I became determined to visit 'the Land of the Lake', and perhaps follow some of the routes taken by David Livingstone during the mid-nineteenth century.

Return to the African Police Training School.
Despite the absence of high mountains and seaside resorts, I was delighted to return to the simple life of sunny, uncomplicated Rhodesia, and memories of crowded, austere Britain soon faded. A busy and interesting eighteen months lay ahead, before a career change beckoned to another African country.

Most of my time was spent with young African recruits, and I learned much about their tribal culture. About a third of the recruits were members of the formerly war-like Matabele tribe, an off-shoot of the Zulu nation of South Africa. Tall, muscular and well-disciplined, their homelands were in arid Matabeleland in the south of the country, and they were rightly proud of their Zulu ancestry and heritage. They needed very little encouragement to demonstrate their dancing skills and war chants, and responded enthusiastically when I suggested forming a dancing troupe. From animal skins and tails, donated by the local abattoir, they quickly fashioned tribal shields, headbands and skirts, and managed to muster spears, knobkerries and beads. Their energy, enthusiasm and harmonious, deep-throated singing and tribal chanting ensured their success. Several shows were given locally, before performing at the prestigious Rhodesian Agricultural Show in Salisbury.

During a lecture on punishments, the young Matabele recruits related their tribal customs, prior to the arrival of Europeans. Warriors of the war impis operated under very strict discipline, and punishments for cowardice or misbehaviour were horrendous: smashing the head with a knobkerrie, being tied to a tree and eventually eaten by hyenas and jackals, and mass spearing by fellow warriors. During the initiation of young warriors, a young bull would be let loose and, with just their bare hands, they had to capture and kill the unfortunate beast, before devouring everything except the bones and horns. They were unanimous in declaring that punishments given by Rhodesian courts were far too lenient.

Grooming the Police horses at the European depot was one duty that most recruits secretly hated. Every afternoon, the duty squad marched to the stables where they mucked out, watered, and groomed the horses. At first, most of the young lads were understandably frightened of these large, unpredictable creatures, that tended to bite and kick, and the chore was more a duty than a pleasure. For those destined to work in the District

Staff sergeant / Linguist

With African Instructors

Recruits' Tribal Dancing Team

Branch, caring for horses was likely to be one of their duties for many years. Africans fed, watered and groomed the station horses, and only the Europeans rode them!

Young boys from our primary school earned pocket money as caddies for Europeans on the Police Golf course, and the annual Caddies' match was a popular event for the youngsters. European golfers acted as their caddies and, playing with just one club, the schoolboys usually produced good scores. It was all good fun and the boys made the most of playfully chastising their 'caddies', and having their single club carried for them. European golfers had their favourite barefooted caddies. Bigger boys, with large feet, were preferred, particularly if they were adept at secretly picking up balls with their toes, and transferring them from the rough to the edge of the fairway! The youngsters' nick-name for a golf ball was 'dammit'; a word they had heard European golfers shout after miss-hitting a ball.

An interesting interlude from recruit training came during the early part of 1950, when I travelled to Serowe, in neighbouring Bechuanaland, as part of a Police contingent from the Rhodesias and Basutoland. Until that time, it was unknown and considered impossible, for an African to have a white wife, and the news of such a marriage sent shock waves through the white communities. Whilst studying law in Britain, Seretse Khama, the young African chief of the Bamangwato tribe, had married a London typist, Ruth Williams, and they were about to return to the tribal homelands. Tsekhedi Khama, who had acted as regent during his nephew's absence in Britain, strongly disapproved of the marriage. It was contrary to tribal custom, and trouble was expected when Seretse returned to Serowe with his white wife. Luckily, there was no serious conflict, and pleasant days were spent riding, target shooting, and playing football with other contingents. Seretse was banished from the country in 1950, but returned in 1956, on his renunciation of any claim to the chieftainship. In 1966, he became the first President of newly independent, Botswana.

Renowned as the premier military band in the country, the Police had an equally famous dance band, which played at important social occasions throughout Rhodesia. As well as practising at the A.P.T.S., the bandsmen and their families lived at the school, and one of its members was a brilliant saxophonist named Musarurwa. Rather plump and slow moving, he was over fond of Kaffir beer and was often in trouble. On one occasion he was unfit to play his instrument through drink, and was paraded before the Officer Commanding. His humiliating punishment was to walk barefoot round the parade ground for a couple of hours, with his Police boots strung round his neck. About this time he composed the acclaimed jazz tune 'Skookian' (a slang word meaning a 'strong, illicitly brewed drink') and became internationally famous.

Football accounted for much of my leisure time during 1950. Considered the best in the country that season, the Police team made a clean sweep of all the country's trophies: the League Cup, the Challenge Cup, the Charity Cup, and Rhodesia's premier trophy, the prestigious Austen Cup. Now in the big city, I caught the eye of the national selectors and gained my first Rhodesian colours, by playing twice for Rhodesia against Australia, before large, sports-loving crowds, in Salisbury and Bulawayo.

Interesting tours to neighbouring territories followed. 1950 was the 50th anniversary of the founding of the Belgian Congo, and the Rhodesian team took part in the celebrations. Flying by Sabena aircraft to Elizabethville (Lumbumbashi), in the rich copper-bearing province of Katanga, was my first experience of air travel. Flying on to the northern boundary of the country, another match was played at Leopoldville (Kinshasa), on the River Congo and only a few degrees south of the equator. Taking advantage of our presence, the French invited us to play their national team in Brazzaville, a short journey across the mighty Congo, in French Equatorial Africa. Despite the heat and humidity, we easily won all our matches, and enjoyed the sumptuous hospitality provided by the rich copper mining companies.

Compared with Rhodesia, the Congo region seemed raw and primitive, and I noted in my diary, '… the Congo Africans are almost jet black, and tend to be surly and unsmiling'.

Another soccer tour was made to the rich copper-belt of Northern Rhodesia, now Zambia, when I captained the Rhodesian team. Travelling entirely by rail, our first game was at Livingstone, near the Victoria Falls, followed by games at Ndola and Mufulira. At Kitwe/Nkhana, we continued our winning streak, when we trounced the Northern Rhodesian national team for the Levy Cup.

Scouting took up some of my leisure time, and our school troop participated in joyous rallies and weekend camps. With no motorised transport, we occasionally cycled or walked to rallies but, more often, I was able to scrounge the use of Police open-sided carts, pulled by mules, and controlled by a whip-cracking African driver. At times our activities took us to Salisbury's main African township, known as the 'Location', and out-of-bounds to the white population. This was another world, where thousands of African workers, from several neighbouring countries and different tribes, lived in mainly shanty-type dwellings. Now free from tribal restrictions and dull village life, most found city life and doubtful western ways attractive and soon became urbanised. Sadly, many male workers took other wives or concubines in the township, to the detriment of their wives and families in the home villages. Despite the comparative squalor and cramped living conditions, the 'Location' always seemed a happy, vibrant place, teeming with people whose social lives were centred round the vast township beer hall.

Now in the city I was able to observe the lives and behaviour of the privileged white community. Most had very little contact with Africans, except their house servants, and lived private, comfortable lives within their own community. New white immigrants rapidly took on the 'white supremacy' mantle, and often Africans were treated as a 'conquered race', whose role was that of 'hewers of wood and drawers of water'. Although very ordinary citizens in their home countries, immigrants quickly slipped into the comfort of their newly found status, and were prepared to fight tooth and nail for the privileged position they had assumed on entering the country. Encouraged and helped, by the many 'foreign' Africans at the school, I became obsessed with learning their language; Chinyanja. New

Off to Scout Rally on mule cart

School Comedians

Prize Giving

Outside Bungalow

Off to Camp on borrowed 'basikoro'

words, heard during my daily duties, were assiduously noted and used to construct my own dictionary. Fortunately, the structure of the language was similar to Chishona and, once able to engage in intelligible conversations, considered myself ready for academic examination. As Chinyanja was not an official language of Southern Rhodesia, I had to travel to Livingstone, Northern Rhodesia, for examination. Combining the exam with a few days' leave at the nearby

Victoria Falls, I managed to 'pass with distinction' in both written and oral exams.

Towards the end of 1950, my abstemious life style made the purchase of a brand new Austin A40 van possible. Now able to undertake more adventurous African journeys, the Nyasaland Protectorate, with its historic David Livingstone connections, became my main objective. With friends Basil and Jack, we took local leave and headed northwards into the unknown. It was October, one of the hottest months of the year, and it took two hot, dusty days to cover the 430 miles journey to Zomba, the picturesque capital of Nyasaland.

From Salisbury, the macadamised 'strip' road passed through the tobacco farming areas of Mrewa and Mtoko, before gradually descending several thousand feet, through flat, parched scrub, to the Mozambique border. Suddenly, the poorly maintained gravel road worsened, and a combination of king-size pot-holes, excessive heat and dust combined to more than halve our rate of progress. Our first delay was at the Mazoe River, one of the many tributaries of the Zambesi. Due to insufficient water, the wooden pontoon ferry had ceased operating, and we watched aghast as a few ramshackle lorries churned their way through sandy mud to the opposite bank. With only a few hundred miles on the clock of my most valuable possession, I was loathe to make the crossing unaided. A Chinyanja speaking lorry driver kindly towed us across the deep mud flats, where a few enterprising African children waited with cans of water to playfully remove a thick layer of sandy mud, for a small reward.

Another 30 miles, through flat, dry and almost uninhabited scrub, brought us to the Zambesi River and the small, sun-baked town of Tete, where we spent the night. The oldest Portuguese settlement in the country, Tete dates from 1505, when Portuguese adventurers, seeking the legendary gold of the Monomatapa Empire, sailed 300 miles up the Zambesi, from its mouth at the Indian Ocean, and founded a small base on the river, which they called Tete. For many years, it was the starting point for several unsuccessful, and often fatal, prospecting and missionary endeavours.

During the mid-nineteenth century, Tete played a part in the Livingstone saga, and was an important collecting centre for the sinister slave trade to Brazil. An exhausted David Livingstone arrived there in March 1856, on the last leg of his epic two years foot-slog across Africa. After spending a month as the guest of the hospitable Portuguese Governor, Livingstone was canoed down river to Quilemane, on the East African coast. There he waited six dreary weeks for a ship to take him to Britain, via the Cape of Good Hope. Two years later, Livingstone returned to Tete as leader of the Zambesi Expedition, which led to the discovery of Lake Nyasa, and the start of missionary activity in the lands that became known as Nyasaland.

In the cool of the evening, we strolled Tete's narrow streets, where swarthy locals filled the numerous smoke-filled wine bars. In Rhodesia, most of Tete's inhabitants would have been classified as 'Coloured' or 'halfcastes'; sure evidence that for hundreds of years the Portuguese had cohabited fruitfully with the indigenous population. Queuing at the ferry before 7 a.m. the next morning, we reached the north bank of the Zambesi before the tropical sun became too hot, and our excitement grew as we gradually climbed out of the hot, dreary Zambesi valley. Passing over the southern end of the Kirk range, with its rugged peaks and rolling foothills, and entering Nyasaland at Mwanza, the scenery became more spectacular, with wooded hills, tidy villages, lush, well-tended gardens and friendly waves from happy children. There were even numerous African cyclists on the dusty road, something we had not witnessed in sparsely populated Mozambique.

Situated in the picturesque Shire highlands, the friendly town of Blantyre, at 3,500 feet, was reached late-afternoon and we were now just 42 miles from our destination. Founded in 1876, by Church of Scotland missionaries, the town grew round the mission station and was named Blantyre, after David Livingstone's birthplace, in Scotland. Blantyre was already well established when Salisbury, Johannesburg and Nairobi were still unknown places in the inhospitable African bush. Now, with its twin town of Limbe, it was the commercial centre of the country, and was connected by rail to Beira and the Indian Ocean.

Confident of reaching Zomba before dusk, we headed northwards through dramatic, rock-strewn hills and small road-side settlements, with their distinctive lean-to Indian stores, and open-air vendors selling small pyramids of fruit and vegetables. After dreary, flat Mozambique, it was a spectacular journey through well-populated villages, and with the majestic peaks of the Mlanje massif towering over 10,000 feet, to the south-east. With the golden sun setting behind the rolling hills of Zomba mountain, we reached Zomba's main street, with its stately blue-gum and jacaranda trees, and a mixture of tin-roofed, Colonial style buildings and small Indian stores. Asking for a 'hotela', a young African boy directed us to Manda's Hotel, a suspect, budget establishment, nestling between a row of open-fronted Indian stores, in the nearby bazaar area.

Although not quite what we had expected, the jovial African proprietor was welcoming, and our large white-washed room was basic but clean. Assured that the car would be safe in the unlit earth road, we settled for a cold shower and scrumptious fish and chips for supper. Before leaving Salisbury, one of the A.P.T.S. instructors had asked if I would deliver a letter to his uncle, Sub-Inspector Thomas Gombera, who worked in Zomba. Mr Manda knew Thomas and kindly sent one of his servants to deliver the letter. Before retiring, a reply, in Chishona, came from Thomas inviting me to have tea with his family the following afternoon.

Next morning, a stroll before breakfast, confirmed that our 'hotela' was in the scruffy market area of town and, although not yet 7 a.m. A fascinating African scenario unfolded. To an all-pervading odour of smoked fish and rotting vegetables, colourful African men and women busily set out their produce in small heaps: red beans, maize flour, monkey nuts and a variety of fruit and vegetables. At the covered section of the market, scraggy chickens, imprisoned in small bamboo cages, squawked noisily and waited their fate, and piles of unappetising meat on concrete slabs, attracted swarms of buzzing flies. Blessed with several large lakes in the country, fish was an important part of the local diet, and smoked and fresh fish was being off-loaded from large bamboo baskets tied to the backs of sturdy, upright cycles. At the nearby Indian stores, traders in comfortable Muslim dress pushed up the shutters of their open-fronted shops, and prepared for business. Chatting with a friendly, bearded trader, he was surprised that we had stayed at Manda's Hotel, and mentioned that Europeans usually stayed at the Government Hostel, further up the mountain side.

After breakfast, we decided to explore Zomba. Despite being the capital of Nyasaland, there was only one bank and a couple of European stores, and much-needed petrol had to be purchased from a Government depot; two four-gallon tins encased in a wooden box. Part way up the mountain, we found the Government hostel, an elegant double-storied Colonial building, set above impressive botanical gardens, and with extensive views of distant

Mlanje mountain and several minor mountains. The abode of single European male and female civil servants, we managed to get a shared room for a couple of nights.

The mountain and plateau are Zomba's main attraction, and can be reached by a narrow motor track. From Zomba Gymkhana Club, the social centre of the small European community, a tarmac road soon gave way to a rough track, which zig-zagged up the mountain side, for about seven miles, to a point known as Kraal Corner. Here a clock had been installed, and a sign advised that the final two and a half miles to the summit, was 'One way traffic only: ascending traffic between the hour and quarter past, and descending cars between half-past and quarter to each hour.' Becoming dramatically narrower, and with perilous drops, we carefully negotiated the roughly hewn mountain track to the top and were rewarded with magical views. In the distance, across the Palombe plain, was the isolated granite massif of Mlanje at nearly 10,000 feet, and nearer were the smaller mountains of Pyupyu, Ntonya and Chiradzulu. To the east, was shimmering Lake Chilwa, an expanse of shallow water some 20 miles in length, and a source of fish for the local population. 3,000 feet below us lay Zomba, comparatively small and spread out, and reputed to be 'the most beautiful capital in the British Empire'. Built precariously on the edge of the plateau, and facing Zomba, were several small bungalows which commanded breath-taking views of the area. Little did I realise that seven years later I270 Thomas Gombera would marry in Zomba, and honeymoon in one of the mountain bungalows!

Returning to Zomba, I made my way to the Police camp, to meet Thomas Gombera and his family at their small Police cottage. In his mid-fifties, and his face scarred by smallpox, Thomas was a gentle, friendly man who seemed delighted to converse in his mother tongue. His buxom wife also spoke Chishona and, as she served tea, biscuits and thick, unbuttered jam sandwiches, she proudly introduced her adult family and a bevy of shy grandchildren. Entertaining a young European to tea was obviously an unusual experience and a novelty to the wide-eyed children. Their eldest son, Snogger Gombera, worked as a detective in Zomba, and probably did not realise the significance of his unusual name.

With over 30 years service with the C.I.D., Thomas was an experienced policeman with a fascinating background. In 1894, Thomas's father was working for Methodist missionaries, and Thomas was born in a lumbering ox wagon as they trekked through Rhodesia, to establish a mission station. A few years later, both his parents died of blackwater fever, and the European missionaries became his guardians.

Speaking fluent English, Thomas attested in the British South Africa Police in 1913, but transferred to the Rhodesian Native Regiment, during the First World War. He fought against the Germans in Tanganyika and, at the end of the war, was stationed in Nyasaland with his regiment. After the war, in 1920, several European members of the British South Africa Police travelled to Nyasaland to establish a police force. Thomas joined them as an interpreter, and became a founder member of the Nyasaland force.

Next day, with insufficient time to visit Lake Nyasa, Africa's third largest lake, and to escape the oppressive October heat, we opted for a longer trip to Zomba mountain. Feeling energetic, we climbed to the plateau, by a steep path which branched off from the mountain track. Known as the 'potato' path, it had been formed by generations of barefooted African potato growers, as they took a short cut to Zomba market. It was a rough, precipitous path but, as we scrambled to the top, we were again rewarded with magnificent views and cool mountain air. Strolling through shady, pine plantations and along tumbling, crystal-clear streams, was a soothing, tranquil experience, and I found myself becoming more and more attracted to Zomba and the Nyasaland Protectorate.

Returning to the hostel mid afternoon, there was an invitation to call on the Deputy Commissioner of Police later that afternoon. Quickly bathing and donning the best of my travel-stained clothes, I hurried to Police Headquarters, a collection of single-storey, green-tinned roofed buildings at the foot of Zomba mountain. Seated in a large, airy office was Geoffrey Morton, a grey-haired, authoritative figure, wearing the insignia of a high-ranking Colonial police officer. A dynamic character, Geoff had spent many years in the Palestine Police, and had gained notoriety when he shot and killed the leader of the Stern gang, the infamous Jewish terrorist group.

As we sipped tea, he quizzed me about my work in the B.S.A.P., and it became obvious that Thomas Gombera had briefed him. Perhaps not convinced that a Rhodesian could speak the language of Nyasaland, Geoff summoned a couple of African orderlies to the office and invited us to converse. Being something I enjoyed, I was quickly chatting and laughing with the friendly orderlies. Geoff, a non-linguist, was obviously impressed and, when the orderlies had been dismissed, he offered me a post in the Nyasaland Force, specifically to assist in the reorganisation of African recruit training. It was a complete surprise, and the thought of a free sea passage to Britain, every two and a half years, was a great incentive to work in this newly found 'Shangri La'.

Our dusty journey back to Rhodesia was uneventful and, within a few days, I gave three months' notice of resignation. My decision caused some sadness, as Rhodesia had been my home for five happy, adventurous years, and I knew I would miss the camaraderie of the 'Regiment', top level sport, and the African Scouts and school children. Despite its faults, Rhodesia had been good to me, and I would always regard the country and its people with great affection.

However, life is an ever-changing pattern and, having experienced another very different, and scenically beautiful, African country, I felt ready for further adventures in the Nyasaland Protectorate – **'The Land of the Lake'**.

www.ingramcontent.com/pod-product-compliance
Lightning Source LLC
Chambersburg PA
CBHW050140170426
43197CB00011B/1905